Deaths Abstracted from

THE CAMP POINT JOURNAL

1873-1882

Camp Point

Adams County
Illinois

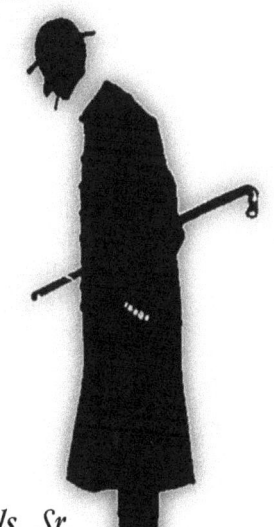

Mrs. Joseph J. Beals, Sr.
and *Mrs. Sandy Kirchner*

HERITAGE BOOKS
2011

HERITAGE BOOKS
AN IMPRINT OF HERITAGE BOOKS, INC.

Books, CDs, and more—Worldwide

For our listing of thousands of titles see our website
at
www.HeritageBooks.com

Published 2011 by
HERITAGE BOOKS, INC.
Publishing Division
100 Railroad Ave. #104
Westminster, Maryland 21157

Copyright © 1999 Mrs. Joseph J. Beals, Sr.
and Mrs. Sandy Kirchner

All rights reserved. No part of this book may be reproduced or transmitted in any form or by any means, electronic or mechanical, including photocopying, recording or by any information storage and retrieval system without written permission from the author, except for the inclusion of brief quotations in a review.

International Standard Book Numbers
Paperbound: 978-0-7884-1229-5
Clothbound: 978-0-7884-8642-5

Contents

Introduction *v*

Map of Adams County, Illinois, 1872 *vi*

Deaths, Alphabetically by Surname *1*

The death related items in this book were abstracted from The Camp Point Journal newspaper of Camp Point, Adams County Illinois. These papers were dated from 1873 through 1882. In the early 1960's while doing research on my own genealogy in Camp Point Journal, we found so much valuable information that we decided to start writing it all on 3" x 5" index cards. We wrote down any items that mentioned a family name. Although this book consists of death related announcements our collection of index cards includes information from advertisements, jury lists, criminal courts and letter remaining at the post office. We hope to prepare these remaining items for publication as time permits. A cross reference in this book contains an additional list of names.

The town of Camp Point was laid off on February 16, 1854 by the order of P.B. Garrett, Benj. Booth, Wm Farlow and Thomas Bailey. It is situated on a beautiful, high, rolling prairie and is at the junction of the C.B. & Q and T.W. and W. Railroads.

In April of 1855 what is known as the original survey of Camp Point was laid out. The following summer James A. Roth came from Quincy and built a store and house, the store is gone and the house was rebuilt by his son, John.

In 1856 the Francis Hotel was built by Thos. Ensminger. At about the same time Moses Bryant erected a part of what is now the Omer House

                        Mrs Joseph J. Beals Sr.
                        Mrs Sandy Kirchner
                        P.O. Box 279
                        Cherokee, IA   51012

ADAMS COUNTY

Illinois

1872

	R5W	R6W	R7W	R8W	R9W	R10W
T2N	Northeast	Houston	Keene	Mendon	Lima	
T1N	Clayton	Camp Point	Honey Creek		Ursa	
T1S	Concord	Columbus	Gilmer	Ellington		
T2S	McKee	Liberty	Burton	Melrose		
T3S	Beverly	Richfield	Payson	Fall Creek		

ACKLEY, HENRY - Neighboring News - July 8, 1880 Last night at 8 the report was that Henry Ackley and John Christian were dead in a coal shaft near Pulaski. Jackson Christian the boys father and Wm Dean found them. They had been sent after the pigs and didn't return. "Augusta Saturday Mail" Extra

ADAIR, MRS - Mendon - Dec. 27, 1878 Mrs Adair, who lived between Mendon and Marcelline died on Saturday, over 90 years old.

ADAIR, JAS. F. - Mendon - March 18, 1880 Died, Mr Jas. F. Adair, one of the earliest settlers and oldest inhabitants of this county. Died at his home about 4-1/2 miles NW of Mendon at 5 A.M. today, age 93 years.

ADAIR, WILLIAM - Supposed Murder - Apr. 3, 1873 On the 16th of January at Loraine, this county, William Adair died under circumstances that created a suspicion in the minds of a few neighbors that his death was caused by poison administered by his wife. After the funeral the widow moved to Hancock County. Wednesday a warrant was sworn out for the arrest of Anne Adair with murder and placed in the hands of Constable John Richards to execute. Mrs Adair was 24 years old, had been married 6 years.

ADAMS, DAVID - Local - Nov 23, 1882 Suicide, David Adams, a constable of Good Hope, McDonough county committed suicide Wednesday.

ADAMS, FREDDIE - Hash - Jul 19, 1878 Freddie, a little son of George B. Adams living in Clayton Twp. drank poison and died.

ADAMS, GEORGE - Local - Jan. 16, 1880 Remember the trial of George Adams in 1876 for robbery and murder of Nancy Ferris. Adams says he is not guilty of murder, but Ira Galloupe is.

ADAMS, GEORGE - Hash - Sep 29, 1876 George Adams was sentenced to the penitentiary for life for the murder of Nancy Ferris last March.

ADAMS, GEORGE - Fowler - Sep 29, 1881 Body of George Adams Jr. came in on the train. He was an engineer running thru Parson's, Kansas and was out about 20 miles when the boiler exploded, killed him and 2 other men. (Mother is mentioned in article)

ADAMS, JOHN - Died - Jun 11, 1875 Died, on the 7th inst at the home of C.A. Easum, John Adams, of consumption.

ADAMS, MR AND MRS W.J. - Personal - Aug 25, 1881 Died, the babe of Mr and Mrs W.J. Adams last Saturday A.M.

AKERS, MR AND MRS A. - Oakwood and Vicinity - Mr and Mrs A. Akers lost their only child on the 18th.

AKERS, BENJAMIN L. - Local - Nov 25, 1880 Died, Benjamin L. Akers an old resident of Columbus twp died Tuesday.

AKERS, MRS JOHN W. - Local - Nov 24, 1881 Died, Mrs John W. Akers of Wyandolte, Kansas, a daughter of A. W. Butts of Columbus twp died last Tuesday. Remains brought here for burial in Pleasant View Cemetery.

AKERS, MRS NANCY P. - Recent Deaths - Nov 21, 1879 Mrs Nancy P. Akers died at her home in Barry, Tuesday of last week. Mr Akers survives her.

ALEXANDER, MRS - Clayton - Mar 11, 1880 Old Mrs Alexander over north was buried last Saturday.

ALEXANDER, MRS WM - Junction - Mar 11, 1880 Died of consumption last Thursday, Mrs Wm Alexander.

ALLEN, ALEXANDER - Hash - Jul 21, 1876 Alexander Allen was drowned in the bay at Quincy, Sunday while bathing.

ALLEN, MR D. SKILLMAN - State News - Aug 26, 1880 Mr D. Skillman Allen of Decatur died near that city at the home of his son in law, Dr Gregory on Saturday night.

ALLEN, EDDIE - Liberty - Jul 25, 1879 Eddie Allen died on Wednesday. Also Mrs A. Ketzler died Sunday night. Leaves Mr Ketzler alone.

ALLEN, MR AND MRS GEO. W. - Independence Notes - Dec 5, 1879 Mr and Mrs Geo. W. Allen lost their youngest child a few days ago.

ALLEN, ISAAC - Local - Jul 11, 1879 Isaac Allen and James W. Simmond's each lost a child this week.

ALLEN, DR J.N. - Death List - Sep 7, 1877 Old settlers death list since last meeting: Dr J.N. Allen, Brown Co., age 62 years.

ALLEN, DR J.N. - Hash - May 11, 1877 Died, Dr J.N. Allen died at his home in Mt Sterling one day last week. Studied medicine under Dr G.O. Pond.

ALLEN, DR J.N. - Hash - May 18, 1877 H.K. Davis of the Brown County Democrat has been appointed postmaster at Mt Sterling to fill the vacancy caused by the death of Dr J.N. Allen.

ALLEN, MARY
    SEE: COLLINS, FREDERICK

ALLEN, MRS MARY E. - Died - Nov 3, 1876 Died of consumption October 23rd at the home of Warren Strickler near Craig, Holt County, Missouri, Mrs Mary E. Allen age 24 years 6 months. She was daughter of Clandius and Elizabeth Cook. Married to Mr Frank Allen, Nov 1, 1874 and moved to Iowa in the fall of 1875 until a short time before her death.

ALLEN, MRS SAMUEL C. - Neighborhood News - Jul 1, 1880 The wife of Samuel C. Allen of Decatur was buried on the 26th instant.

ALLISON, AUGUSTUS - Hash - Nov 19, 1875 Augustus Allison, a resident of Ursa twp committed suicide last Friday by hanging himself to a tree.

ALLISON, LEOIDAS M. - Obituary - Oct 5 1882 Died at Coatsburg, Sept 23rd, Leoidas M. Allison age 20 years 6 months 15 days. Born near Perrinsville, Clermont county Ohio. Came here with parents when 6 years old. Leaves father, mother, sister and brothers.

ALLISON, LOYD - Coatsburg - Sep 28, 1882 Died, Loyd Allison, Saturday A.M. Services by Rev J.S. Dinsmore on Sunday.

ALLISON, LOYD - Paloma - Oct 5, 1882 Rev A.M. Danely will preach the funeral sermon of Loyd Allison Sunday next at Coatsburg.

ALSPAUGH, SOLOMON AND MARTHA J. - Sale - Sep 8, 1876 Trustees sale of real estate of Solomon and Martha J. Alspaugh, his wife of Adams Co. dated Mar 30, 1869. Recorded in Box 5 of mortgages page 254. W.L. Oliver, trustee.

AMBLER, "OLD MAN" - Clayton - Dec 19, 1879 Old man

Ambler, whose wife died last summer, is going east to his son's and will exhume her remains and take them with him.

AMBLER, MRS – Clayton – May 23, 1879 Mrs Ambler and Mrs Marion Foster have died suddenly of heart disease within a few days.

ANDERS, JOHN – Died – Apr 21, 1881 Died at his home on Camp Point twp April 4th, John Anders in his 63rd year. Born in Hamilton County Ohio Apr 15, 1819. Married Elvy Woods Feb 10, 1840. In 1849 they moved to Adams County Illinois. Mrs Anders died Apr 12, 1854. They had 4 children, 3 still living. Jan 7, 1855 he married Mildred Kelley. They had 1 child, she and child survive him. Buried Pleasant View, April 6th.

ANDERS, JOHN – Probate Notice – Apr 28, 1881 John Anders, deceased 3rd Monday of June (6th) Benj. Cummings, ex.

ANDERS, JOHN – Died – Apr 7, 1881 Died Monday eve, April 4th, John Anders in his 63rd year. Buried Pleasant View Cemetery, Wednesday at 11 A.M.

ANDERS, JOHN – Apr 20, 1882 John Anders, deceased petitioner vs. George Anders, Martha J. Anders, Elvy Sammons, Wesley Sammons, Samuel K. Lewis, Elizabeth A. Lewis, William Sammons, Abram Landers, Theresa Geise and Theodore Siebers defendants.   Benjamin Cummings, ex.

ANDERSON, CORNELIA – Died – Sep 16, 1880 Died on Sept 13th A.M., Miss Cornelia Anderson, daughter of William W. Anderson, age 20 years.

ANDERSON, MAJOR – Hash – Jul 6, 1877 Died, Major Anderson died Tuesday morning. He was a native of Kansas wilds.

ANDERSON, MORRIS – Neighborhood News – Aug 3, 1877 Died-Hurt Thursday at 5 P.M. Morris Anderson a farmer who lived in Hancock County twp, 8 miles east of Carthage was killed in a farm accident. Died Friday at 12:20 A.M.   "Carthage Gazette"

ANDERSON, MRS NEAL – Clayton – Jun 13, 1879 Mrs Neal Anderson was buried Sunday eve.

ANDERSON, THOS. W. – Personal – Sep 16, 1880 Thos. W.

Anderson of Mechanicsburg came over Tuesday A.M. to attend the funeral of his sister.

ANDERSON, WM W. - Died - Jul 31, 1873 Died, July 27th of inflammation of the stomach, Mary Jane, daughter of Wm W. Anderson age 16 years.

ANDREW, SAMUEL J. AND ELIDA - Trustee's Sale - Sep 6, 1878 Samuel J. Andrew and wife Elida Andrew recorded book of mortgages #22 page 310. Joel Benton, trustee dated Sept 3, 1878

ANDREWS, MRS ADA - Died - Jan 13, 1881 Died in Houston twp, Adams County, Mrs Ada Andrews, consort of R.R. Andrews and daughter of William and Dollie Brown. Died Jan 6th, 1881, age 25 years. Married Mar 4, 1880. Her sister Alice died 7 months ago. Was a member of Ebenezer Church over 10 years.

ANGLE, LEWIS - Hash - Mar 22 1878 Lewis Angle, of Barry, died Wednesday.

ANGLE, LEWIS - Neighborhood News - Mar 29, 1878 Mr Lewis Angle who died in Barry last Thursday was buried Thursday. Odd Fellows helped in services.

ANTRIM, ELIZA ANN - Columbus - Aug 24, 1882 Died, Eliza Ann Antrim on August 15th, age 71 years. Services by Bro. Bryant.

APSLEY, MRS - Local - Feb 17, 1881 Mrs Apsley a wife of a merchant of Kingston, Adams County, became deranged about 3 weeks ago and taken to Jacksonville where she died last Friday. Buried Kingston. "Barry Adage"

ARMSTRONG, MRS MARY
    SEE: WALLACE, ALLEN

ARTUS, JOSEPH - Death of Capt. Joseph Artus - Mar 28, 1879 Capt. Joseph Artus and old citizen of Quincy died at Blessing Hospital Sunday at 11 A.M., 84 years old. Born near Paris, Kentucky. Was Capt. on the lower Mississippi and Ohio Rivers. Never married. "Herald"

ASHCRAFT, LAURA A. - Columbus - Dec 15, 1881 Died, at the home of their parents in Columbus of scarlet fever December 1st, Laura A. age 5 years 11 months. Also on December 5th Jesse A. age 3 years 8 months. Both children of Jas. Ashcraft.

ASHER, JASPER
    SEE: JOHNSON, SARAH A.

ATER, MRS - Clayton - Apr 20, 1882 Buried, Mrs Ater was buried on last Friday.

AULL, JAMES - Hash - Aug 9, 1878 James Aull, a well known Irishman died at the home of his grandson, Joseph Aull of this twp Saturday, 3rd inst., age 86 years. In his younger years Mr Aull was an Irish smuggler.

AUSMUS, CALVIN - Clayton - Jan 2, 1880 Died, Calvin Ausmus died a few miles south of town last week.

AUSMUS, CALVIN - Clayton - May 20, 1880 Elder Thompson preached the funeral of Calvin Ausmus at the Old Baptist Church last Sunday.

AUSMUS, PHILIP - Death List - Sep 7, 1877 Old settlers list of death's since last meeting: Mr Philip Ausmus, 72 years old of Brown County.

AUSTIN, DANIEL - Mendon - Feb 9, 1882 Died, one of Daniel Austin's children last Wednesday of Small Pox.

AUSTIN, JOHN C. - Local - Aug 1, 1879 Died, John C. Austin an old citizen of the county died on the 25th inst at his home 3-1/2 miles NE of Mendon. Was a resident of Mendon since 1848, 66 years old.

AVEY, JOHN - Murder Trial - Oct 3, 1879 Thomas Avey says he is half brother to the defendant. Wm M. Herring bought out the cigar store the day before the murder of John Avey. John Avey is father of defendant. John Hetrick Jr is a brother of Marion. Aggie Hetrick is a half sister of Marion. Carrie Hetrick another sister. John Hetrick is father of Marion. Jury returned "not guilty".

AVISE, WM E.
    SEE: RICHARDSON, MRS CHARLES H.

AYERS, JOHN H. - Death - Dec 10, 1875 Died, John H. Ayers, chief engineer of the fire department of Quincy died at his residence Saturday A.M. from hemorrhage of the lungs. Was a native of New Hampshire born Sept 30, 1830. Settled in Quincy in 1855. Served in the war on the 151st Ill. Infantry. Buried Monday.

BACON, WM - LaPrairie - Sep 20, 1878 Died this week, a son, 12 years old of Mr and Mrs Wm Bacon near Pulaski.

BAGBY, NATHANIEL AND MARY J. - Trustee's Sale - May 24, 1878 Trustee's sale of real estate, Nathaniel Bagby and wife, Mary J. Bagby recorded Aug 9, 1876 Book 22 mortgages page 35 to Henry R. Motter. Henry R. Motter, trustee Clayton, Ill. May 23, 1878

BAGBY, ROBERT B. - Hash - Jan 4, 1878 Died, Robert B. Bagby, a well known miller and citizen of Quincy died in Quincy Sunday.

BAILEY, EDDIE - Oct 2, 1874 Eddie Bailey about 8 year old son of Isaac Bailey of Griggsville was killed while playing around the cars at the depot. His skull was fractured and his neck broken.

BAILEY, JAMES - York Neck - Mar 14, 1879 Died, James Bailey one of the pioneers of Adams Co. died at his home in Honey Creek twp March 5th in his 76th year. Born in North Carolina in 1803. Moved to Tennessee where he married Rebecca Maynard. When about 30 years old he came to Illinois and settled in Adams County. Leaves a son and daughter and wife.

BAILEY, JENNIE - Died - Sep 2, 1880 Died at DeSota, Iowa, August 20th, Jennie, youngest daughter of Silas and Eleanor A. Bailey.

BAILEY, LEVI
    SEE: SAWYER, MRS ESTHER

BAILEY, NABBY
    SEE: SAWYER, MRS ESTHER

BAILEY, REBECCA
    SEE: KELLEY, ELEANOR B.
    SEE: SEATON, RICHARD

BAILEY, THOMAS
    SEE: KELLEY, ELEANOR B.

BAIRD, JOHN F. - Died - Oct 12, 1877 Died, on the 1st inst, John F. Baird, age 45 years.

BALLARD, MRS ELIZABETH ADELINE - Obituary - Feb 13, 1873 Died, Feb 8, Mrs Elizabeth Adeline, wife of H. Ballard, M.D. after 8-1/2 hours of painful illness. She was baptized early in life at Ursa, Illinois in the Christian Church. She was born in Madison County Illinois Jan 11, 1828, being 45 years 27 days when she died. Leaves a husband and son.

BALLARD, JERRY – Local – Mar 11, 1880 Died–"Uncle Jerry" Ballard of this county and many years proprietor of various hotels in Quincy died in that city last week.

BALLENGER, BENJAMIN – Neighborhood News – Jul 26, 1878 Benjamin Ballenger of Montezuma twp, Pike County fell from a load of wheat and died.

BALTZER, DANIEL – Liberty – Jan 9, 1880 Died–Mrs Baltzer, mother of Daniel Baltzer of McKee getting quite old drowned Saturday (suicide). Mr Baltzer was buried about 3 months ago.

BALZER, MR A.E. – Liberty – Jun 13, 1879 Last Sunday Mr A.E. Balzer, a son of Valentine Balzer of McKee was in a scuffle with Henry Dissler and hurt badly. Died Tuesday evening. Was his father's only help and leaves him in a rather helpless condition.

BANKS, MRS LYNN SR. – Livingston – Dec 29, 1881 Mrs Lynn Banks Sr. is not expected to live.

BARBOUR, DR J.W. – Died – Mar 27, 1873 Died suddenly, Dr J.W. Barbour after a brief illness at his residence on 3rd Street between Maine and Jersey yesterday A.M. He was an old resident of Columbus and well known to the citizens of the county. He moved to the city 2 or 3 months ago. Herald 22nd.

BARCLAY, MRS – Mendon – Apr 27, 1882 Died, Mrs Barclay one of our old residents died yesterday A.M. from cancer, age 65 years. Leaves an aged mother.

BARGER, CYRUS – Criminal Court – Jan 1, 1875 Cyrus Barger, manslaughter, stabbing Robert McGinley, jury sentenced 3 years.

BARGER, CYRUS – Hash – Dec 25, 1874 Trial of Cyrus Barger for the murder of Robert McGinley began today in circuit. Jury was as follows: James Griffin, Wm Bangert, Geo. W. Montgomery, John Bassett, Thomas Marshall, Francis Dougherty, L. Altmix, Wm McWherter, C. Baker, F. Hodgon, A. Baker and Geo. M. Ross. Just as we go to press we learn that the jury found Barger guilty of manslaughter and sentenced him to the penitentiary for 3 years.

BARKER, MRS - Burton - Oct 28, 1880 Mrs Barker died Thursday. Funeral following day by Rev. Murphy, of Payson. Leaves a husband and 7 children.

BARKER, SAM - Burton - Nov 25, 1880 Infant daughter of Sam Barker's aged 5 weeks died last Wednesday.

BARNES, MRS MARY A. - Jun 17, 1880 Died, Mrs Mary A. Barnes of Macomb, age 57 years, was killed by lightning last Wednesday A.M.

BARR, ELIZABETH - Supplement - Sep 1, 1876 Died since last years meeting of old Settlers of Adams and Brown Counties: Elizabeth Barr of Ellington.

BARR, HIRAM - Supplement - Sep 1, 1876 Died since last years meeting of Old Settlers of Adams and Brown Counties: Hiram Barr of Ellington.

BARTELL, GEORGE C. - Died - May 30, 1879 Died at the home of his parents in Quincy George C., son of E.C. and H. Bartell's, age 19 years.

BARTON, OTIS B. - Personal - Feb 12, 1880 Otis B. Barton, a postal clerk from Quincy and Louisiana died last Thursday night at his home in Quincy.

BASS, JOHN W. - Hash - Nov 26, 1875 John W. Bass, a Prominent commission merchant of Quincy died last Friday.

BATES, "UNCLE BILLY" - Local - Jan 2, 1880 Died, the Mt Sterling papers announce the death of "Uncle Billy" Bates of Brown County. Mr Bates was a resident of Camp Point for a short time over 20 years ago.

BATES, CAPT D.E. - Local - Aug 26, 1880 Died, Capt. D.E. Bates, a retired army officer committed suicide on the 17th inst at Pittsfield. He was deranged. He had lost an arm at the siege of Vicksburg.

BATES, J.H.
    SEE: HARRIS, HATTIE B.
    SEE: SHARP, MRS PERMELIA JANE

BATES, NANCY
SEE: HARRIS, HATTIE B.
SEE: SHARP, MRS PERMELIA JANE

BATES, HON T.J. - Personal - Jun 16, 1876 Hon. T.J. Bates has gone to Lincoln on a visit to his parents and a sister who is lying very ill.

BATES, WALLACE A. - Died - Oct 12, 1877 Died, on the 9th inst of membranous croup, Wallace A., son of Frank H. and Mary J. Bates, age 5 years 8 months 21 days. Mt Sterling Papers, please copy.

BATLEY, EVAN - Neighborhood News - Jul 26, 1878 Evan Batley, of Vermont, Fulton County was thrown from a buggy Saturday 13th, died that evening, 76 years old.

BATTELL, MRS
SEE: REES, MRS WM

BATTELL, JOHN F. - Hash - Oct 1, 1875 John F. Battell died at his residence in Quincy Tuesday eve. No clue has been obtained to the murderer.

BATTELL, WM - Death - Mar 3, 1876 Died, Wm Battell of the firm of Battell and Collins at 5 Sunday eve. He had been ill with typhoid pneumonia about a week. Mr Battell came to Adams County in 1835 and was in business in Quincy 20 years. 66 years old.

BAUMAN, MARY - Died - Feb 12, 1874 Died on the 9th inst of Tetanus, Mary, daughter of John Bauman.

BEAVER, MISS - Hash - Dec 15, 1876 Shepherd Cox and Mrs Sarah Beaver of Lima were indicted last week for abortion and murder. It is alleged that Cox seduced Miss Beaver, daughter of the woman indicted and the 2 undertook to produce an abortion from the effects of which the girl died. Mrs Beaver is in jail and Cox cannot be found.

BEAVER, SARAH JANE - Local - October 1879 Shep Cox was acquitted by the jury at Carthage last week where he was tried for the murder of Sarah Jane Beaver of this county by producing an abortion on her in October 1876.

BECK, MRS E.E. - Died - May 30, 1879 Died near Industry, Illinois May 28th, Mrs E.E. Beck, sister of Jas. J. Earl of this place.

BECKETT, C.R. - Death of C.R. Beckett - May 19, 1881 S.T. Herron of La Prairie received an Oregon paper containing the following: Last Thursday, April 28th, C.R. Beckett fell 11 feet to his death from a scaffolding. Buried by Odd Fellows. He was a brother of Mrs Herron and lived at Weston, Umatilla Co.

BECKETT, FRANKIE P. - Died - Nov 15, 1878 Died on the 2nd inst, Frankie P., son of George R. and Mary S. Beckett, age 2 years 6 months 8 days.

BECKETT, GEO. R. - Died - Apr 4, 1879 Little Edith, daughter of Geo. R. and Mary S. Beckett born Sept 24, 1878 and died March 29th, 1879.

BECKETT, GEORGE R. - Local Hash - Nov 8, 1878 A 3 year old son of George R. Beckett died last Saturday. Buried Sunday at Hebron.

BECKETT, JAMES - Personal - Apr 21, 1881 Died - News received by R.A. Beckett that his brother, James Beckett died in Defiance, Kansas.

BECKETT, JANE
    SEE: DAILY, JACOB

BECKETT, JOHN - Died - Feb 14, 1879 Died at his residence near La Prairie on the 8th inst, John Beckett, age 74 years.

BECKETT, MRS JOHN - La Prairie - Oct 27, 1876 Mrs John Beckett and Mrs Wm Choate, both well known and highly respected, have died within the last 2 weeks.

BECKETT, JOSEPH S.
    SEE: THOMAS, MRS WM R.

BECKETT, JOSEPH S. - Hash - Oct 25, 1878 Joseph S. Beckett died Saturday. Buried Hebron Cemetery Sunday.

BECKETT, JOSEPH S. - Probate Notice - Nov 8 1878 Joseph S. Beckett 3rd Monday of December 1878 Wm. T. Beckett, Ex.

BECKETT, JOSEPH S. - Local - Feb 28, 1879 Mrs E.F. Beckett will sell the personal property of the late Joseph S. Beckett at public sale March 8th.

BECKETT, LOLA FRANCES - Died - Jan 28, 1876 Died, on

the 24th ult, Lola Frances, only child of Geo. R. and
M.S. Beckett with croup, age 4 years 11 months 13 days.
Grandmother Beckett and mother were at her bedside, also
papa.

BECKETT, LUKE - Hash - Jul 20, 1877 Died, Rev T.J.
Bryant will preach the funeral of the late Luke Beckett
at Hebron Church Sunday at 11 A.M.

BECKETT, MARY E.
     SEE: JOSLYN, JOHN

BECKETT, WILLIAM T.
     SEE: DOWNING, CELESTINE

BECKINBAUGH, JOHN - Local - Jun 24, 1880 John
Beckinbaugh, a brakeman on the Louisiana line of the
C.B. & Q. Railroad met with a probably fatal accident
Wed. Lives at Louisiana and has a wife and 2 children.

BEEBE, ALBERT - Local - Oct 10, 1879 Albert Beebe of
the firm of Harris and Beebe, tobacco manufacturers of
Quincy, died at his home on S. 4th Street, Sunday A.M.

BEHAN, LOTT - Apr 3, 1873 Died on the 8th inst, Lott
Behan of pneumonia in the 62nd year of his age.

BELDON, MRS - Neighborhood News - Dec 28, 1877 Mrs
Beldon, whose husband was killed at Gilson last August
by Frank Rande, was married some weeks ago to Mr Henry
Graham of Kewanee.

BELL, FRANK - Neighborhood News - Oct 18, 1878 Last
Tuesday night Frank Bell about 18 years old living in
Fulton County was killed by lightning while in bed.

BELL MRS MARY A. - Death List - Sep 7, 1877 Old
Settlers death list since last meeting: Mrs Mary A.
Bell, Brown County age 63 years.

BELLEW, WILLIAM
     SEE: KEENAN, JOSEPH
     SEE: SMITH, MRS LETITIA

BELTS, MRS NORA - Mar 31, 1881 Died, Mrs Nora Belts
from consumption.

BENNESON, MRS S.E. - Recent Deaths - Nov 21, 1879 Mrs
S.E. Benneson died at her home in Quincy, Saturday morn

in her 70th year. Came to Quincy in 1839 and married Mr Benneson in 1840.

BENNETT, C.S. - Local - Aug 19, 1880 One of C.S. Bennett's children was buried at the village cemetery Sunday.

BENNETT, MRS J. - La Prairie - Feb 3, 1881 Died, Mrs Bennett (late Miss Lou Elliott) on the 29th inst. She married J. Bennett only a month ago.

BENNETT, JEFF - Personal - Nov 2, 1877 Jeff Bennett of Adair, McDonough County was in town Wednesday, was called down to attend the death bed of his father.

BENNETT, THOMAS - Died - Nov 2, 1877 Died on the 31st ult at his home in Houston twp of typhoid fever, Thomas Bennett, age 70 years.

BENNETT, THOMAS H. - Probate Notice - Jan 25, 1878 Thomas H. Bennett 3rd Monday of Mar. Alvin Bennett, adm.

BENNETT, MRS Z.F.
    SEE: MARRETT, MRS CATHERINE

BENTON, MR - Local - Mar 11, 1880 Died, Mr Benton, the postmaster at Ripley died last Sunday night.

BENTON, ABRAHAM
    SEE: COOK, D.A.
    SEE: COOKE, MRS

BENTON, JOEL - Mendon - May 4, 1882 Died, Joel Benton at 11 A.M. yesterday, 71 years old. Native of North Guilford, Conn. Came to Mendon in 1834 or 35.

BENTON, JOEL
    SEE: COOK, D.A.
    SEE: COOKE, MRS

BENTRUP, WM - Mar 20, 1873 Wm Bentrup, son of Wm Bentrup residing on the corner of Ohio and 6th Street was accidentally shot (by himself) yesterday in the bay while on a hunting trip. Buried from his father's residence this P.M. (Whig 18th).

BERNARD, JAMES C. - Local - Mar 18, 1880 Died, James C. Bernard, one of the old citizens of Quincy died Monday A.M. Came to Quincy in 1834 and was in his 73rd year.

BERRY, GREEN - Mendon - Feb 9, 1882 Died, Green Berry an old citizen who lived 3-1/2 miles south of this village died Friday of typhoid pneumonia.

BEST, JOHN H. - Local - Apr 13, 1882 Died, John H. Best of Quincy Sunday age 69 years. Born Ireland. Came to America when about 20 years old and a few years later came to Quincy. In 1857 he moved to Clayton and back to Quincy in 1873. Leaves a wife and 7 grown children.

BIDAMON, MRS EMMA - Local - May 16, 1879 Died in Nauvoo, Mrs Emma Bidamon age 76 years. She was the first wife of Joseph Smith, the founder of Mormonism and the mother of Joseph Smith Jr, the head of the anti polygamy branch of the church. After the Morman's departed Nauvoo she stayed. Married in 1847 to Major L.C. Bidamon.

BILLINGS, JONATHAN - Obituary - May 15, 1874 Died at his residence near Clayton on the 5th inst, Mr Jonathan Billings, age 62 years. Born Conway, Mass. Came to Ill. 1833 first settled in Schuyler County. Served in Mexican War as a private in Col. Wm A. Richardson's Co. and took part in the notable battle of Buna Vista. Moved to Clayton vicinity 14 years ago. He leaves 4 sons and one daughter.

BINKERT, MRS THERESA - Local - May 25, 1882 Died, Mrs Theresa Binkert, mother of Anton Binkert, county treasurer, in Quincy Friday, age 80 years.

BIRDSALL, ABRAHAM - Local - Nov 21, 1879 Died, last Tuesday the young wife of Abraham Birdsall. Buried on Wednesday.   "Barry Adage"

BIRDSALL, MR P. - Newtown - Apr 18, 1879 Mr P. Birdsall formerly of Camp Point left for Colorado last week for his health. Gone 5 days and his infant daughter died.

BIRKS, JOHN - Killing of a Coal Miner at Colchester - Sep 28, 1877 Died, John Birks a native of Cornwall England was killed in a coal mine accident Tuesday of this week. Leaves a wife and 4 children. "Macomb Journal"

BISSELL, ISAAC - Killed by an Engine - Sep 7, 1877 Killed, ran over by the Wabash train, Isaac Bissell of Washington, Kansas appeared to be about 60 years old. Killed near Camp Point (1/2 miles east of town).

BLACK, JOHN H. - Hash - Mar 16, 1877 A daughter of John H. Black, county superintendent of schools, aged 2 years was buried Friday in Quincy.

BLAKE, JOHN - Hash - Jan 12, 1877 John Blake, for many years foreman of the Whig job rooms, died in St Louis Wednesday. He was one of the finest job printers in the west. He left a wife and 1 child.

BLAKESLEE, ACHSA
    SEE: GAY, VIXEN P.

BLICKHORNE, LOUIS - Liberty - Oct 17, 1879 A daughter of Louis Blickhorne was killed by lightning Sunday morning.

BLOCK, MRS MAGGIE - Golden - Jun 9, 1881 Died, Mrs Maggie Block, daughter of Herman Sartorus was buried today. Died Sunday. Married just 6 weeks to Ulfort Block.

BLUM, ROBERT - Local - Jul 14, 1881 A infant child of Robert Blum, Coatsburg died Tuesday.

BOBBITT, MRS BARBARA - Local - Apr 27, 1882 Died, Mrs Barbara Bobbitt age 86 years Tuesday A.M. Buried Wednesday A.M. at Pittsfield.

BOND, GEORGE - Death List - Sep 7, 1877 Old settlers death list since last meeting: George Bond, Quincy, age 62 years.

BOND, GEORGE - Hash - Aug 24, 1877 George Bond, business man of Quincy and director of the First National Bank died Tuesday.

BOND, GRANVILLE - Death List - Sep 7, 1877 Old settlers death list since last meeting: Granville Bond, Brown County, age 72 years.

BOON, JOHN T. - Neighborhood News - Dec 21, 1877 Died, John T. Boon was killed by a German named Jacob Horton near Kohoka, Missouri last week.

BOOTH, BENJAMIN - Sale of Lots - Feb 6, 1873 Sold at auction February 1st by P.A. Sawyer, Esq. Adm of the estate of Benjamin Booth deceased, subject to widows dower and homestead, family residence on lots 9, 10, 11, 12 block 1 Booth's addition sold to J.T. Baker for

$43.00. Lots 3 and 4 block 28 sold to J.T. Baker $1.00. Lot 1 block 1 Dehaven's addition to Jos. Cromwell for $1.00. 2 acres adjoining Jas Robertson's land sold to W.L. Oliver for $40.00.

BOOTH, GEORGE L. - Obituary - Feb 11, 1876 Died at his home in Clayton, Feb 6th, George L. Booth of consumption. Leaves a wife and child. He was a mason.

BOOTH, GEORGE L. - Supplement - Sep 1, 1876 Died since last years meeting of Old Settlers of Adams and Brown counties: George L. Booth of Clayton.

BOOTH, IDA - Died - Feb 20, 1873 Died on the 18th inst, of cerebro spinal meningitis, Ida, daughter of Wm Booth, of Gilmer, aged 1 year.

BORAN, MR - Liberty - Jul 1, 1880 Died, Mr Boran died at his sons, B. Boran's June 20th. He was one of the oldest persons in this township nearly 80 years old. Buried in Walker graveyard.

BORTTOFF, MR - La Prairie - Sep 20, 1878 Among the deaths this week: Mr Borttoff, a mile or so west of town.

BOSCOW, GEORGE
    SEE: JACKSON, STEPHEN

BOSTIC, WILLIAM E. - Local hash - Nov 8, 1878 William E. Bostic committed suicide at the home of his brother in law, Chas. W. Harris in Quincy, Monday.

BOSWELL, MISS
    SEE: WARREN, CALVIN A.

BOTTORFF, CHARLES EDWARD - Died - Apr 18, 1879 Died, April 18th, 1879 at the home of Geo. Beer, Charles Edward Bottorff, age 27 years 1 month 15 days.

BOTTORFF, JOHN - Golden - Feb 24, 1881 Died, John Bottorff last Monday eve. Leaves a wife and several children.

BOTTORFF, JOHN STRANGE - Died - Feb 24, 1881 Died at his home 2 miles SW of Golden in Camp Point twp, John Strange Bottorff, of consumption, age 51 years.

BOTTORFF, MRS THOMAS - Hash - Aug 25, 1876 Mrs Thomas

Bottorff of Keokuk Junction died Sunday of flux.

BOWEN, FANNY - Probate Notice - Mar 6, 1875 Fanny Bowen 19 April 1875 L.F. Walden, adm.

BOWERS, MRS ADA - Clayton - Oct 27, 1876 Mrs Ada Bowers, wife of Prof. Z.B. Bowers of Princeton died at the home of her father, Mr Wm B. Smith of this place last Thursday. Funeral held at the Christian Church on Saturday.

BOWLES, WILLIAM - Local - Nov 3, 1881 Died, William Bowles, son of the late Gus Bowles of Ellington. Committed suicide in Brooklyn last week, left a letter to his brother in Quincy.

BOWLES, WM - Killed by Lightning - May 11, 1877 Killed by lightning a boy named Wm Bowles age 14 years, a grandson of John Pence with whom he lived. Taken from the Barry Adage.

BOWLING, WM - Died - May 14, 1875 Died on the 7th inst William Bowling age 57 years. Remains taken to Quincy for burial in Woodland Cemetery.

BOWMAN, ANDERSON J. - Trustee's Sale - Dec 3, 1875 By virtue of a deed of trust made by Anderson J. Bowman and Ellen M. Bowman his wife to David Wright as trustee bearing the date of November 1874 in Box 14 of mortgaged at page 585. Will sell Monday January 3rd, 1876 David Wright Camp Point, Ill. December 1st.

BOWMAN, JOSEPH - Public Sales - Feb 16, 1877 J.A. Hendrix, adm of the estate of Joseph Bowman, deceased will sell personal effects of the estate of deceased 3 miles south of Bowen March 6th.

BOWMAN, JOSEPH - Probate Notice - Feb 16, 1877 Joseph Bowman 3rd Monday of April J.A. Hendrix, adm

BOYER, MRS PROF.
    SEE: COOK, D.A.
    SEE: COOKE, MRS

BOYLE, HENRY - Local - Feb 5, 1880 Henry Boyle, alias John Cox was arraigned last week in Warren Co. on charge of murder of Wm P. Ketchum and plead guilty.

BOYLE, MRS JOHN - Local - Dec 12, 1879 A typographical

error last week made the notice of the death of Mrs John Boyle read December instead of November.

BOYLE, MRS JOHN – Personal – Dec 5, 1879 Mrs S.E. Smart, St Louis and Mrs J.H. Garrison arrived on Sunday A.M. to attend the funeral of their sister, Mrs John Boyle. Returned home Tuesday.

BOYLE, MRS JOHN – Personal – Dec 5, 1879 Silas Garrett of DeSota, Iowa arrived Sunday to attend the funeral of Mrs Boyle.

BOYLE, MRS SUSAN – Died – Dec 5, 1879 Died, <u>December 29th</u>, 1879 at her home near Camp Point, Mrs Susan Boyle, wife of John Boyle age 39 years 1 month. Daughter of the late Peter B. Garrett. Leaves 5 small children and her husband. Services Sunday at 11 A.M. at Christian Church. Buried Pleasant View Cemetery where other members of the family have been buried.

BRADLEY, MRS – Local – Jan 9, 1880 Mrs Bradley of Quincy committed suicide Tuesday, had 2 children.

BRADLEY, MISS CLARINDA – Liberty – Mar 16, 1882 Died, Miss Clarinda Bradley on the 9th. Born October 13, 1815 in New London, Conn.

BRADY, JAMES – Obituary – Mar 10, 1881 Died, James Brady Esq. died at the parsonage in Paloma, Adams County Illinois March 8, 1881, father of Mrs T.J. Bryant. Born Leesburg London County Virginia October 28, 1801. Went to Missouri in 1837. Was 1st mayor of Hannibal.

BRAY, JULIA
    SEE: YOUNG, WM

BRAY, ROBINSON & JOSEPHINE – Mendon – Feb 26, 1880 An infant son of Robinson and Josephine Bray died last Friday.

BRAY, THOMAS W. – Adm Sale of Real Estate – Apr 20, 1882 Thomas W. Bray, deceased vs petitioner and Lucinda W. Bray, widow, defendant. Howard Ogle, adm.

BRAY, THOMAS W. – Probate Notice – May 9, 1879 Thomas W. Bray 3rd Monday of June 1879 Howard Ogle adm with will annexed.

BREWER, DOW – Suicide – Sep 4, 1874 Dow Brewer a very

eccentric plasterer, well known in this vicinity hung himself Saturday eve at Samuel Witt's in Big Neck. He was nearly 65 years old.

BREWER, MRS E. - Hash - Jun 19, 1873 Mrs E. Brewer has received notice that her family are heirs to a large property in New York City.

BRIMSON, HENRY - Obituary - Apr 7, 1881 Died, Henry Brimson an old resident of Kingston died March 21st.

BRISTOL, GEO. W. - Local - May 4, 1882 Geo. V. Bristol, of Quincy dropped dead last Wednesday eve. His family lives in Massachusetts. Remains taken to Massachusetts for burial.

BROADY, MRS - Liberty - Nov 14, 1879 Died, Mrs Broady died Sunday. Buried Monday the same day her brother, Mr Wigle of Clayton was brought here for burial. She leaves a large family.

BROADY, JOHN C. - Liberty - Apr 5, 1878 Died, Mr John C. Broady Sr. at his home near Liberty March 27th of heart disease. Born Kentucky in 1812. Married in 1836 to Miss Wigle, near Liberty and resided there since. Was a good husband and father.

BROCKER, WESLEY - Neighborhood News - Oct 18, 1878 A child of Wesley Brocker living north of Fairburg was kicked to death by a horse Thursday.

BROCKMAN, J.R. - Local - oct 31, 1879 Death of J.R. Brockman, an old resident of Mt Sterling occurred a few days ago.

BROOKER, THOMAS - Local - Oct 10, 1879 Thomas Brooker, a well known local politician in Quincy died Saturday afternoon.

BROOKS, MR - La Prairie - May 24, 1878 Died, Mr Brooks, U.S. Mail carrier between here and Elm Grove (was quite old).

BROOKS, WILLIAM - Died - Oct 17, 1879 Died, October 9 at his home in Payson, William Brooks in his 20th year. Leaves parents, 3 brothers and 2 sisters.

BROWN, MRS
    SEE: WALKER, MR

BROWN, MRS - Local Hash - Dec 20, 1878 A death certificate was filed with the county clerk last week by Dr W.M. Landon, setting forth that Mrs Brown of Burton, age 115 years, died December 6th. She was a native of Indiana and had resided in this county 35 years. Cause of death was old age.

BROWN, MR AND MRS - La Prairie - Jan 13, 1881 Mr and Mrs Brown's daughter, Adie's, funeral was Friday. This leaves them only 2 daughters.

BROWN, CHARLES N. - Hash - Jun 16, 1876 Charles N. Brown committed suicide in Quincy, Tuesday, by taking morphine.

BROWN, DOLLIE
    SEE: ANDREWS, MRS ADA

BROWN, MRS JOSIAH - Died from Neglect - Jul 16, 1875 last Sunday morn Mrs Josiah Brown was delivered, a daughter at the home of her mother's, Mrs Mary Omer in Clayton township, where she had been living since her marriage in April. The child was born at full term, alive, on Sunday July 11th and died from want of care and apparent willful neglect. Alexander Brown, coroner of Adams County.

BROWN, NETTIE - Hash - Sep 18, 1874 Miss Nettie Brown of Warsaw age 13 attempted to hasten a fire by pouring coal oil upon it. The can exploded and enveloped her in flames. Her clothes were all burned from her body. She died in horrible agony at 1 o'clock next morning.

BROWN, PAUL - State News - Aug 26, 1880 Paul, son of Hon. C.C. Brown of Springfield died Sunday.

BROWN, MRS ROBERT - Clayton - Feb 26, 1875 Died, the wife of Mr Robert Brown of our city died very suddenly on Wednesday eve February 17th. Services at the ME church on last Friday. Leaves husband and children.

BROWN, DR W.J. - Died - Nov 27, 1873 Died at Mendon, in this county on the morning of the 1st, Dr W.J. Brown aged 62 years and 2 months.

BROWN, WILLIAM
    SEE: ANDREWS, MRS ADA

BROWN, WM - Death of Wm Brown - Jul 15, 1880 Died, Wm

Brown Sr. of this city while on his way to Scotland to visit the home of his youth. Left to visit Paisley, Scotland went from New York in the Georgia, died before arrival in Scotland on the 8th inst. Remains taken to Paisley for burial. Was 74 years old and a native of Scotland. Came to this country as a young man and lived Quincy since 1840 or 41. "Herald 18th"

BROWN, WM
    SEE: SHERRICK, MRS DARRAH

BROWNELL, MRS
    SEE: LANOIX, DR

BROWNING, ASA M. - Riceville - Dec 22, 1881   Died, Asa M. Browning at the home of his brother, Jef, November 30th from consumption. Leaves 2 children.

BROWNING, O.H. - Death of O.H. Browning - Aug 18, 1881   Died, Hon. Orville H. Browning at his home in Quincy Wednesday August 10th, 75 years old. Born Kentucky, educated there. Came to Illinois in 1831 and settled in Quincy. Leaves a wife and adopted daughter, Mrs O. Skinner, an adopted son died in the army. Buried Woodland Cemetery on Saturday.

BRYANT, JOHN H. - Died - May 22, 1873   Died in Chicago on the 14th inst of consumption, John H. Bryant formerly of this place. His remains were brought to Camp Point and interred Friday the 16th.

BRYANT, JOSEPHINE - Death of Josephine Bryant - Jul 6, 1882   Died, Mrs Josephine Bryant, June 22nd, 68 years old. Born Kentucky in 1814 stayed there until 1842 when with her husband Moses O. Bryant came to Illinois and located at Clayton. In 1856 they came to Camp Point. Had 11 children, 4 of whom and her husband preceded her in death. Buried Clayton Cemetery beside her husband.

BRYANT, MRS T.J.
    SEE: BRADY, JAMES

BUCK, MR - Columbus - Dec 15, 1881   Died, a child of Mr Buck last Thursday of scarlet fever.

BUCKHEIT, CHRISTIAN - Neighborhood News - Oct 19, 1877   Fatal accident on the Louisiana division of the C.B. & Q. Railroad. Christian Buckheit who lived between Washington and Jefferson on the 6th Street in Quincy was killed. He was deaf. "Herald"

BUCKINGHAM, MRS GILPIN - Burton - Nov 23, 1882 Died - News received last Tuesday noon of the death of Mrs Gilpin Buckingham of Humbolt, Kansas requesting the members of the family living here to come at once. One of the daughters left on the evening train.

BUCKLEY, EDWARD H. - Notice of Trustee's Sale - May 25, 1877 Recorded March 16th, 1875 at pages 157 et. Seq. In book 13 of mortgages, Adams County.

BUCKLEY, GEO. H. - Hash - Nov 3, 1876 Geo. H. Buckley, son of E.H. Buckley of Quincy died in that city of consumption last Saturday.

BUDDEE, LOUIS - Local - Aug 4, 1881 Louis Buddee, an old merchant of Quincy died in Colorado Sunday.

BUFFINGTON, JACOB - Obituary - Mar 3, 1881 Died, Jacob Buffington died, one of the old residents of this township, about 70 years old. Died on the 4th inst. Buried Kingston Cemetery.

BUFFINGTON, JAMES - Obituary - Apr 7, 1881 Died, March 27th, James Buffington, age 20 years. Seventh of that family to die of consumption in 2 years.

BUMP, WM - Keokuk Junction - Jul 22, 1880 Died, one of Wm Bump's children died last week.

BURBRIDGE, W.R. - Clippings - May 22, 1873 The only son of W.R. Burbridge, of Burnside, Hancock County a bright boy 7 years old while playing with a kite last Wednesday fell into a kettle of boiling lye. Died a few hours later.

BURK, JESSE & ELIZABETH A. - Sale - May 12, 1876 Trustee Sale of Real Estate of Jesse Burk and Elizabeth A. Burk his wife, October 26th. Dated Camp Point May 1st Wm Howell, trustee   Geo. Simmons, attorney

BURKE, FLEMING - Death List - Feb 19, 1875 Death of old settlers during last week in Adams County: Fleming Burke of North East.

BURKE, SARAH - Died - Jul 28, 1881 Died at her home in North East township near Elm Grove Church, Adams County Illinois Mrs Sarah Burke, widow of the late Fleming

Burke on July 6, 1881 in her 70th year. Sarah Horney was born in North Carolina Feb 1, 1812. Came with parents to Schuyler County in 1828. Married Mr Burke Dec 12, 1832. Leaves 5 children, 3 sons and 2 daughters.

BURNETT, JOHN - Exchange Notes - Jan 10, 1879 Mr John Burnett who resided just east of Roodhouse, Illinois and his wife both died of lung fever leaving a 16 year old son, had just inherited money from a aunt in Ohio.

BURNS, JOHN - Died - Jul 31, 1874 Died, Capt. John Burns, father of Maj. George Burns and one of Quincy's oldest citizens died at his residence at 20 minutes past 9 Wednesday eve.

BURNS, WILLIE - Beverly - Jul 20, 1882 On Friday the 9th Willie Burns died, age 4 months of cholera infantum.

BUSHNELL, NEHEMIAH - Obituary - Feb 6, 1873 Died January 31st at his residence in Quincy, Hon. Nehemiah Bushnell of erysiphilas, 50 years old. Native of Connecticut and graduated from Yale College in 1835 and Law Department of Harvard University in 1837. Came west same year and located in Quincy. Was formerly a law partner of hon. O.H. Browning.

BUSKIRK, Mrs Amy - Local - Feb 9, 1882 Died, Mrs Amy Buskirk of Liberty township who came to this county in 1834. Died on the 2nd inst of dropsy, age 78 years.

BUTLER, NOAH B. - Died - Sep 29, 1876 Died at his home in La Harpe, Ill. on the 17th inst of congestion of the lungs and brain, Dr Noah B. Butler age 51 years. He was a former citizen of Adams County and son of Hezekiah Butler of Columbus and a brother of Mrs Wm Groom. He was a prominent doctor and citizen of La Harpe.

BUTLER, S.C.
    SEE: FEREE, MRS JANE

BUTTS, A.W.
    SEE: AKERS, MRS JOHN W.

BUTTS, M.R. - Hash - Nov 26, 1875 M.R. Butts, formerly of Liberty and later an attorney in Quincy died at his residence in Burlingame, Kansas last week of consumption. His remains arrived at Liberty Tuesday where they will be buried.

BUTTS, MICHAEL R. - Obituary - Dec 10, 1875   Michael R. Butts belonged to Liberty Lodge #380 A.F. and A.M. Leaves a wife.

BUTZ, HENRY - Liberty - Mar 14, 1879   Died, Mrs Henry Butz.

BUTZ, MRS HENRY - Livingston - Mar 14, 1879   Died, Mrs Henry Butz, of Liberty died last Saturday in her 36th year. Born south west of Livingston. Nee Harriet Foster. Leaves her parents.

BUTZ, JOHN - Liberty - Jul 11, 1879   Mr and Mrs John Butz mourn the loss of their little son, who died with cholera infantum on the 26th ult.

BYINGTON, CHARLIE - Obituary - Sep 2, 1880   Died, Charlie, 3 year old son of Mr and Mrs Byington on Saturday the 21st.

BYLER, JOHN - Death List - Feb 19, 1875   Old settlers death list during last week in Adams Co.: John Byler of Honey Creek.

BYLER, JOHN - Sale - Apr 1, 1880   Estate of John Byler, deceased property to be sold by adm of John Byler estate, 3rd Monday of April, 1880   John Byler and Jas. M. White Executor's.

CADOGAN, JACOB - Fowler Fancies - May 25, 1877   Died, at his home at Cliola Monday morn, Mr Jacob Cadogan from asthma and pneumonia. Leaves widow and children.
Buried in Quincy by Odd Fellows of Fowler. Resident of Adams County for 40 years. Parents moved here from Pennsylvania in 1837. He was 55 years old. Services by Rev Haff.

CADOGAN, JACOB - Fowler - May 25, 1877   Died, Jacob Cadogan at his home near Cliola on Monday A.M. at 7 (May 14th), 56 years old. Was old pioneer of Adams County. Came here in 1836. Leaves a wife and 7 children. Buried Woodland Cemetery near Quincy.

CADOGAN, JOHN P.
    SEE: MOORE, JOHN S.

CADWALLADER, SAM - Shooting - Sep 11, 1874   Sam Cadwallader of Stone's Prairie, Adams County shot James Winget in the head causing death in a short time on

Wednesday 2nd inst.

CAMPBELL, A.B. - Mendon - Mar 23, 1882 Funeral of Rev. A.B. Campbell at the Congregational Church last Thursday by Rev Walker of Payson.

CAMPBELL, A.B. - Mendon - Mar 9, 1882 Died, Rev A.B. Campbell at Dallas City.

CAMPBELL, JAMES
    SEE: OMER, JACOB

CANNELL, MRS ROBERT - Mendon - Nov 10, 1881 Died, the wife of Robert Cannell who lived a few miles NW of this village, yesterday.

CARAHAN, P.J. - Hash - Apr 21, 1876 P.J. Carahan from the neighborhood of Macomb accidently shot himself near Booth's in Gilmer township last Thursday. He died Friday. Leaves a wife and several small children. Body returned to Macomb. He was on his way to Kansas.

CARD, BENJ. M. - Death List - Sep 7, 1877 Old settlers death list since last meeting: Benj. M. Card, Mendon, age 77 years.

CARLIN, FLORENCE E. - Died - Jul 20, 1882 Died, July 13th, Florence E., infant daughter of William and Matilda Carlin, age 4 months 17 days.

CARLIN, JOSIAH - Livingston - Jul 26, 1878 Mr and Mrs Thompson attended the funeral of Josiah Carlin near Camp Point yesterday.

CARLIN, WILLIAM - Local - Nov 30, 1882 Died, William Carlin's babe. Was buried at Hebron Cemetery on Saturday.

CARNEY, JOHN - Killed - Jan 8, 1875 A man named John Carney supposed under the influence of liquor was killed while riding on a hand car on the T.W. and W. Railroad near Keokuk Junction.

CARPENTER, ARMENIA P. - Died - May 5, 1876 Died, in Henry County Missouri April 10, 1876, Armenia P. wife of Edward Carpenter in her 57th year.

CARTER, MARTIN - Local - Jul 4, 1879 Martin Carter, formerly of this county was killed by the falling in of a well he was digging in Reno County Kansas May 9th.

CARTER, THOMAS - Hash - Jun 22, 1877 Died, Thomas Carter, the veteran miller of the Eagle Mills, Quincy died Monday. Buried by Masonic frat. Wednesday.

CARTER, THOMAS - Death List - Sep 7, 1877 Old settlers death list since last meeting: Thomas Carter, Quincy age 73 years.

CASEY, ROBERT - Local - Jun 23, 1881 Died, Robert Casey was killed at Mt Sterling when a smoke house fell in on him.

CASTLE, MARY E. - Died - Dec 28, 1877 Died on the 24th inst, of consumption, Mary E., wife of William H. Castle, age 26 years.

CASTLE, E.G. - Local - Sep 23, 1880 Died-Dr E.G. Castle of Quincy died Monday. Came to Quincy in 1851 and in 1867 was sent to England his native country as a consulor agent for 2 years. Was 66 years old.

CASTLE, RIAL - Died - May 1, 1873 Died on the 28th inst of inflammation of the lungs, Rial Castle, age 39 years. He was a resident of Camp Point and vicinity for a great number of years. Leaves a wife and 6 children almost destitute. Being an Odd Fellow he was buried with all the honors of the order. (The age in this article was hard to read it might have said 89 years)

CASTLE, TIMOTHY H. - Local - Jun 24, 1880 Died, Timothy H. Castle of Quincy, died Wednesday age 66 years. Born in Vermont and came to Illinois in 18 5 (this is either 25 or 35) settling in Columbus where he stayed until 1859.

CATE, WALTER - Died - Sep 21, 1882 Died near Columbus, Illinois September 8th, Walter, infant son of Walter and Jane Cate age 2 months 16 days. Funeral at the family home on Saturday the 9th inst. Services by Rev A.M. Danely.

CATES, MRS PATIENCE - Died - Nov 16, 1882 Died at Perryville, Arkansas November 10th, Mrs Patience Cates, daughter of Samuel Curless, age 37 years.

CECIL, WILFRED - Hash - Feb 22, 1878 Wilfred Cecil, an old resident of Big neck died February 10th, age 90 years. Father of 15 children, 96 grandchildren and 74 great grandchildren.

CHAMBERLAIN, ROSALIE - Died - Jul 7, 1881 Died, June 26th near Canton, Missouri Rosalie, infant daughter of John T. and Cora A. Chamberlain age 7 months 14 days.

CHANDLER, CHARLES - Exchange Notes - Jan 3, 1878 Charles Chandler, a citizen of Macomb died a few days ago at San Diego, Calif. Was one of the oldest and wealthy citizens of the county.

CHAPMAN, CYNTHIA
    SEE: MORRISON, H.H.

CHARLES, CLARK - Personal - May 8, 1874 Clark Charles formerly cashier of the Union Bank Quimby, died of consumption Monday.

CHASE, CHAS. - Death List - Sep 7, 1877 Old settlers death list since last meeting: Chas. Chase, Ellington, age 73 years.

CHASE, LETTIE
    SEE: POWELL, MRS J.S.

CHASE, SUSAN - Fowler - Apr 21, 1881 Died, April 10th at her home near Fowler, Mrs Susan Chase. Leaves 2 sons.

CHASE, W.
    SEE: POWELL, MRS J.S.

CHATTEN, IDA
    SEE: WHITE, MRS FRANK

CHATTEN, WILLIAM - Local - May 20 1880 William Chatten of Quincy died last week and was buried Sunday. He was the oldest son of the late B.I. Chatten and a brother of Mrs Z.S. Pratt.

CHILDERS, ROBERT - Newtown - Apr 25, 1879 Robert Childers, living west of this place died and was buried at Burton last week.

CHILDS, DANIEL T. - Died - Apr 8, 1880 Died, <u>April 30</u>, 1880 at his home in Camp Point townhsip, Daniel T. Childs in his 68th year. Native of Rhode Island. Came to Illinois in 1855 and settled in Camp Point. Funeral at Christian Church by Elder Wm Stewart.

CHILDS, GRACIE - Died - Sep 20, 1878 Died on the 5th inst, Gracie, daughter of C.L. and Josephine Childs, age 2 years.

CHILDS, MR AND MRS H.W. - Local - Aug 18, 1881 Died, the babe of Mr and Mrs H.W. Childs Monday. Buried Tuesday.

CHILDS, HARVEY W. - Local Hash - Nov 15, 1878 A son of Harvey W. Childs aged 1 year died last Thursday night.

CHILDS, WILLIAM O. - Death in a Well - Sep 1, 1881 Died, William O. Childs of this place while digging a well on the farm of James T. DeHaven about 3 miles NW of town. Leaves a wife and 3 children. 34 years old.

CHILDS, WILLIAM THOMAS - Died - Dec 21, 1877 Died, William Thomas, son of Hervey W. and Lydia Childs on the 15th inst., age 10 years 8 months 27 days.

CHITTENDEN, JOHN - Neighborhood News - Dec 28, 1877 John Chittenden has fallen heir to an estate in England, thru the death of an aunt near London. "Whig"

CHOATE, MRS WM - La Prairie - Oct 27, 1876 Mrs John Beckett and Mrs Wm Choate, both well known and highly respected have died within the last 2 weeks.

CHRISTIAN, JACKSON
    SEE: ACKLEY, HENRY

CHRISTIAN, JOHN
    SEE: ACKLEY, HENRY

CHRISTIE, J.B.
    SEE: STONE, MRS

CHURCHILL, CHESTER R. - Neighborhood News - Jul 19, 1878 Chester R. Churchill, of Barry died at the insane hospital, Jacksonville a week ago Friday. Was a prominent citizen of Pike County.

CLAIR, MR - Local - Jul 18, 1879 Clair, the man stabbed on the train on the 4th died at his home near Mendon last Friday.

CLAIR, ELIJAH
    SEE: MCCORMICK, MICHAEL

CLARE, ELIJAH - Whiskey & Blood - Jul 11, 1879 Mike McCormick and Elijah Clare from the vicinity of Mendon got into a fight on the train near Ursa on the 4th. McCormick stabbed Clare 3 times.

CLARE, ELIJAH - Mendon - Jul 18, 1879 Elijah Clare, who was stabbed by Mike McCormick on the 4th died Saturday A.M. McCormick held in jail for willful murder.

CLARK, ANN M. - Death of Mrs E.B. Curtis - May 2, 1879 Died at her home in Camp Point on the 28th inst Mrs Ann M. Clark, wife of E.B. Curtis. Born in Wiloughby, Ohio in 1818. After her first marriage she moved to Lake County Illinois and on November 11, 1856 she married E.B. Curtis and lived in Camp Point.

CLARK, EUGENE - Neighborhood News - Feb 8, 1878 Eugene Clark, for many years connected with wholesale drug house of Sommer, Lynds and Company, Quincy died at the Furlong House last week.

CLARK, FREDDIE - Mendon - Jan 17, 1879 Freddie Clark, a son of Mr John Clark, engineer at the Pearl Mills, died on Saturday, age 5 years.

CLARK, MRS MARY ELLA - Local - Oct 12, 1882 Died, Mrs Mary Ella Clark nee McClintock, in Schuyler County, September 28th in her 28th year. Was daughter of James McClintock who formerly lived on the Wyle farm north of town.

CLARK, PHEBE - Newtown - Sep 26, 1879 Died-Phebe Clark, wife of John Clark living 1 mile north of town died at her home last Thursday . Buried at Burton. Leaves a husband.

CLARK, S.P. - Local - Oct 5, 1882 Died, S.P. Clark from congestion of the brain in the hospital.

CLAYTON, BERTHA - Mendon - Nov 28, 1879 Died Miss Bertha Clayton. Remains taken to Bowen for burial (her old home).

CLING, ADAM - Fowler - Feb 2, 1877 Mr Adam Cling Sr. a worthy citizen and the wife of Adam Cling Jr. died at the same residence, the former died at 6 P.M. the latter at 12 midnight. Both funerals at the same time. Both members of the German Methodist Church.

CLINGINGINGSMITH, SOL - Burton - Jan 9, 1880 Died, Sol Clingingingsmith, an old resident of the vicinity died on December 26th, about 60 years old.

CLINTON, STEPHEN P. - Supplement - Sep 1, 1876 Died since last years meeting of Old Settlers of Adams and Brown County: Stephen P. Clinton of Concord.

CLOSE, MR - Local - Aug 4, 1881 A man named Close, a brakeman on the C.B. & Q. Railroad was killed in a train accident between St Augustine and Avon Saturday A.M. Lived in Kewanee and his body returned there to relatives.

COATS, HARLOW - La Prairie - Feb 23, 1882 Died in La Prairie February 11th Harlow Coats, age 3 years, son of Rev S.K. Coats.

COATS, WILLIAM A. - Local - Nov 10, 1881 Died, William A. Coats of Liberty township, Tuesday.

COATS, WILLIAM A. - Tribute of Respect - Nov 17, 1881 Liberty Lodge #380 AF & AM to William A. Coats, deceased.

COATS, WILLIAM A. - Probate Notice - Dec 15, 1881 William A. Coats   1st Monday of February 1882 (6th)   Wm A. Coats, Jr. Executor

COBER, MRS H.H.
    SEE: CRAWFORD, MRS ABIGAL S.

COBER, MRS J.H.
    SEE: CRAWFORD, MRS ABIGAL S.

COBURN, A.S. - Hash - Aug 17, 1877 Died A.S. Coburn, a prominent business man of Quincy died Saturday.

COFFEY, WM
    SEE: NORRIS, MRS

COLEMAN, ADDA - Neighborhood News - Aug 23, 1878 La Crosse August 12th - Miss Adda Coleman died of burns received when she was starting a fire. About 22 years old. Buried in Pilot Grove Cemetery. "Cor. Carthage Republican"

COLLINS, FREDERICK - Obituary - Feb 22, 1878 Died, Frederick Collins an old citizen of Quincy at his home in Quincy on the 15th inst., 74 years old. Born Litchfield, Connecticut in 1804. Settled in Columbus about 1837. Went to Quincy in 1850. Married Miss Mary Allen, sister of the late Dr Allen of Mt Sterling who survives him. Leaves 5 children: Mrs A.L. Harrington of Camp Point, Mrs J.H. Stewart of Quincy, Mrs C.W. Keyes of Quincy, Miss Louisa Collins of Quincy and George Collins of Hannibal, Missouri.

COLLINS, FREDERICK G. - Recent Deaths - Nov 21, 1879 Frederick G. Collins of Liberty died Sunday, former resident of Quincy an a nephew of the late Frederick Collins, age 81 years.

COLLINS, HENRY - Legal Notes - Jan 1, 1875 Chancery-Henry Collins in his own right and as executor of Michael Collins vs. Frederick O. Collins, et al bill for relief.

COLLINS, MORRIS - Liberty - Feb 24, 1881 Died, Morris Collins buried his babe on Sunday.

COLLISTER, JOSEPH - Hash - May 1, 1873 Joseph Collister was drowned in back waters of the Illinois River near Frederick on Sunday the 20th inst.

COLTON, D.D. - Neighborhood News - Oct 18, 1878 General D.D. Colton of San Francisco who died on Wednesday night was a former resident of Galesburg and a relative of the Colton family of that city. He was one of the richest men in California.

COMER, JOHN - News Shortened - Oct 18, 1878 John Comer of Macomb a brakeman on the CB & Q railroad beat his girls brother and killed him, hurt her mother. He was arrested.

COMSTOCK, ENOCH - Personal - Jul 16, 1875 Enoch Comstock, one of the oldest and most prominent business men of Quincy died Tuesday P.M. He was the founder of the extensive stoneworks bearing his name.

CONNER, DANIEL H.
    SEE: RICHARDS, JAS.

CONOVER, JOHN - Local - Jul 14, 1881 Died-John Conover, attorney at Quincy died Sunday of consumption.

COOK, CELESTIA A. - Probate Notice - Mar 29, 1878

Celestia A. Cook, deceased 3rd Monday of May 1878
David Mack, executor.

COOK, CLANDIUS
    SEE: ALLEN, MRS MARY E.

COOK, D.A. - Mendon - Jan 13, 1881 Died, D.A. Cook died Wednesday A.M. almost 80 years old. Lived Mendon 45 years. Leaves a wife of more than 50 year and one son D.B. Cooke of our village and 2 daughters, Mrs C.H. Hoffman and Mrs Prof. Boyer. Mrs Cook is a sister of Joel and Abraham Benton.

COOK, ELIZABETH
    SEE: ALLEN, MRS MARY E.

COOK, V. - Liberty - Apr 14, 1881 Died, Mrs V. Cook at her residence ½ mile east of Liberty, Thursday the 7th ult.

COOKE, MRS - Mendon - Aug 11, 1881 Died, Mrs Cooke at 5 A.M. Monday in her 76th year. She was a sister of Abraham and Joel Benton and was one of the first settlers of Mendon. Husband died last winter. Leaves 3 children: Mrs C.H. Hoffman, D.B. Cooke and Mrs Prof Boyer.

COOKE, D.B.
    SEE: COOK, D.A.

COON, ELISHA - Exchange News - Nov 29, 1878 "Augusta Herald" Elisha Coon who resides in the NW part of town met instant death Wednesday. First accident in this place since a team ran away with Jacob Mickle about 3 years ago. Mr Coon leaves a wife and daughter.

COOPER, JOHN D. - State News - Feb 12, 1880 John D. Cooper, one of Morgan Counties oldest citizens died at Chapin on the 5th.

CORKINS, P.G.
    SEE: CRAIG, C.H.

CORLEY, WM H. - Hash - Mar 6, 1875 Wm H. Corley, Supt. of the Quincy Gas Works died last week.

CORNELIUS, ALBERT
    SEE: HUTMACHER, FRANK

CORRELL, E.D. - Sales - Feb 25, 1876 Public sale at the residence of the late Edward Sharp, 5 miles SW of Clayton today and E.D. Correll 3-1/2 miles NE of this place March 11th James T. Omer 2-1/2 miles SE next Monday.

COUGHLIN, WILLIAM - Local - Aug 11, 1881 Killed, William Coughlin, a switchman in the CB & Q yards at Quincy was crushed to death last week while coupling cars.

COUNCILMAN, MARY - Local - Nov 10, 1881 Died, Miss Mary Councilman died in Bushnell recently, age 100 years 8 months 4 days.

COUREY, KATE
    SEE: ROBERTSON, JOHN B.

COX, JOHN
    SEE: BOYLE, HENRY

CRABB, WM - Exchange Notes - Mar 7, 1879 Wm Crabb of Macomb has lost 3 children in the past few days with scarlet fever.

CRAFTON, WM T.
    SEE: MANARD, WM G.

CRAIG, MRS AGNES - Local - Aug 22, 1879 Died, Mrs Agnes Craig of Liberty, died last week, age 65 years.

CRAIG, C.H. - Liberty - Sep 27, 1878 Mr C.H. Craig of Clayton died of typhoid pneumonia last Tuesday eve at the home of his father in law, Dr P.G. Corkins in Liberty. Services by Rev Lierle on Wednesday. Leaves a wife and parents.

CRAIG, C.H. - Hash - Sep 20, 1878 C.H. Craig, of the banking house of Montgomery and Craig, Clayton died Tuesday eve.

CRAIG, JOHN - Neighborhood News - Aug 17, 1877 John Craig who lives about 3 miles from Liberty, this county, was badly injured when his team ran away. It is thought he will not recover.

CRAIG, MRS JOHN - Liberty - Aug 22, 1879 Died, Mrs John Craig, a sister of Mrs H.C. Craig of Clayton died on the evening of the 16th. Leaves a large family all of which

are grown up. Services by Rev Cornelius of Kingston.
Buried in Boyer graveyard where Mr John Craig was buried
2 years ago on the 28th of this month.

CRANE, REV J.L. - Death's Doing's - Aug 1, 1879 Died,
Rev J.L. Crane of Shelbyville, Illinois died Tuesday
July 29th at his home, 58 years old.

CRANK, MRS ELIZA - Mendon - Feb 3, 1881 Died, Mrs Eliza
Crank, widow of the late Jesse Crank of this township
died of pneumonia last Thursday eve age 70 years.

CRANK, MRS JAMES - Mendon - Jul 28, 1881 Died, Mrs
James Crank last week. Lived some 4 miles north of
Mendon.

CRAVER, MISS
         SEE: HARRIS, JAMES M.R.

CRAWFORD, MRS ABIGAL S. - Obituary - May 10, 1878 Mrs
Abigal S. Crawford, wife of Wm Crawford and sister of Wm
Marsh Esq., Quincy, died at her home on N. 5th Street,
Thursday eve at 7. Born in Moravia, New York November
20, 1815. Came to Illinois with her husband in 1858,
resident of Quincy nearly 10 years. Leaves a husband,
and 4 children: Mrs H.H. Cober, Mrs J.H. Cober, Henry
and George Crawford all of Quincy.

CRAWFORD, JAMES M. - Neighborhood News - Jan 18, 1878
Died, James M. Crawford one of the old settlers of Adams
County died at Abingdon, Friday on the 11th inst. Lived
in Ursa 40 years. Buried in Ursa. Sister is Mrs
Cordelia Wilks of this place.

CRAWFORD, JOHN
         SEE: HEDGES, MRS M.J.

CRAWFORD, THOMAS - Hash - Apr 30, 1875 Died, Thomas
Crawford recently died in Hancock County, age 63 years.
Born in Nicholas County Kentucky. Came to Illinois with
his father in 1832, stayed briefly in Quincy and then to
Woodville, Adams County and then on to Hancock on a
tract of government land in Walker township.

CRESSWELL, MRS WM
         SEE: JUDY, PARIS T.

CRIPPIN, MRS
         SEE: WILKES, DANIEL

CROMWELL, CHARLIE - Obituary - Feb 12, 1875 Died, January 19th Charlie, age 18 months 12 days, infant son of Joseph and E.J. Cromwell.

CROMWELL, CHARLIE R. - Died - Jan 22, 1875 Died, on the 18th inst, of scarlet fever Charlie R., son of Joseph and Elizabeth J. Cromwell, age 18 months 12 days.

CROMWELL, HATTIE - Local - Jan 19, 1882 Died, Miss Hattie Cromwell, daughter of Joseph Cromwell of La Prairie about 15 years old last week. Buried here Friday.

CROMWELL, HETTIE - In Memoriam - Jan 26, 1882 Died, in La Prairie January 14th, Hettie Cromwell in her 15th year.

CROMWELL, MARY
    SEE: WALLACE, ALLEN

CROMWELL, MATTIE - Died - Jan 19, 1882 Died in La Prairie, Illinois January 11th Mattie, daughter of Mr and Mrs Joseph Cromwell age 14 years 5 months 18 days.

CROSBY, GEO. L. - Neighborhood News - Jul 6, 1877 Geo. L. Crosby, his wife and 2 children, were drowned at Hannibal Wednesday afternoon when a bridge broke and their buggy went in a creek. All bodies recovered.

CROSBY, MATTIE - Neighborhood News - Jul 13, 1877 The body of Mattie Crosby, who was drowned at Hannibal last week has not been found.

CROSS, CHARLES - Local - Aug 4, 1881 Killed - Charles Cross, 11 years old, was killed in Quincy Monday by a 12 year old boy named George Love.

CROSS, HARRY- Local - Apr 1, 1880 Harry Cross of Kinderhook was killed last week while working with a stump puller used to tighten wire fence.

CUNNINGHAM, GEORGE - Beverly - Jun 8, 1882 James Sykes Sr. and wife are staying at Barry while he is settling the estate of the late George Cunningham of that place.

CUPP, H.C. - Local - Feb 2, 1882 Died, 4 year old daughter of Mr and Mrs H.C. Cupp last week.

CURL, CHARITY - Died - Feb 28, 1879 Died on Sunday

February 23rd Charity Curl, widow of Elder John B. Curl, age 86 years.

CURLESS, FREDDIE - Local - Aug 17, 1882   Died, Little Freddie Curless Sunday night of typhoid fever.

CURLESS, SAMUEL
    SEE: CATES, MRS PATIENCE
    SEE: SWAIN, MRS RACHEL

CURLESS, SARAH - Died - Sep 30, 1880   Died on the 22nd, Sarah, wife of Samuel Curless, age 67 years.

CURLESS, SARAH - Trustee's Sale - Jun 8, 1877   Sarah Curless, October 13, 1873 deed dated, recorded in Adams County Book 18 of mortgages page 16   Geo. W. Cyrus trustee.

CURRY, A.A. - Hash - May 19, 1876   A.A. Curry, an old citizen of Mt Sterling died on the 13th inst.

CURRY, ANNIE M. - Obituary - Feb 5, 1875   Died, January 30th of congestion of the lungs, Annie M. daughter of Richard S. and Virginia Curry, age 17 years 18 days.

CURRY, ELIZA
    SEE: WISEHART, JAMES

CURRY, JOHN R. - Local - Nov 23, 1882   Died, John R. Curry an old resident of Mt Sterling, Friday.

CURRY, LOTTIE - Died - Dec 26, 1879   Miss Lottie Curry daughter of R.S. Curry of Clayton township died Tuesday.

CURRY, MRS LUCY - Local - Oct 13, 1881   Died, Mrs Lucy Curry, wife of B.A. Curry of Clayton died Sunday A.M. the 2nd inst.

CURRY, PAULINE - Died - Jan 1, 1875   Died, on the 28th ult, of membranous croup, Pauline, daughter of H.H. and Ella Curry, age 14 months 9 days.

CURRY, SUSAN
    SEE: SMITH, JOHN K.

CURRY, MRS THOMAS - Local - Apr 25, 1879   Mrs Thomas Curry, of Clayton, mother of Mrs Richard Seaton died Wednesday A.M. Buried at Pleasant View Cemetery yesterday.

CURRY, MRS THOS. - Clayton - Apr 25, 1879 Mrs Thos. Curry died Wednesday A.M.

CURRY, VIRGINIA - Death's Doings - Dec 14, 1882 Died, at her home near Clayton, December 9th Virginia, wife of Richard S. Curry of consumption.

CURTIS, AMOS - Local - Mar 16, 1882 Died, Amos Curtis, an old resident of Augusta died recently, age 66 years. Came to Augusta in 1845 from New York.

CURTIS, ANN M. - Probate Notice - Apr 15, 1880 Ann M. Curtis, deceased   3rd Monday of May 1880   E.B. Curtis, adm.

CURTIS, E.B. - Adm. Sale - Jan 1, 1881 Adm. Sale E.B. Curtis, deceased by Thos. Bailey, adm.

CURTIS, E.B.
    SEE: CLARK, ANN M.
    SEE: LASLEY, MATTIE J.

CURTIS, ELAM B. - Died - Dec 16, 1880 Died at his home in Camp Point, Illinois on December 7th, 1880 Mr Elam B. Curtis, 62 years old.

CURTIS, ELAM B. - Local - Dec 9, 1880 Died, Elam B. Curtis died Tuesday afternoon, 62 years old and was a old settler here after the village was laid out, coming from Columbus where he lived for several years. Funeral today in Presbyterian Church.

CURTIS, ELAM B. - Probate Notice - Jan 13, 1881 Elam B. Curtis, deceased 3rd Monday of March 1881 Thomas Bailey, adm.

CURTIS, ELAM B. - Aug 10, 1882 Thomas Bailey as adm of estate of Elam B. Curtis, deceased petitioner vs. Mary Stevens, Maria Francis, Louisa S. Curtis, Arthur B. Seymour, Curtis J. Lyon, Emily Linn, Wilkes Warren, Charles B. Warren defendants. August term of county court Adams County.

CYRUS, CLEMMIE
    SEE: ROSS, WILLIAM C.

CYRUS, GEORGE W. - Trustee Sale - Dec 8, 1876 Trustee Real Estate Sale Emma Ashenfelter by her deed of trust dated Aug 16, 1873 recorded in Book 17 of Mortgages P.

65 did convey unto George W. Cyrus as trustee to secure payment of one certain promissory note payable to John T. Hagerty ($200.00) George W. Cyrus, trustee.

CYRUS, JOHN M. - Obituary - Feb 12, 1874 Capt. John M. Cyrus died of consumption on the 4th inst at Franklin, Louisiana where he had gone for his health. Born November 9, 1838 some 5 miles NW of this town in Houston township and was the 2nd son of the late Elder Henry A Cyrus and the next older brother of Geo. W. Cyrus of the Journal. His father died in 1847. He taught school for awhile. In 1861 he joined a call for volunteers in Capt Hanna's Co. E, 50th Reg. Illinois Volunteers. After discharge he worked in treasury department at Washington and studied law and graduated at the law dept. of that city. In 1868 he returned home and in winter of "69" he opened a law office in Quincy. In June 1872 he married Emma A. Maertz of Quincy. Left with wife for Louisiana last winter for southern Louisiana. He had stopped to rest at Franklin.

DAILEY, MRS - Mendon - Aug 26, 1880 Mrs Dailey long a resident of Mendon but some months past a resident of the county house as a distracted person was buried here today, age 72 years.

DAILY, AMANDA - Real Estate Transfers - Nov 17, 1881 Amanda Daily, deceased by adm's to Hiram F. Denny lot 41 Fowler addition to Mendon $110.00. Heirs of P.F. Leach, deceased to Wm Terry lot 12 Block 2 original Camp Point $376.00.

DAILY, JACOB - Died - Feb 28, 1879 Died February 23rd near Bowensburg, Hancock County, Jacob Daily nearly 67 years old. Born Clark County Indiana February 26, 1812. Married Jane Beckett in 1833 and came to Adams County in 1840. Member of Hebron Church.

DALLAM, WILL - Local - Aug 26, 1880 Will Dallam of Warsaw was killed last Monday while coupling cars at Downing, Missouri. He is a brother of Phil Dallam of the Warsaw "Bulletin".

DANLEY, JOHN S.
    SEE: KEENAN, JOSEPH

DANLEY, ZEREIDA C.
    SEE: KEENAN, JOSEPH

DARK, ROBERT L. - Local - May 30, 1879 Robert L. Dark, one of the early settlers of McDonough County died at Industry on the 15th inst., age 75 years.

DARRAH, JOEL - Adm's Sale - Aug 25, 1881 Adm's sale of real estate Joel Darrah deceased in interest of Maria Darrah, widow of Joel. Maria Darrah, adm.

DARRAH, JOEL - Adm Sale of Real Estate - Nov 3, 1881 Maria Darrah adm of the estate of Joel Darrah, deceased was petitioner and Adam C. Kropp and other unknown owners and others were defendants will sell property Saturday November 19, 1881 at the Post Office in Coatsburg. Maria Darrah, adm.

DARRAH, JOEL - Apr 7, 1881 State of Illinois, Adams County, Arpil Term, Maria Darrah adm of the estate of Joel Darrah, deceased vs the unknown owners of south 1/2 of NE 1/4 of section 12.

DARRAH, JOEL - Probate Notice - Nov 15, 1878 3rd Monday of December 1878 Joel Darrah, Maria Darrah, adm.

DARRAH, JOEL - Hash - Sep 27, 1878 Died Dr Joel Darrah died at his residence near Coatsburg Sunday at the age of 72 years. 30 years ago Dr Darrah had the most extensive practice probably in Adams County extending from Mendon to Schuyler County and from Chili to Liberty.

DAVENPORT, E.L. - Latest News - Sep 7, 1877 E.L. Davenport, the tragedian, died at his summer home at Canton, Pennsylvania on the 1st.

DAVIDSON, I.G. - Neighborhood News - Jan 25, 1878 I.G. Davidson, of Lewiston, father of the editor of the Carthage "Republican" died on the 17th inst, age 76 years.

DAVIS, ANNIE - Local - Apr 28, 1881 Died, Miss Annie Davis died Sunday A.M. of consumption age 18 years.

DAVIS, MRS E.C. - Local - Jun 23, 1881 Died, Mrs E.C. Davis died Wednesday A.M. of consumption. Third in family to die within the past year, all from consumption.

DAVIS, EARNEST – Hash – Jul 21, 1876 Earnest Davis was killed at Barry Sunday night, 20 years old about, son of C.S. Davis'.

DAVIS, ELVA – Fowler – Aug 1, 1879 Died, Elva, beloved wife of Allen Davis, of this place died suddenly Friday eve July 18th. Services at ME Church Sunday. Leaves husband and motherless child.

DAVIS, MRS ELVA L. – Death's Doing's – Aug 1, 1879 Died at Fowler, Illinois July 18th, Mrs Elva L., wife of E. Allen Davis and daughter of John Stewart, age 20 years. Was known to students at Maplewood as she attended there 1 year.

DAVIS, JAS C. – Hash – Jul 19, 1878 Infant daughter of Jas C. Davis of Coatsburg died Wednesday. Remains brought here for burial Thursday A.M.

DAVIS, JOSEPH S. – Died – Jan 27, 1881 Died, Monday A.M. January 24th Joseph S. Davis age 28 years of consumption. Services Wednesday at Presbyterian Church by Rev T.D. Davis.

DAVIS, THOMAS – Local – Jan 5, 1881 Died, Thomas Davis of this township Sunday eve at his home 4 miles NW of town from pneumonia.

DAVIS, V.D. – Local – Jun 9, 1881 Died, V.D. Davis of Concord township last week from cancer. Was one of the old settlers of Concord.

DAVIS, V.D. – Concord – Jun 9, 1881 Died, V.D. Davis an old settler of Concord died last Monday and was buried at Clayton.

DEAKIN, ALBERT – Hash – Aug 24, 1877 Albert Deakin committed suicide in Quincy Tuesday by cutting his throat. He was insane.

DEAN, ELIZABETH – Neighborhood News – Mar 29, 1878 Elizabeth Dean, deceased bills presented for probate and used as a witness her husband, John Dean. "Mt Sterling Democrat"

DEANE, DR – Neighborhood News – Dec 28, 1877 A young physician by the name of Deane formerly of Pittsfield was found dead in his bed at a hotel in St Louis, heart disease.

DEATHS IN ADAMS COUNTY - 1879-499, 1880-709, 1881-542

DEGROSSE, MRS BARBARA - Exchange Notes - Dec 13, 1878 Mrs Barbara Degrosse committed suicide at Jerseyville, Tuesday night. She went to the river at Alton last August and drowned her 10 year old daughter.

DEHAVEN, D.J. - In memoriam - Dec 30, 1880 In memoriam Camp Point Lodge #215 100F for brother D.J. De Haven.

DEHAVEN, D.J. - Local - Jan 20, 1881 Richard A. Wallace has been appointed adm of the estate of D.J. De Haven, deceased.

DEHAVEN, D. JAY - Local - Sep 16, 1880 D. Jay De Haven has bought the interest of William McClintock in his fathers estate.

DEHAVEN, DANIEL J. - Probate Notice - Jan 20, 1881 Daniel J. De haven, deceased 3rd Monday of March, 1881 R.A. Wallace, adm.

DEHAVEN, JAMES T. - Local - Aug 11, 1881 A infant child of James T. DeHaven died Monday eve.

DEHAVEN ,JAY - Personal - Dec 30, 1880 Hon. Chas. Ballow of Clayton was in town Friday attending the funeral of Jay De Haven.

DEHAVEN, MARIA J. - Died - Feb 14, 1879 Died, February 10, 1879 Maria J., daughter of James T. and Laura L. Dehaven, age 18 years.

DEMOSS, ANNA - Columbus - Apr 13, 1882 Died, Tuesday April 4th at the home of her father in Columbus township, Miss Anna DeMoss age 17 years of dropsy. Funeral at Pleasant View Church Wednesday at 2 P.M.

DEMOSS, ANNIE - Obituary - Apr 13, 1882 Died, Annie, daughter of James and Margaret DeMoss, Born March 3, 1865 and died April 4, 1882, age 17 years 29 days. Leaves parents. Services by Rev J. Cornelius, buried cemetery at Pleasant View Church 3 miles east of Camp Point.

DEMPSEY, ED - Local - Feb 10, 1881 Died, Ed Dempsey who lived a few miles from Bloomfield, this county died suddenly on his way home Friday eve.

DEMPSEY, THOMAS - Accident - Oct 30, 1874   Thomas and Edward Dempsey residing on a farm near Fowler, Illinois while driving along the Columbus road about 4 miles east of Quincy their horses became frightened and ran away, throwing both from the wagon killing Thomas and injuring Edward.

DENMAN, M.B. - Supplement - Sep 1, 1876   Died since last years meeting of Old Settlers of Adams and Brown counties: M.B. Denman of Quincy.

DENNEY, WESLEY - Hash - Jul 27, 1877   Died, Wesley Denney, an old resident of Camp Point. Died at Canton, Illinois on the 15th inst of dropsy of the heart.

DENNY, ROBERT - Local - Jun 24, 1880   Robert Denny lost a little child with whooping cough last week.

DENSLOW, E.L. - Neighborhood News - Jul 26, 1878   E.L. Denslow of Clarksville, Missouri was drowned in the Mississippi Sunday A.M.

DERRICK, CLARA J. - Died - Jan 9, 1880   Died December 30th, 1879, Clara J., youngest daughter of Jacob L. and Caroline Derrick age 14 years 11 months 9 days.

DEUMAN, MRS SARAH - Local - May 18, 1882   Died, Mrs Sarah Deuman at her home in Quincy Tuesday, age 64 years. Lived in Quincy since 1842.

DEVORE, MRS ANDREW - Mendon - Jul 28, 1881   Died, Mrs Devore wife of Andrew Devore on Wednesday of last week.

DEWEY, MRS L.
    SEE: PERRIN, OLIVER

DEXTER, GEORGE - Local - Nov 30, 1882   Suicide, George Dexter shot himself thru the head in Macomb last week. Hopeless love thought to be the cause.

DEXTER, JOHN - Local - Jun 23 1881   Died, a son of John Dexter of Augusta was run over by a load of hay Saturday and killed. Was about 8 years old.

DILLEY, J.W. - Local - Oct 7, 1880   Died, J.W. Dilley of Macomb died at the Adams House Friday A.M. Buried in Macomb this eve.

DISMORE, MISS NANCY - Junction - Apr 22, 1880   Died,

Miss Nancy Dismore died on last Friday night, was an invalid many years. Buried at Hebron last Sunday A.M.

DISMORE, ROBERT - Death of Robert Dismore - May 5, 1881 Died at his home in Houston, Apr 30, 1881 Robert Dismore, age 67 years and 1 day. Born in state of Kentucky and moved with parents to Clark County Indiana when a child. Was left a orphan when a small boy. Married Elizabeth Schwartz in 1840 and came to Adams County same year. Services at Hebron. Leaves a wife and 5 children; 1 son and 4 daughters. One daughter died about 1 year ago.

DISMORE, ROB'T - Golden - May 5, 1881 Several of our citizens attended the funeral of Rob't Dismore yesterday. Rob't Dismore died of heart disease last Saturday A.M. Leaves a wife and several children, one daughter died about 1 year ago. Services at Hebron by Rev L.F. Walden.

DISSLER, HENRY - Hash - Aug 23, 1878 Henry Dissler was arrested in Quincy for the murder of Officer Seehorn. Was a former resident of Camp Point where he worked at blacksmithing. His family lives in McKee township near the covered bridge.

DITMER, JOHN - Local - Jul 14, 1881 Died, John Ditmer, a farmer north of Coatsburg died last Tuesday of consumption.

DODD, W.D. - Death List - Sep 7, 1877 Old settlers death list since last meeting: W.D. Dodd.

DOLE, GEORGE - Clayton - May 27, 1880 A little daughter of George Dole living near Kellerville was choked to death in a few minutes last week by getting a young peach in her throat.

DONLEY, J. - Fowler - Oct 4, 1878 September 13th J. Donley was hit by a train and killed, 80 years old. Leaves a wife and 2 children.

DORAN, MADISON - Death from Poison - Oct 5, 1882 Madison Doran, Supt. of the county poor farm died Sunday afternoon from accidently taking poison.

DOUGLAS, JAMES - Supplement - Sep 1, 1876 Died since last years meeting of Old Settlers of Adams and Brown Counties: James Douglas of Concord.

DOUGLASS, MRS JAS.
    SEE: GRIFFITH, JEFFESON

DOUGLASS, WILLIAM B. - Trustees Sale - Dec 7, 1877 Deed made by William B. Douglass and Jane Douglass his wife to Henry R. Motter dated March 1872 recorded Book 10 of mortgages page 252. Dated Clayton Nov 28, 1877.

DOWNING, ALMA EMMA - Died - Aug 18, 1881 Died, Alma Emma, wife of Geo. Y. Downing and daughter of Wm L. and Z.E. Oliver. Born in Rockcastle county Kentucky Dec 19, 1854. Came to Illinois when a child with her parents. Married her husband Nov 7, 1876 and died Aug 10, 1881. Services at the home of her parents by Rev T.D. Davis. Leaves a wife, sister and daughter.

DOWNING, CELESTINE - Died - Nov 30, 1882 Died on Wednesday, November 22nd of quick consumption Celestine, daughter of John and Elizabeth Downing and wife of William T. Beckett, 33 years old. Leaves an aged mother, brothers, sisters, a husband and 5 children. United with ME Church at Hebron early in girlhood.

DOWNING, E.C.
    SEE: HUGHES, MRS W.M.

DOWNING, MR AND MRS J.E. - Local - Aug 18, 1881 Died, the baby daughter of Mr and Mrs J.E. Downing, Friday.

DOWNING, JOHN - Died - Jul 31, 1874 Died at his residence in this twp on the 29th inst, John Downing. He was the oldest son of Rezin Downing and born in London county Virginia Sep 7, 1810. Moved with his father's family to Clark County Indiana in 1822. In 1830 he married and lived 1 year in Kentucky and moved his family to Morgan County Illinois. In spring of 1833 he settled in this township where he died. Member of ME Church.

DOWNING, JOHN - Probate Notice - Aug 21, 1874 John Downing, 3rd Monday of September 1874 James E. Downing, Executor.

DOWNING, JOHN - Hash - Aug 21, 1874 James E. Downing, ex. of the John Downing estate will sell the personal property of the estate at public sale September 10th.

DOWNING, JOHN - Aug 14, 1874 Geo. Rhea, Henry M. Lewis and Daniel Omer were appointed appraisers of John

Downing's estate.

DOWNING, MARIA - Died - Feb 1, 1878 Died of diptheria on the 30th inst, Maria, daughter of James E. and Jane R. Downing age 3 years 4 months.

DOWNING, MARIA JOSEPHINE - Obituary - Feb 8, 1878 Died, January 30th, Maria Josephine, daughter of James E. and Jane R. Downing, age 4 years 4 months 2 days.

DOWNING, MARTHA - Mendon - Nov 29, 1878 We learn that Mrs Martha Downing, wife of William Downing, formerly of this vicinity died at her home in Chariton County Missouri the 21st inst. Mrs L. was we think related to several parties in the vicinity of Camp Point.

DOWNING, NANCY
    SEE: HUGHES, NATHAN

DOWNING, REZIN
    SEE: TURNER, NANCY

DOWNING, REZIN - Probate Notice - Jan 20, 1881 Rezin Downing, deceased 3rd Monday of March 1881 R.H. Downing, Executor.

DOWNING, REZIN - Died - Jan 6, 1881 Rezin Downing died Monday eve at the age of 91 years, surviving his wife only 6 weeks. Settled in Camp Point in fall of 1835. Had 12 children, 8 still living and residents of this vicinity. Buried Wednesday at Hebron Cemetery.

DOWNING, SARAH E. - Died - Jun 8, 1877 Died on the 2nd inst, Mrs Sarah E., wife of W.H. Hughes and daughter of Ebon C. Downing age 29 years of consumption. By T.J. Bryant.

DRUMMON, CHARLY - Obituary - Sep 2, 1880 On the 18th inst, Charly Drummon age 19 years dropped dead.

DUCY, ANTHONY - Local - Aug 29, 1879 Died, Anthony Ducy, living near Griggsville dropped dead on the 15th.

DUDLEY, A.E. - Local - Apr 18, 1879 A.E. Dudley, of Quincy died last Friday had lived Quincy 25 years.

DUDLEY, JEPTHA - Hash - Aug 2, 1878 Jeptha Dudley of Ellington was drowned in Cedar Creek in the suburbs of Quincy Thursday night.

DUDLEY, JEPTHA
    SEE: SHERMAN, SETH C.

DUFF, MRS - Liberty - Mar 25, 1880 Died, on Tuesday March 16th at the home of her son, Thomas Duff, Mrs Duff died in her 62nd year. Leaves many friends.

DUFF, MRS SARAH - Liberty - Mar 25, 1880 Died, Mrs Sarah Duff died at her son's home in this place on Tuesday eve 16th inst.

DUFF, THOMAS - Hancock County Murder - Sep 2, 1880 Thomas Duff found guilty of murdering Salisbury at Fountain Green, Hancock County last week.

DUFFY, A.N. - Mendon - Jul 1, 1880 A.N. Duffy lost his little babe last week from cholera infantum.

DUFFY, WILLIAM - Local - Jan 6, 1881 Word received Tuesday A.M. that William Duffy one of our railroad boys had been killed Monday on the Peoria branch of the C.B. & Q. while coupling cars. Married but a few months ago.

DUNCAN, HARVEY - Columbus - Jul 13, 1882 Infant child of Harvey Duncan died Sunday and buried Monday. Services by Rev A.M. Danely.

DUNCAN, HATTIE MAURINE - Died - Jul 13, 1882 Died, Hattie Maurine, daughter of Mr and Mrs R.H. Duncan July 2nd, age 3 months 15 days. Services following day at Mt Pleasant by Rev. A.M. Danely.

DUNLAP, JANE
    SEE: MCFARLAND, LEWIS

DUNLAP, DR W.B. - Local - Jan 5, 1882 Died, Dr W.B. Dunlap of Liberty lost a babe this week by some brain afflection.

DUNN, CAPT JAMES E. - Local - Sep 15, 1881 Capt James E. Dunn an old resident of Quincy died Sunday at Decorah, Iowa where he was visiting a daughter, about 84 years old. Buried at Quincy.

DUNN, MRS JAS E. - Local - May 16, 1879 Died, Mrs Jas E. Dunn of Quincy. Died Tuesday A.M. was in her 75th year.

DUNWIDIE, ALMA SMITH
    SEE: WALLACE, ALLEN

DURANT, GEORGIA - Hash - Nov 9, 1877 Miss Georgia, daughter of Dr J.F. Durant, Quincy died last Saturday.

DURANT, THOMAS - Hash - Aug 9, 1878 Thomas Durant, an old settler of Columbus, father of Thos E. and Dr J.F. Durant died in Quincy Wednesday, age 86 years. Burial in Columbus.

DWYER, J.A.D. - Jan 16, 1880 A stage driven by J.A.D. Dwyer was overturned by a sharp wind in Boulder Canyon, Colorado the other A.M. and fell down an embankment 70 feet. Dwyer was killed, others not seriously hurt.

EARL, ARTHUR T. - Died - Aug 6, 1875 Died, July 29th of cholera infantum, Arthur T., youngest son of James J. and Sarah M. Earl, age 16 months.

EARL, JAS. J.
    SEE: BECK, MRS E.E.

EARL, JOHN W. - Died - Jan 10, 1879 Died January 5th at Clayton of consumption, John W., son of John T. and Rebecca Earl, age 31 years 6 months. Buried in Camp Point on the 6th.

EASUM, ELMIRA
    SEE: MURPHY, ELMIRA

EATON, CHARLES SIMEON - Died - Dec 23, 1880 Died at the home of his father in North East twp December 21st Charles Simeon, eldest son of Lorenzo D. and Maria Eaton aged 28 years, 2 months 7 days. Buried in Simm's Cemetery today at 2 P.M. by Rev B.D. Hawk.

EBERT, MRS MARY - Liberty - Oct 12, 1877 Died, Mrs Mary Ebert age 73 years a resident of Liberty more than 40 years. Died Saturday, September 29th. Funeral Sunday.

ECKERT, AUGUST - Hash - Oct 23, 1874 The case of Chas. Bellow, adm vs. The Camp Point Mfg Co. for $5,000 damages for causing the death of August Eckert, will be tried the 2nd time during the present term of court.

ECKERT, AUGUST - Hash - Apr 3, 1873 The suit of Chas. Bellew, adm of the estate of August Eckert vs. the Camp Point Mfg Co. for causing the death of Eckert by the

bursting of an emery wheel, resulted in a verdict for
the plaintiff for $2,800. The defendants take an appeal
to the Supreme Court.

EDGAR, MRS - Local - Nov 12, 1880 Died, Mrs Edgar,
mother of Col. W.H. Edgar died at her home in
Jerseyville on Monday of last week.

EDMONSTON, ARCHIBALD - Sale - Sep 21, 1882 U.H. Keath,
Salie for Petitioner October term of court Henry R.
Motter, adm of the estate of Archibald Edmonston,
deceased vs. Archie B. Edmonston, Stephen D. Edmonston,
Louis C. Edmonston and Jesse L. Francis defendants.
Public sale of land. (Stephen D. lives Iola, Allen
County Kansas) Willis Haselwood, clerk by W.T. Head,
deputy.

EDMUNSON, MR - Clayton - Jan 23, 1880 Old man Edmunson,
the stone man of Missouri Creek died after a few day
illness last week.

EDWARDS, MR - Local - Oct 28, 1880 Judge Edwards a
pioneer of Keokuk died last week. <u>One</u> a brilliant legal
light, he wrecked himself by drink.

EDWARDS, MARGARET - Probate Notice - Aug 7, 1874
Margaret Edwards 3rd Monday of September 1874 George
Simmons, adm.

EDWARDS, MARGARET - Died - Jul 17, 1874 Died, Mrs
Margaret Edwards of this town on the 5th inst of dropsy,
age 64 years. She was a native of Tenn. And a
consistant member of the ME Church 35 years. In her
last sickness her 4 children were absent from her.

EDWARDS, MARGARET - Legal Notice - Jun 24, 1875
Petition of Geo. Simmonds, adm of the estate of Margaret
Edwards, decease. Petitioner vs Caroline Moore, John
Edwards, Thomas Edwards and the unknown heirs of
Margaret Edwards, dec. Willis Haselwood, clerk county
court dated June 8, 1875.

ELLIOTT, E.H. - Neighborhood News - Jul 12, 1878 E.H.
Elliott, a Wabash brakeman living at Mounds was struck
by a train a few days ago and was probably fatally
injured.

ELLIOTT, ELMER - Livingston - Aug 25, 1881 Died, Elmer,
infant son of Samuel and Fannie Elliott near Paloma on

the 19th inst.

ELLIOTT, F.N. - Neighborhood News - Aug 9, 1878 Dr F.N. Elliott of Quincy was killed last evening, 35 years old. Born in Willimantic, Connecticut. Came to Quincy about 14 years ago and engaged as a dentist. Leaves a wife and child. "Whig 3rd"

ELLIOTT, J. - Burton - Dec 1, 1881 Died, youngest child of J. Elliott, 6 months old. Services in Burton by Mr King of Newtown.

ELLIOTT, LOU
    SEE: BENNETT, MRS J.

ELLIOTT, ROBERT
    SEE: STRICKLER, MRS MAGGIE B.

ELLIOTT, SARAH L.
    SEE: STRICKLER, MRS MAGGIE B.

ELLIS, CHAS M. - Local - Dec 2, 1880 Died, Chas M. Ellis, son of O.T. Ellis, proprietor of the Ballard house, Quincy. Died last Friday.

ELLIS, O.T. - Local - Dec 9, 1880 Died, O.T. Ellis, proprietor of the Ballard House, Quincy, died Sunday. Lived Quincy since 1862.

ELY, MR - Mendon - Dec 22, 1881 Died, a little son of Mr Ely.

ELY, WALLACE - Mendon - Dec 29, 1881 Died, Wallace Ely, eldest son of Jared Ely last Thursday night of spasmodic croup. Only a week before they buried their second son who was stricken with diptheria croup.

EMMONS, JUDGE SYLVESTER - Local - Dec 1, 1881 Death of Judge Sylvester Emmons occurred at Beardstown on the 15th in his 74th year. Was founder of a newspaper at Nauvoo in 1843 which was mobbed and destroyed by Mormons.

ENGLE, ELIAS - Local - Apr 20, 1882 A report reached Quincy that the vigilants of Durango, Colorado hung Elias Engle Saturday night. Engle was a well known gambler in Quincy and has been in Colorado for a few years.

ENGLISH, JOHN H. - Local - Mar 2, 1882 Killed, John H.

English was run over by a train and killed near Baylis, Pike County last week.

ENLOW, SENECA - Burton - Oct 7, 1880 Died, Seneca Enlow died on the 22nd at his father's, Riley Enlow.

ERIE, ADAM - Local - Jul 8, 1880 We learn as we go to press that Adam Erie, who lives about 5 miles SW of Bowen was seriously stabbed maybe fatally at Bowen Saturday eve.

ERNST, CHRIST - Local - Nov 12, 1880 Christ Ernst, Quincy died Sunday.

ERSKINE, JAMES P. - Local - Apr 14, 1881 Died, James P. Erskine an old resident of Quincy died Saturday, age 87 years. He came to Quincy in 1844.

ERTEL, MRS - Coatsburg - Feb 16, 1882 Died, Mother Ertel on Tuesday night. Buried Quincy in Woodland Cemetery on Thursday.

ERTEL, MRS MARIE - Local - Feb 16, 1882 Died, Mrs Marie Ertel, wife of Daniel Ertel of Columbus township last week. Buried in Quincy.

ERTZ, FREDERICK - Fatal Accident - Jul 22, 1880 Monday at 11 a German farmer from Columbus township named Frederick Ertz was killed in a wagon accident at Casco Mills. Died at 8 P.M. Was 66 years old. Leaves an aged wife and family.

ERTZ, FREDERICK JOHANN - Probate Notice - Aug 5, 1880 Frederick Johann Ertz, deceased 3rd Monday of September 1880 Mary Ertz, ex.

ERTZ, FREDERICK JOHANN - Probate Notice - Sep 16, 1880 Frederick Johann Ertz, deceased 3rd Monday of September 1880 Mary Ertz, Ex.

EUBANKS, S. - Neighborhood News - Jun 28, 1878 S. Eubanks of Edina, Missouri was kicked by a horse last Wednesday eve. Died Friday, was 22 years old. "Herald"

EUBANKS, MRS SARAH E. - Local - Jun 15, 1882 Died, Mrs Sarah E. Eubanks in Quincy Saturday, resident of this county since 1836, 82 years old.

EVANS, JOHN J. - Chatten - May 15, 1874 John J. Evans

committed suicide at Bowen last Friday.

EVERSON, J.N. - Various Squibs - Aug 3, 1877 Died, J.N. Everson, an old gentleman and one of the pioneers of Schuyler county. Died at his home in Huntsville, Saturday week before last.

EVERSON, WILLIAM - Hash - Jun 15, 1877 Died, a daughter of William Everson living near Coatsburg and about 20 years old committed suicide on the morning of the 14th inst.

EWING, MRS - Local - Oct 19, 1882 Died, Mrs Ewing, mother of Mrs Frank Parker Saturday A.M. at Clayton.

EWING, SAM'L - Jul 27, 1877 Sam'l Ewing a resident of Ferris was struck by lightning and killed in his home Sunday night.

FAIRFAX, HENRY - Livingston - Jul 26, 1878 Little Henry, son of Dr and Mrs Fairfax died. Born yesterday.

FAIRFAX, MRS HENRY - Livingston - Apr 22, 1880 Died, Mrs Henry Fairfax died in Quincy on the 16th inst. Buried in family graveyard near Mr Samuels on the following day. Born Virginia and came west with her husband.

FARNER, DR W.H. - Local Hash - Dec 20, 1878 Dr W.H. Farner of Loraine died last Saturday.

FELHABER, HENRY - Local - Jun 23, 1881 Died, Henry Felhaber, a wealthy farmer of Clark county Missouri committed suicide Tuesday. Domestic trouble was the cause.

FELT, MRS ALEY - Obituary - Oct 12, 1882 Died, Mrs Aley Felt, one of the oldest residents of Quincy, on Sunday at her home on Broadway, east of 4th Street. Came to Quincy with her husband Mr Francis Tanner March 14, 1831 accompanying the Hon Archie William, wife and sister, the last named Mrs Loughlin, still alive. Mr Tanner died 6 months after coming to Quincy and Mrs went to Liberty township with their children and in 1841 she married Col Peter Felt who died 16 years ago. She was 86 years old last April. One son by her second husband survives her. Leaves 13 grandchildren, 18 great grandchildren and 5 great great grandchildren. Was mother of 2 of her grandchildren, one being Mrs W.C.

Winget living with her all her life until 5 years ago. "Whig"

FERBER, FRANK - Hash - Dec 28, 1877 Frank Ferber living near Burton beat his wife and shot himself to death Friday.

FEREE, MRS JANE - Local - Jun 15, 1882 Died, Mrs Jane Feree, Tuesday, at the home of her daughter, S.C. Butler, Quincy, 77 years old. Lived in Camp Point about 15 years ago.

FERGUSON, ED - Ed Ferguson Convicted - Mar 18, 1880 Ed Ferguson (colored) found guilty of murder of Dr Pierson in Augusta November 1878. "Herald"

FERGUSON, ALLEN - Probate Notice - Dec 18, 1874 Allen Ferguson 3rd Monday of February 1875 Seldon G. Earel, Ex.

FERGUSON, EDNA - Livingston - Nov 22, 1878 Edna Ferguson died November 14th in her 4th year of age. Services at the church by Rev Dinsmore.

FERGUSON, MR AND MRS RUSSEL - Livingston - Nov 15, 1878 Little Edna, youngest daughter of Mr and Mrs Russel Ferguson still lingers on.

FERRINGTON, DOC - Neighborhood news - Oct 12, 1877 Doc Ferrington a citizen of Industry township was found dead in a hayloft of I.N. Beaver's. "Macomb Eagle" He was brother of Osmus Ferrington and 50 years old. Leaves no family. Lived with Osmus 15 years.

FERRIS, ANNA - Hash - Mar 17, 1876 Anna Ferris, the girl beaten by George Adams, died Wednesday afternoon.

FERRIS, ANNA - Murder in Q - Mar 17, 1876 Anna Ferris was murdered in her bed at the home of her step mother on Vermont St. between 9th and 10th in Quincy Tuesday morn. She was about 25 years old. She was killed by George Adams, age 19 or 20 years, a nephew of George Adams a well known business man and pork packer of Quincy.

FERRIS, E.S. - Neighborhood News - Aug 9, 1878 A young man named E.S. Ferris of Galesburg was drowned in the Spoon River, near Ellisville, Fulton County, Tuesday about 8 P.M.

FERRIS, NANCY
    SEE: ADAMS, GEORGE

FINCH, MISS LUCY - Supplement - Sep 1, 1876 Died since last years meeting of Old Settlers of Adams and Brown Counties: Miss Lucy Finch of Brown County.

FINDLEY, JAMES - Clayton - Jun 8, 1882 Died, at Augusta May 30th of typhoid fever, James, son of John and Martha Findley.

FINLAY, MRS L.E.
    SEE: JUDY, PARIS T.

FINLAY, MRS WM
    SEE: JUDY, PARIS T.

FINLEY, M.B. - Local - Mar 30, 1882 Died, M.B. Finley, one of the merchants of Quincy of the olden times, Monday in his 62nd year.

FISHER, RUDOLPH - Liberty - May 5, 1881 Died, Rudolph Fisher on the 29th.

FISHER, CHARLEY - Liberty - Jun 3, 1880 Charley Fisher, son of Henry and Catherine Fisher died last Tuesday A.M. about 13 years old.

FISHER, WM V. - Obituary - Aug 24, 1882 Died, at Paloma, Ill, August 18th of consumption Wm V. Fisher. Born Ohio May 13, 1840. Came to Illinois with parents when 8 years old and settled near Paloma. Enlisted in Co. E. 50th Reg. Ill Vol. October 17, 1869 he married Miss Mary L. Ogle who with 5 children survive him. Funeral at ME Church at Columbus by Rev A.M. Danley. Buried Columbus Cemetery.

FISHER, WILLIAM - Columbus - Aug 24, 1882 Died, William Fisher of Paloma in Friday August 18th. Remains taken to Columbus on the 19th. Services by Bro. Danely. Was Lieutenant of Co. E. of the 50th Reg. Ill. Vol.

FLAGG, NEWTON - Hash - Feb 8, 1878 Died, Newton Flagg, formerly of Quincy died at Yonkers, N.Y. Tuesday. Was one of the early merchants of Quincy and senior member of the old banking firm of Flagg & Savage.

FLAGG, WILLARD C. - Neighborhood News - Apr 5, 1878 Death of Hon. Willard C. Flagg, Saturday at his home near More in Madison County. Was a native of Madison County, age in his 49th year.

FLEMMING, MR - Clayton - Sep 7, 1882 Died, Mr Flemming of Columbus, Kansas a former resident of Clayton township was buried here today. Died of heart disease.

FLETCHER, JOHN - Murder - May 28, 1875 John Fletcher (colored) of Quincy brutally murdered his adopted son, 3 years old, Tuesday A.M. Later: Name of child was John W. Gibbs, 3-1/2 years old.

FLYNN, JAS - Clayton - Jul 18, 1879 Jas Flynn who went to Colorado for his health died there and was buried at Mt Sterling.

FOLCKEMER, FRANKIE - Died - May 28, 1875 Died, on the 24th inst of heart disease, Frankie Folckemer age 8 years and 10 months.

FOLCKEMER, JOHN C. - Johnnie Flockemer - Nov 2, 1877 Died, Sunday A.M. October 29th John C. Folckemer son of Henry and Ellen Folckemer age 8 years 7 months 13 days.

FOLEY, ALICE - Neighborhood News - Oct 26, 1877 Died, Alice Foley a young woman, age 19 years, who lived with her brother in Hire township, McDonough County committed suicide in the presence of her lover, George Hainline. They were to be married about Christmas. She died Saturday.

FOLTZ, GEORGE - Probate Notice - Dec 5, 1879 George Foltz 3rd Monday of January 1880 Elias Stahl, Ex.

FORSYTHE, MISS - Mendon - Nov 30, 1882 Died, a Miss Forsythe, a young colored lady about 16 years old. Died Sunday of consumption, buried Monday.

FORSYTHE, ROBERT - Death List - Feb 19, 1875 Old settlers death during last week in Adams County: Robert Forsythe of Ursa.

FOSTER, MRS ELLA - Liberty - Dec 2, 1880 Mrs Ella Foster died of consumption Monday the 22nd at her fathers, Mr Edmund Grubb.

FOSTER, H.C. - La Prairie - Jan 6, 1881 Died, H.C. Foster on December 30th.

FOSTER, HARRIET
    SEE: BUTZ, MRS HENRY

FOSTER, MRS MARION - Clayton - May 23, 1879 Mrs Ambler and Mrs Marion Foster have died suddenly of heart disease within a few days.

FRANCIS, MRS J.T. - Personal - Jul 21, 1881 Col Wm Hanna of Golden attended the funeral of Mrs J.T. Francis.

FRANCIS, JOHN - Clayton - Aug 12, 1880 A young man named John Francis who was suspicioned of stealing some 2 years ago a horse of Robert McLain, the old man who hung himself was captured last week and sent to jail.

FRANCIS, JOHN H.
    SEE: SEYMOUR, HATTIE

FRANCIS, MARIA
    SEE: CURTIS, ELAM B.

FRANCIS, WILLIAM - Local - Aug 12, 1880 William Francis was arrested last week on charge of stealing a horse from Robert McLain about 2 years ago. At the time McLain was found dead in his pasture. People suppose McLain was hung by the thief.

FRANKS, THOMAS - Probate Notice - Mar 16, 1877 Thomas Franks 3rd Monday of May Thomas M. Lawler, Ex.

FRASIER, JAMES
    SEE: TINDALL, MRS JOSEPH

FRASIER, WM - Mendon - Dec 13, 1878 Wm Frazier, son of the late Geo. Frasier of Mendon township is supposed to be accidentally drowned near Belmont, Missouri October 9th.

FRAZIER, GEORGE - Died - Apr 2, 1874 Died on Sunday night March 29th George Frazier of pneumonia. He was an old and respected citizen of Mendon township.

FRICKE, CHARLES - Probate Notice - Jun 15, 1882 Charles Fricke 3rd Monday of June (21st) Wm F. Fricke, Ex.

FRICKE, CHARLES - Probate Notice - Jul 20, 1882 Charles Fricke 3rd Monday of August (21st) Wm F. Fricke, Ex.

FRICKE, EDITH - Coatsburg - Jul 6, 1882 Died, little Edith Fricke on Friday of spotted fever. Funeral by Rev Coats of the U.B. Church.

FRIDAY, GEO. - George Friday Shot - Apr 18, 1879 Yesterday eve at 5 Geo. Friday was shot by Sheriff. Leaves a wife and 4 children, oldest a boy of 12 years. "Mt Sterling Message"

FROMME, GEORGE - Local - Nov 28, 1879 George Fromme of Marblehead was found dead Wednesday.

FRY, J.J. - Mendon - Feb 14, 1879 Mr J.J. Fry of Loraine died on the 8th inst of dropsy. Was a member of Co. D. 78th Illinois Infantry and lost a leg in service at Jamestown, Georgia.

FUNK, CHARLES - Suicide - Apr 27, 1877 Charles Funk, a man age 33 years and unmarried who lived with his father in Beverly township committed suicide there Saturday A.M. by shooting himself. He was a school teacher and member of ME Church. "Herald"

FUNK, EFFIE - Obituary - Sep 28, 1882 Died, at Beverly on the 18th of September, Effie, daughter of James and Annette Funk, age 5 years (blood poison).

FURRY, MRS - Mendon - Feb 28, 1879 Died, Mrs Furry. Died Saturday night age 73 years. Several of her sons are among the best citizens of Mendon and vicinity.

FURRY, JESSE - Mendon - Aug 11, 1881 Died, Mr Jesse Furry's little son on Friday night. Buried Sunday.

GAGE, FRANK - Hash - Aug 31, 1877 Frank Gage, Supt. of Hannibal stock yards shot and is thought fatally wounded Geo. Hawkins, a citizen of that place.

GALASPIE, MR - Fall Creek - Jul 15, 1880 Yesterday a man named Galaspie was run over and killed a short distance east of the Hannibal bridge, was deaf and didn't hear the train. He was a painter and lived at Payson. Taken to Fall Creek and taken on to Payson for burial. Leaves a wife, no children.

GALLEHER, CARVEL
    SEE: KEENAN, JOSEPH

GALLEHER, CYNTHIA
   SEE: KEENAN, JOSEPH

GALOUPE, DAVID - County News - Feb 19, 1875 David Galoupe was killed by a man named Hart in Quincy. On Friday eve the 5th they had a fight and Mr Galoupe died on the 12th.

GANT, CADOR - Probate Notice - Apr 13, 1882 Cador Gant, deceased 1st Monday of June 1882 Rezin H. Downing, adm.

GARDNER, MRS JEMIMA - Hash - Mar 29, 1878 Died, Mrs Jemima Gardner, wife of H.J. Gardner, of the Herald died last Thursday, age 47 years. Born in England.

GARLETT, DAVID - Local - Apr 13, 1882 Died, David Garlett of this township Friday A.M. from erysipelas. 62 years old and a resident here 20 years.

GARLETTS, DAVID - Adm Sale - Jul 26, 1883 Adm. Sale of Real Estate Thomas J. Bates, adm of David Garletts deceased petitioner and Elizabeth J. Walcott, Mary Husted, James R. Garletts, Adaline Garletts, Nancy Tuxford, Alexander Garletts, David Garletts, Joseph Garletts, Anna L. Garletts, Philip Garletts and Lafayette Garletts, defendants   C.M. Gilmer attorney.

GARLETTS, DAVID - Probate Notice - Apr 27, 1882 David Garletts, deceased   3rd Monday of July (17th)   T.J. Bates, adm.

GARNER, NATHAN - Supplement - Sep 1, 1876 Died since last years meeting of Old Settlers of Adams and Brown Counties, Nathan Garner of Clayton.

GARNER, NATHAN - Clayton - Mar 24, 1876 Nathan Garner, a well known and highly respected farmer residing about 1-1/2 miles north of Clayton died very suddenly Saturday about 11 A.M. with heart disease. He owned a large farm and leaves a large family.

GARNER, NATHAN L. - Probate Notice - Mar 31, 1876 Nathan L. Garner   3rd Monday of May 1876 Nancy M. Garner, adm.

GARNER, NATHAN L. - Adm Sale - Dec 20, 1878 Adm Sale of Real Estate Nathan L. Garner deceased, against Nancy M. Garner widow and others minor children, William A. Garner, Elizabeth A. Garner and Nathan A. Garner. Nancy

M. Garner, adm   Camp Point, Illinois.

GARNER, OTTIE - Clayton - Apr 28, 1881   Died, Ottie Garner age 15 years died in Clayton on the 15th inst, brother of G.A. Garner, formerly of Camp Point.

GARNER, ROBERT - Supplement - Sep 1, 1876   Died since last years meeting of Old Settlers of Adams and Brown Counties, Robert Garner of Clayton.

GARNER, Robert - Probate Notice - Oct 22, 1875   Robert Garner   3rd Monday of December 1875   Rezin H. Downing, adm.

GARNER, ROBERT - Hash - Oct 15, 1875   Rev A.M. Pilcher will preach the funeral of Robert Garner, deceased, by especial request Sunday October 31st at Hebron Church at 11 A.M.

GARNER, WARREN - Clayton - Apr 27, 1882   Died, Warren Garner this A.M.

GARRETT, BENJAMIN - Local - Dec 9, 1880   Died, Benjamin Garrett, switchman in the C.B. & Q yards Quincy was killed Saturday A.M.   Leaves a wife and 1 child.   His mother lives at Plymouth.

GARRETT, JOHN - Local - Oct 7, 1880   John Garrett, a citizen of Littleton, Schuyler County committed suicide by hanging himself in a apple tree.

GARRETT, PETER B.
    SEE: BOYLE, MRS SUSAN

GARRETT, ROBERT - Died - Nov 20, 1873   Died on the morning of the 19th inst, Robert, son of R.W. Garrett, age 5 months.   Funeral today (20th).   Leave residence of Mr Garrett for Pleasant View Church at 10:30.

GARRISON, J.H.
    SEE: BOYLE, MRS JOHN

GARTNER, JACOB - Hash - Jul 21, 1876   Jacob Gartner, a lad of 9 years was drowned in the river at Quincy Monday eve.

GAUNT, SMITH - Probate Notice - Apr 14, 1876   Smith Gaunt   3rd Monday of June   Thomas Marshall, adm.

GAY, VIXEN P. - Hash - Oct 12, 1877 Albert P. Gay was appointed adm of the estate of Vixen P. Gay, deceased.

GAY, VIXEN P. - Obituary - Sep 28, 1877 Died, in Camp Point township on the 20th inst, Mr Vixen P. Gay, 63 years old. Born near Zanesville, Ohio July 31, 1814. Came to Illinois in 1837 stopped in Brooklyn, Schuyler county. On to Adams in 1839 with his cousin Robert Gay. Married twice, first to Lydia A. Knight Jan 5, 1840 she died Nov 5, 1852. Second to Achsa Blakeslee June 3, 1855.

GAY, VIXEN P. - Died - Sep 21, 1877 Died, at his home in Camp Point township September 19th, Vixen P. Gay, 63 years old. Services at York Neck Church Friday 21st.

GAY, VIXEN P. - Probate Notice - Nov 2, 1877 3rd Monday of December Albert P. Gay, adm.

GEBHARDT, CHRISTOPHER - Neighborhood News - Aug 24, 1877 Christopher Gebhardt of Peoria, hung himself in his barn on the 1st inst.

GEISE, H.A. - Local - Dec 9, 1880 Died, H.A. Geise, Quincy died Monday. Came to Quincy 1855.

GEISE, THERESA
    SEE: ANDERS, JOHN

GEMMILL, JAS D. - Personal - Sep 27, 1878 Jas D. Gemmill of Columbus left for Pennsylvania Wednesday. Called there by the death of his father.

GENTLE, BENJAMIN F. - Probate Notice - Jul 20, 1882 Benjamin F. Gentle, deceased 3rd Monday of August (21st) W.R. Graham, adm.

GERHARD, MR - Identified - Sep 28, 1882 Remains of a man identified as Gerhard was found below the city Thursday (drowned). He left his home a week ago left a note of his intention. Lived Burton township and leaves a family. It is said he belonged to German nobility of Prussia and that his real name was Baron Fritz Von Goetzen, that his barony was situated in West Prussia. He left his native country because of family difficulties and came west at once and settled in Burton township. "Whig"

GERHARD, MR - Burton - Sep 28, 1882 Suicide, Mr Gerhard

of Newtown was a high military officer in Germany in rebellion of "48". Came to this country as a refugee along with Carl Schurz and others.

GHARKEY, A.M. - Local - Jun 1, 1882 Killed, A.M. Gharkey, wife and a hired man were going home from Quincy Friday when near La Grange a tree fell and killed Mrs Gharkey and the hired man, seriously injured Mr Gharkey.

GIBBS, ALICE - La Prairie - May 24, 1878 Died, Alice Gibbs of consumption.

GIBBS, CORDELIA - Coatsburg - Jul 27, 1882 Died, Cordelia Gibbs at the home of her father Wm Gibbs, 17 years 4 months old. Funeral by Rev H.C. Coats.

GIBBS, HARRY - Mendon - Jul 27, 1882 Died, Master Harry, son of W.H. Gibbs of our village last Thursday (oldest of the family).

GIBBS, JOHN W.
    SEE: FLETCHER, JOHN

GIBSON, JACK - Local - Oct 31, 1879 Sheriff Ritter had hardly returned from taking Jack Gibson to jail when Gibson was reported dead. Died last Friday in the penitentiary and buried at Joliet. Leaves a wife and family here in this city. "Mt Sterling Message"

GICK, EDWARD - Local - Oct 5, 1882 The motion for a new trial in the case of Edward Gick of Macomb was overruled and Gick was sentenced to hang.

GILBIRD, COL. - Local - Dec 21, 1882 Prof and Mrs S.F. Hall attended the funeral of Col. Gilbirds at Mt Sterling Friday.

GILBIRDS, COL. - Clayton - Dec 28, 1882 Died, Col Gilbirds was buried on Friday from Masonic fraternity. Remains taken to Mt Sterling.

GILBIRDS, CHARLES H. - Probate Notice - Dec 28, 1882 Charles H. Gilbirds, deceased 3rd Monday of March 1883 Henry R. Motter and John H. Carver Executors

GILKEY, JOHN S. - Local - Nov 17, 1881 Died, John S. Gilkey a young lawyer of Quincy, last week in his 26th year. Born Richfield township. Funeral Wednesday the

16th inst.

GILKEY, JOHN S. - Riceville - Nov 17, 1881 Died-Heard of death of John S. Gilkey of Quincy who died 8 A.M. Thursday. Born in Richfield township, about 27 years old. Had 2 brothers, their mother was insane. Buried Quincy Wednesday.

GILL, MRS - Death List - Sep 7, 1877 Old settlers death list since last meeting: Mrs Gill, Brown County age 80 years.

GILLILAND, DR W.E. - Local - Feb 24, 1881 Died, _____ Gilliland, son of Dr W.E. Gilliland of Coatsburg died recently in Colorado.

GILLMAN, JESSE - Local - Nov 7, 1879 Jesse Gillman, an early settler of Hancock county died a few days ago.

GILLMORE, NASHUA - Death List - Sep 7, 1877 Old Settler death roll since last meeting: Nashua Gillmore, Keene, age 80 years.

GILMER, JOHN B. - John B. Gilmer - Jul 15, 1880 Died in Honey Creek township, John B. Gilmer age 42 years 8 months 17 days. Born in Gilmer township ___ 20, 1838. Was a good husband and father.

GILMER, MRS LYDIA - Neighborhood News - Jan 25, 1878 Died, Mrs Lydia Gilmer of Quincy died at her home Saturday, age 66 years. Born Kentucky came to Adams County 1833. Buried in Fowler.

GILMER, MRS DR T. - Fowler - Jan 25, 1878 Funeral of Mrs Dr T. Gilmer, of Quincy was preached at the Christian Church of this place yesterday.

GILPIN, JOSEPH B. - Obituary - Jul 12, 1878 Died, Joseph B. Gilpin of Quincy died Wednesday night. Sick several weeks. Born Leesburg, Virginia in 1824. Afterwards lived in Annapolis, Maryland and Washington City. In 1842 he came to Quincy, went into real estate, admitted to bar in "44". In "62" he went into army as a major. Married in Van Buren County, Iowa in 1852. His wife and 3 children survive him.

GITTER, MRS - Neighborhood News - Aug 23, 1878 Accident with buggy, Mrs Gitter was killed and her daughter hurt, Mrs F. Lohrman.

GITTINGS, MISS ELLA - Neighborhood News - Feb 8, 1878
The funeral of Miss Ella Gittings, victim of the
Burlington tragedy was Wednesday at her fathers home at
La Harpe.

GITTINGS, MISS ELLA - Neighborhood News - Feb 1, 1878
Died, Miss Ella Gittings of La Harpe. Died at
Burlington, Iowa from abortion. Dr Jacob Paul of
Blandenville, Illinois is under arrest.

GOODING, D.W. - Local - Jun 10, 1880 The Mendon
"Dispatch" reports the death of D.W. Gooding of Honey
Creek township on Wednesday of last week from pneumonia.

GOODRICH, R.E. - Neighborhood News - Jul 20, 1877 Died,
Mr R.E. Goodrich died suddenly Sunday A.M. of heart
disease. Lived on Spring Street between 2nd and 3rd.
"Whig"

GORDLEY, JAMES - Exchange Notes - Mar 7, 1879 James
Gordley a well known citizen of Mt Sterling died
Thursday.

GORDON, MRS - Liberty - Nov 3, 1881 Died, Mrs Gordon
Thursday night at her old home, about 70 years old.

GORDON, MRS ELIZABETH - Liberty - Nov 10, 1881 Died,
Mrs Elizabeth Gordon whose death was recorded last weeks
Journal was 73 years 11 months 5 days old. Was the
mother of 12 children, 6 now living. Had 48
grandchildren and 9 great grandchildren.

GORDON, MRS O. - Local - Feb 10, 1881 Died, Quincy
papers announce the death on Sunday night of Mrs O.
Gordon of that city. Mrs Gordon was a daughter of J.C.
Wright of York Neck.

GORMAN, ANTHONY - Liberty - Mar 25, 1880 Anthony
Gorman, of Philadelphia came back this week to look
after his interest in his brothers estate.

GORMAN, JOHN - Liberty - Apr 13, 1882 Mr A. Gorman of
Philadelphia, brother of the late John Gorman of Liberty
called on us last week. He is here settling up his
brothers estate.

GORMAN, JOHN - Liberty - Jun 13, 1879 Mr Anthony Gorman
of Philadelphia made us a short visit last week. We
suppose he was looking after his interests in the John

Gorman estate.

GRAFF, PETER - Mendon - May 6, 1880   Died, Peter Graff Jr. died at his fathers home last Friday.

GRAHAM, HENRY
    SEE: BELDON, MRS

GRAVES, NELLIE - Neighborhood News - May 3, 1878   Nellie Graves, eldest daughter of Mr Graves, the blind man committed suicide yesterday A.M. "Rushville Times"

GRAY, MARIE
    SEE: SMYTH, THOMAS

GREER, THOMAS - Neighborhood News - Dec 28, 1877   A farmer of Mercer County named Thomas Greer age 45 years committed suicide at Galva, Henry County on the 15th.

GREGG, KATIE L. - Died - Dec 2, 1880   Died youngest daughter of Rev R. and Fannie M. Gregg at Camp Point November 27th, 1880.

GREGORY, DR
    SEE: ALLEN, MR D. SKILLMAN

GRIDLEY, TIMOTHY - Neighborhood News - Sep 28, 1877   Died, Timothy Gridley, an old citizen of Hancock County living near Elveston died a few days ago. Buried in Colchester.

GRIFFITH, JAMES - Coatsburg - Aug 11, 1881   Died, James Griffith an old citizen of this place died here Thursday eve last of paralysis. Confined to his bed the last 6 years. Services by Rev Gregg of Camp Point.

GRIFFITH, JEFFERSON - Clayton - Dec 2, 1880   Died, Jefferson Griffith, 79 years old died at his daughters, Mrs Jas. Douglass last Sunday eve.

GRIFFITH, LIZZIE
    SEE: WALLACE, JASON

GRIFFITH, OLIVER
    SEE: WALLACE, JASON

GRIMSHAW, COL. - Hash - Dec 17, 1875   The funeral of Col. Grimshaw took place Tuesday afternoon.

GRIMSHAW, HON JACKSON - Obituary - Dec 17, 1875 Hon. Jackson Grimshaw died at his home in Quincy Monday A.M. Born in Philadelphia November 22, 1822. Came to Illinois in 1843 and located at Pittsfield, Pike County about 1857 he moved to Quincy. He was a republican.

GROOM, MRS WM
    SEE: BUTLER, NOAH B.

GROVES, STEPHEN E. - Died - Apr 6, 1882 Died, March 28th of cerebro spinal meningitis Stephen E. son of Jacob and Margaret Groves of Big Neck age 9 years 6 months.

GRUBB, MRS DANIEL - Liberty - Jun 16, 1881 Died, Mrs Daniel Grubb one of the early settlers of Liberty township died at her home 2 miles NW of Liberty Saturday the 11th. Had been blind 2 years. Leaves a husband and children.

GRUBB, EDMUND
    SEE: FOSTER, MRS ELLA

GRUBB, JONAH
    SEE: WOLF, MRS EMMA

GUENTHER, C.F.C. - Local - Jan 26, 1882 Died, C.F.C. Guenther of Coatsburg last week at 88 years. Was father of Dr Guenther of Quincy and Louis Guenther of this township.

GUNTHER, CHARLES - Probate Notice - Feb 2, 1882 Charles Gunther 3rd Monday of March   Julius Gunther, Ex.

GUTHRIE, MRS - Mendon - Mar 14, 1879 Died, Mrs Guthrie, formerly a resident of this vicinity and a sister of Mr John Johnson, one of our oldest citizens died at her home near West Point, Hancock County a few days ago.

GUTHRIE, MOSES - Died - Aug 7, 1874 Died on the 1st inst in Columbus township in this county, Moses Guthrie. He was born near Louisville, Kentucky Apr 6, 1796. As a youth volunteered in the War of 1812 and was at the Battle of New Orleans in 1815. Came to Illinois in fall of 1831 and settled near the village of Columbus several years before the town was laid out.

HACKNEY, MARY E. - Keokuk Junction - Aug 19, 1880 Died, Mary E. wife of W.D. Hackney of this place Sunday eve at 4, age 42 years.

HACKNEY, MRS MARY H. - Died - Aug 19, 1880 Died in this town last Sunday, Mrs Mary H. Hackney wife of W.D. Hackney Esq. in her 47th year. Husband, sister and children survive her. Formerly of North Carolina. Keokuk Junction, Illinois   Aug 17, 1880

HADSELL, NATHAN A. - Neighborhood News - Dec 28, 1877 On the 13th inst Nathan A. Hadsell, of Barry was killed by being run over by a wagon.

HAFLAN, MARY - Died - Mar 26, 1875 Died from exposure, Mary Haflan formerly of Quincy, found frozen to death in the main road near the farm of Linus Moore about 4 miles SE of Columbus last Wednesday. Buried on Thursday.

HAGERTY, MRS CLARA B. - Died - Aug 7, 1874 Died, August 1st of consumption, Mrs Clara B. Hagerty, wife of George T. Hagerty, age 19 years.

HAGERTY, MRS J.T.
    SEE: PENNEY, SAMUEL

HAGERTY, JOHN T. - Death of John T. Hagerty - Mar 3, 1881 News received Monday of the death of John T. Hagerty at Stanberry, Missouri age 53 years. His family accompanied body back here and buried in Camp Point Cemetery. Born Harrison County Kentucky March 21, 1828 came when very young with parents to Rushville where his father died. Mother then moved to Houston near Marcelline and one to Chillicothe, Missouri. When Mr Hagerty returned to Adams County as a young man he married Miss Georgiana Penny of Rushville and lived there till 1855 when he came to Camp Point. Went to Stanberry last fall and opened a dry goods store. Leaves a wife, a son and 2 daughters. Member of Odd Fellows Lodge 215 IOOF.

HAHN, MRS H.S.
    SEE: SWAN, DORA B.

HAINES, GEO. R.
    SEE: LASLEY, MATTIE J.

HAINES, MRS GEORGE R. - Local - May 2, 1879 Died, Mrs George R. Haines died Sunday at Bayliss, Pike County. She was a sister of Joseph P. Lasley.

HAINLINE, MRS VICTORIA - Mar 5, 1874 Mrs Victoria Hainline, wife of the junior editor of the Macomb

Journal died on the 27th ult in her 29th year of age.

HAIR, LIZZIE - Hash - Jun 9, 1876 Lizzie Hair living on Kentucky Street between 5th and 6th, Quincy was badly burned by a lamp explosion Saturday A.M. No hope for her.

HALEY, MRS JESSE - Mendon - Feb 26, 1880 Died, Mrs Kate Haley, wife of Jesse Haley and daughter of Meshach Wilcox of your city died on February 16th.

HALEY, JESSE - Mendon - Jan 16, 1880 Jesse Haley's little child died last Friday.

HALEY, MRS JESSIE - Obituary - Feb 26, 1880 Died, February 16th, Kate Wilcox, wife of Jessie Haley, age 19 years. Buried Mendon Cemetery.

HALL, E.D. - Neighborhood News - Oct 28, 1878 Mrs E.K. Whitcomb of Elgin received word on Wednesday of the death from yellow fever of her brother, E.D. Hall revenue collector at Okolona, Mississippi.

HALL, GEORGE K. - Hash - Mar 3, 1876 A man named Willard George was arrested Monday in Quincy for the murder of George K. Hall, prop. Of the Opera House Bowling Alley on the night of May 25th, 1875.

HALL, HARRY MAXWELL - Died - Aug 5, 1880 Died, in Camp Point August 1st Harry Maxwell, son of Prof S.F. and Mrs E.A. Hall age 10 months 14 days. Services by Rev Thos. D. Davis, pastor of the Presbyterian Church.

HALL, NATHAN K. - Neighborhood News - Jul 27, 1877 Died, Mr Nathan K. Hall of Sonora township. Died Sunday night. "Carthage Republican"

HALLER, MIKE - Coatsburg - Jun 26, 1873 Mike Haller a farm hand working for Dr Guenther came here the eve of June 16th and drank to much beer. He was thrown from the track by the train engine. Injured severely, if not fatally.

HALSEY, MR W.
    SEE: REED

HAM, JOHN
    SEE: KEMP, MRS RHODA C.

HAMILTON, MRS - Clayton - May 25, 1877 Died, Mrs Hamilton whose been suffering from consumption 2 years died last Friday.

HAMILTON, JOHN - Local - Nov 5, 1880 John Hamilton who took the place of Sullivan (the brakeman on the Wabash who got his hand mashed a few weeks ago) on Thursday A.M. met his death at Hamilton in a train accident. Remains taken to his home town, Clayton, Illinois. "Carthage Gazette"

HAMMER, FRANCIS - Neighborhood News - Jan 11, 1878 Francis Hammer was killed at a dance near Nebo, Pike county, New Years eve by a man named Fowler.

HAMRICK, FARROW
    SEE: WILKES, DANIEL

HAMRICK, JOHN S. - Died - Feb 2, 1882 Died, Sunday eve January 29th John S. Hamrick age 33 years 6 months 21 days. Son of Farrow Hamrick one of the early settlers of the county and lived with parents. Died from typhoid fever.

HANDERSON, HENRY A. - Local - Jul 14, 1881 Died, Henry A. Handerson, of New York committed suicide in the Occidental Hotel.

HANLY, - Neigboring notes - Jul 8, 1880 Coroner Seehorn did not hold any inquest upon the remains of Hanly, the insane inmate of the county poor house who was killed Sunday night.

HANLY, GEORGE - Local - Jul 1, 1880 George Hanly of the county poor farm was killed Sunday night by an insane man at the poor farm.

HANNA, COL. - Golden - Mar 17, 1881 Col. Hanna leaves tonight for Indiana to attend the funeral of Mrs Mitchell the lady who kindly cared for the Colonel when a child.

HARBISON, MR - Clayton - Mar 23, 1882 Conductor Harbison was run over by the train and killed at Springfield Junction Saturday eve. Remains brought to his father's in Clayton Sunday A.M. Funeral in the M.E. Church today.

HARBISON, CHAL. - Local - Mar 23, 1882 Killed, Chal.

Harbison, formerly of Clayton and a brother of Capt W.H. Harbison and Robert Harbison, late of Houston was killed at Springfield Junction Saturday eve by the train. Remains brought to Clayton.

HARBISON, J.C. – Clayton – Feb 7, 1879 Mr J.C. Harbison buried his youngest child here this week.

HARDY, BAPTIST – Hash – Jul 31, 1873 Baptist Hardy, an old citizen of this county died on Thursday after a protracted illness.

HARDY, BAPTIST – Mendon – Apr 27, 1882 Mr and Mrs Baptist Hardy near Loraine lost 3 children last week of scarlet fever or diptheria.

HARDY, MRS BAPTIST – Death List – Sep 7, 1877 Old settlers death list since last meeting: Mrs Baptist Hardy, Keene, age 70 years.

HARDY, JOHN – Mendon – Jan 19, 1882 Died, John Hardy, one of the old settlers of this township at his home some 5 miles north of this village Friday eve. Wife died 9 days ago.

HARNESS, PROF A.P. – Local – Nov 14, 1879 Prof A.P. Harness who spent several weeks here at D.H. Wyle's in the summer of "78" was shot and killed at Harper, Kansas October 22nd.

HARRINGTON, MRS A.L.
    SEE: COLLINS, FREDERICK

HARRIS, CHAS W.
    SEE: BOSTIC, WILLIAM E.

HARRIS, HATTIE B. – Died – Aug 4, 1876 Died, at Lincoln, Illinois July 29th Hattie B. Harris, age 72 years youngest daughter of Rev J.H. and Nancy Bates, formerly of Camp Point.

HARRIS, JAMES M.R. – Obituary – May 19, 1876 Died, James M.R. Harris in Quincy on the morn of the 15th. Born in Massillon, Ohio March 20, 1841 lived there till 15 years old when he lost his parents. Then he went to Mazareth, Pennsylvania to school and stayed 3 years and on to Chicago 1 year then to Peru, Illinois for 1-1/2 years. Entered the service at Chicago "F" 62 Penn. Volunteers and was badly wounded in the Battle of Gaines

Mill and captured and kept 35 days. After discharge he
went to Chicago an worked for C.B. & Q. Railroad till
1868 when he took charge of that companies office here.
While here he married Miss Craver, daughter of M.D.L.
Craver Esq. Leaves a wife and one child.

HARRIS, JAMES M.R. - Memoriam - May 19, 1876 Benjamin
Lodge #297 AF & AM   James M.R. Harris leaves a family.

HARRIS, MRS NANCY ELLEN - Obituary - Jun 29, 1877 Died,
at her home 3 miles west of Camp Point June 20th of
consumption, Mrs Nancy Ellen Harris, 32 years old. Born
in Adams County March 22, 1846. Leaves a husband and 3
children. By W.T. West

HART, AMOS - Horrible Tragedy - Feb 15, 1878 The home
of Amos Hart, an aged resident of Big Neck, Keene
Township was destroyed by fire Sunday and his charred
remains were found the next A.M. nearly 70 years old.
Leaves 4 children.

HART, MRS HANNAH M. - Died - Nov 24, 1874 Died in Big
Neck, Illinois November 10th Mrs Hannah M. Hart age 37
years 5 months 28 days.

HART, NICHOLAS BAILEY - Died - Oct 23, 1873 Died
October 17th Nicholas Bailey, only son of G.W. and Rhoda
Hart, age 10 months.

HARTMAN, AMOS - Probate Notice - Mar 15, 1878 Amos
Hartman, deceased May 20th 1878 Alfred K. Bailey, adm.

HARTMAN, GEORGE - Neighborhood News - Feb 1, 1878 Died,
George Hartman, citizen of Versailles, Brown County died
last week.

HASTING, MRS WM - Fowler - Aug 9, 1878 Died, Mrs
Hasting, wife of Wm Hasting Sr., July 28th. Came to this
country with her husband in 1839 and settled near their
present home, raised 7 sons. Buried at N. Stahls
Cemetery July 30th.

HAUBACK, MR - Hash - Jan 18, 1878 A man named Hauback
was killed by the Wabash passenger train near Bluffs
last week.

HAUPTNER, FRANCIS - Local - Nov 10, 1881 Died, a German
named Francis Hauptner of Columbus died from a wagon
accident Thursday.

HAUSEMAN, PHILLIP - Local - Aug 25, 1881 On Sunday eve last the body of Phillip Hauseman, a Swiss laborer about 60 years old was found with 2 bullet holes in his forehead on the bank of the bay a short distance above an ice house. Gun found beside him. "Quincy Herald"

HAWKINS, GEO.
    SEE: GAGE, FRANK

HAXEL, MRS JOHN F. - Hash - Apr 7, 1876 Mrs John F. Haxel died suddenly Monday A.M. in Quincy of apoplexy.

HAYES, JOHN - Neighboring News - Jul 15, 1880 Three boys, John Hayes, Theodore Routt and Willie Shelton were drowned at Gibson City one day last week.

HAYES, JOHN - Neighborhood News - Nov 2, 1877 John Hayes was run over by the train this side of Milville Saturday night, had lived in Columbus township at one time. 38 years old. Leaves a wife and 2 children.

HAYS, HUGH - Clayton - Feb 17, 1881 Died, Hugh Hays, an old irishman who has been here many years dropped dead on the streets last week.

HEAD, MR - Local - Jan 23, 1880 An old man named Head, was run down and killed by the Keokuk train in Quincy Saturday afternoon. The deceased was a rag picker.

HEAD, DAVID E. - Death of David E. Head - May 4, 1877 David E. Head of Carthage died at his home Tuesday afternoon. The Herald says: Mr Head was for many years circuit clerk at Hancock County being appointed by Stephen A. Douglas.

HEAD, DON - Quincy - Nov 17, 1881 Died, Don, youngest son of Wm T. and E.A. Head age 11 years of gastric fever November 11, 1881 at his fathers home, Quincy, brother Emmett, 2 years his senior.

HEANEY, EDWARD - Mendon - Dec 15, 1881 Died, Edward Heaney's child, 4 years old. Died Saturday.

HEASON, SAMUEL - Probate Notice - Apr 3, 1873 Samuel Heason 3rd Monday of May 1873 (19th) George Rhea, Ex.

HEATON, SAMUEL - Probate Notice - Apr 10, 1873 Samuel Heaton 3rd Monday of May 1873 (19th) George Rhea, Ex.

HECKRODT, MARTIN A. - Probate Notice - Aug 31, 1882
Martin A. Heckrodt, deceased 1st Monday of October (2nd)
Henry A. Heckrodt, adm.

HECKROOT, A.M. - Liberty - Jul 20, 1882 Died, A.M.
Heckroot of Lost Prairie in his chair Saturday night of
dropsy of the heart. Leaves an aged wife and children,
63 years old.

HECOX, MRS - Hash - May 8, 1873 A sister of Mrs Hecox
lost her life in the Dixon bridge trap.

HEDGECOCK, MRS ANNA
    SEE: TOTTEN, MARIA N.

HEDGES, MRS M.J. - Mendon - Nov 3, 1881 Died, Mrs M.J.
Hedges, daughter of John Crawford of our village, last
evening. Leaves a husband and 4 children.

HEDGES, RUFUS M. - Died - Jul 22, 1880 Died in
Whitehall, Tuesday A.M. June 29th, 1880 of old age, Mr
Rufus M. Hedges, 71 years 7 months 29 days. Born Exeter,
Otsego, County New York. Came to Illinois at an early
age. Moved to Michigan about 15 years ago. Whitehall,
Michigan Forum.

HEDGES, WM - Death List - Sep 7, 1877 Old Settlers
death list since last meeting: Wm Hedges, Ellington, age
73 years.

HEILWAGON, MRS - Newtown - Jan 10, 1879 Mrs Heilwagon
of Burton died very suddenly Tuesday A.M.

HEILWAGON, WILLIAM - To Be Hung - Feb 2, 1882 William
Heilwagon, formerly of Burton township, Adams County was
found guilty Friday of the murder of his daughter in
law, Dora Heilwagon in Rock Island County. Killed Dora
on Sept 5, 1881. She was wife of Otto Heilwagon, his
son. The doomed man has a brother living just south of
the city limits. "Herald"

HEINS, HENRY - Local - Mar 30, 1882 Funeral Monday of
Henry Heins was attended by Roll and Oscar Strickler.

HEINS, HENRY - Coatsburg - Mar 30, 1882 Johnie Hart and
wife one of our well known conductors was in town Monday
attending the funeral of Henry Heins.

HEINS, HENRY - Caught in a Frog - Mar 30, 1882 Killed,

Henry Heins of this township was breaking train 111. While at Macomb engaged in switching caught his foot in a frog and was knocked down and ran over. Mother lives west of town. Funeral at Coatsburg Monday. Leaves a widowed mother who buried her husband only a short time since.

HEITZMAN, MR - Local - Apr 1, 1880 From Rushville "Citizen" we learn that a German farmer named Heitzman was shot Monday night. Lived 18 hours and said his brother in law, Jake Morrill shot him.

HEMPSTEAD, MRS CHARLES S. - State News - Aug 26, 1880 Died, Mrs Hempstead, wife of the late Hon. Charles S. Hempstead, died at Galena on the 21st inst. Was about 80 years old and lived Galena nearly 50 years.

HENDERSON, MR - Mendon - Jan 20, 1881 Died, Grandpa Henderson died Sunday A.M. in his 78th year. Was father of G.H. Henderson and was buried beside his wife at Coatsburg. Wife died 13 years ago.

HENDERSON, BENJAMIN - Mendon - Apr 4, 1879 Benjamin Henderson 16 years old, son of Harry Henderson shot himself while hunting Thursday. Funeral Sunday.

HENDERSON, FANNIE - Coatsburg - Dec 22, 1881 Died, little Fannie, youngest child of Mr and Mrs Henderson on Sunday A.M. December 18th.

HENDERSON, REV G.D. - Neighborhood News - Nov 30, 1877 Rev G.D. Henderson a resident of Monmouth died in that city last week, age 59 years.

HENDERSON, NED - Keokuk Junction - Jan 31, 1879 Dr Cushenbery reports from the county farm that Ned Henderson (colored) died last week. Was 106 years old. He was at one time George Washington's hostler.

HENDRICKS, RICHARD - Neighborhood News - Oct 12, 1877 Richard Hendricks was shot by his father in law, George B. Kennedy. Mr Hendricks died. Buried Adams County.

HENDRICKS, STEPHEN - Death List - Sep 7, 1877 Old Settlers death list since last meeting: Stephen Hendricks, McKee, age 55 years.

HENDRICKS, STEPHEN M. - Probate Notice - Jun 15, 1877 Stephen M. Hendricks 3rd Monday of July 1877 W.R.

Baker, adm.

HENDRICKSON, JOHN - Local - Dec 14, 1882 Died, John Hendrickson, a resident of the county 40 years, Sunday at the home of his son James H. at Breckenridge. Buried Mendon.

HENDRICKSON, MRS PHEBE - Mendon - May 9, 1879 Mrs Phebe Hendrickson, eldest daughter of the late Amos Scranton died a few days ago, brought here for burial. Her mother is very sick.

HENNICK, ARTHUR E. - Died - Jul 21, 1876 Died on the 17th inst, Arthur E., son of C. and A. Hennick age 18 months of flux.

HENRY, J.F. - Clayton - May 4, 1882 Died, Mr J.F. Henry on Friday of congestion of the lungs.

HENRY, O.M. - Supplement - Sep 1, 1876 Died since last years meeting of Old Settlers of Adams and Brown County, O.M. Henry of Brown County.

HENSLEY, GEO. - Local - Feb 26, 1880 Killed, a Camp Point man, Geo. Hensley was killed while coupling cars at Decatur a few days ago. "Quincy Papers" The residence is a mistake, no such person known here.

HERKROOT, A.M. - Local - Jul 20, 1882 Died, A.M. Herkroot a farmer of Columbus township Saturday night of heart disease. He was a German and lived in the township many years.

HERMAN, MRS CHARLES - Local - Apr 15, 1880 The report in the Warsaw "Bulletin" of the death of Mrs Charles Herman is an error. The parties live near Camp Point instead of Clayton as reported.

HERMAN, M.M. - Exchange Notes - Jan 3, 1879 Dr M.M. Herman of Galesburgh committed suicide last week by taking morphine.

HERMETET, MRS PETER - Clayton - Dec 9, 1880 Died, Mrs Peter Hermetet died Saturday. Services at the ME Church Monday.

HERNDON, JOHN R. - A Pioneer Gone - Nov 30, 1882 Died, John R. Herndon in Galesburg last Thursday, age 76 years, known as "Uncle Row" in Columbus 40 years ago.

HERRING, WM M.
SEE: AVEY, JOHN

HERRON, MRS
SEE: BECKETT, C.R.

HERRON, SAMUEL T. - Local - Oct 27, 1881 Died, a daughter Samuel T. Herron, La Prairie died last Wednesday. Funeral Thursday by Rev L.F. Walden.

HERRON, SARAH - La Prairie - Oct 27, 1881 Died, Miss Sarah Herron on the 18th inst, daughter of S.T. Herron. Member of ME Church and was 18 years 6 months old.

HESS, GRANDERSON M. - Hash - Nov 30, 1877 Died, Granderson M. Hess of Camp Point died at Mt Sterling Tuesday.

HESTER, FREDERICK - Nov 12, 1880 Frederick Hester of Iroquois Co. wife murderer has been sentenced to be executed on January 21st.

HETRICK, AGGIE
SEE: AVEY, JOHN

HETRICK, CARRIE
SEE: AVEY, JOHN

HETRICK, JOHN
SEE: AVEY, JOHN

HETRICK, MARION - Murder Trial - Sep 26, 1879 Trial of Marion Hetrick, John S. Avery, and Leroy Working for the murder of Dr Daniel Pierson began in Quincy last week.

HICOX, MRS R. - La Prairie - May 25, 1877 Died, Mrs R. Hicox, sister of E. Lancaster, of Chattan died on the 19th.

HIGGINS, CHARLES - Identity of the Printer Killed under the Cars - Sep 1, 1881 Saturday Mr Berry, J.H. Kirkpatrick and Mrs J.N. Higgins of Carthage identified the tramp printer who was killed on the Wabash freight here Wednesday morning as Charles Higgins, son of Mr and Mrs J.N. Higgins.

HIGGINS, CHARLES - Mendon - Sep 8, 1881 Mrs Higgins of Carthage received a telegram from Springfield yesterday and signed by Charles Higgins saying it was not him who was killed at Camp Point by the cars and would be home today.

HIGGINS, CHARLEY - Local - Sep 8, 1881 Charley Higgins who was supposed to have been killed a couple of weeks ago arrived at his mothers in Carthage.

HIGGINS, J.N. - Mendon - Sep 1, 1881 Died, J.N. Higgins of Carthage and before the wife and children had scarcely reached home after the funeral comes the news that there oldest son was killed by the cars Wednesday A.M.

HIGGINS, JOSEPH N. - Local - Sep 1, 1881 Died, Joseph N. Higgins at Carthage Tuesday eve August 3rd. Lived many years in Mendon, moved to Carthage about 4 years ago. Buried Wesley Chapel Thursday.

HIGHLAND, HENRY M. - Local - Nov 18, 1880 Henry M. Highland, formerly steward of the Tremont House Quincy committed suicide Sunday eve in Kansas City, no cause.

HIGHTOWER, MR - Mendon - Apr 8, 1880 Died, another of our oldest citizens died last week, Mr Hightower.

HILGENBRINK, JOSEPH - Hash - Oct 13, 1876 Joseph Hilgenbrink, of Quincy was killed Sunday by falling from a hickory tree near W. Quincy. He was a carpenter by trade, age 48 years. Leaves a wife and several children.

HINKSON, SAMUEL
        SEE: WILSON, WILLIAM

HINKSON, SAMUEL - Adm Sale - Oct 7, 1880 Adm Sale of Real Estate Saturday Nov 6th, 1880 John W. Stormer, adm estate of Samuel Hinkson, deceased Oct 5, 1880.

HINKSTON, SAMUEL
        SEE: WILSON, WM

HIRTH, JACOB JR. - Local - Jul 29, 1880 Jacob Hirth Jr. of Ellington, 12 years old, was killed in an accident last Wednesday.

HIRTH, JACOB - Burton - Jul 29, 1880 Little Jacob Hirth of Ellington was killed in an accident last week. Father, Jacob Hirth Sr. was not home at the time. Jacob was 11 years old. Services by Rev Foot and also in

German by Rev Newman at the German ME Church in Quincy.

HOAR, SAMUEL L. - Hash - Nov 16, 1877 Died, Samuel L. Hoar an old resident of Quincy died at the home of his son, Benjamin F. Hoar, Saturday eve, 80 years old. He settled in Quincy in 1837 and later moved to Payson for 20 years. Returned to Quincy to live with his son.

HOBBS, DAVID - Death List - Sep 7, 1877 Old settlers death list since last meeting: David Hobbs, Liberty, age 68 years.

HOFFMAN, BLUEFORD - Newtown - Dec 20, 1878 Mr Blueford Hoffman died suddenly Sunday from paralysis. He leaves a large family with no means of support.

HOFFMAN, MRS C.H.
    SEE: COOK, D.A.
    SEE: COOKE, MRS

HOFFMAN, MRS H.O. - Local - Jul 13, 1882 Mrs H.O. Hoffman died at Bloomington Thursday. Been an invalid many years.

HOFFMAN, MRS JOHN - Hash - Sep 21, 1877 Died, Mrs John Hoffman last Saturday. A resident of Richfield township. John beat her August 18th, in jail in Quincy.

HOFFMAN, JOHN - Neighborhood News - Nov 30, 1877 Died, John Hoffman of Canton, Missouri died Monday.

HOFFMAN, RICHARD - Mendon - Sep 20, 1878 Mr Richard Hoffman, Quincy died at the home of is brother, C.H. Hoffman our postmaster on Sunday last.

HOKE, EVERETT W. - Death's Doings - Dec 14, 1882 Died, Sunday December 10th of typhoid pneumonia Everett W. Hoke age 21 years. Remains accompanied to the old home in Kentucky by his brother Jacob Hoke and Daniel Omer left on the Wabash train Sunday night.

HOLMES, MRS SAMUEL - Neighborhood News - Feb 1, 1878 Died, Mrs Samuel Holmes died at Marysville, Missouri last Saturday, daughter of Joshua Streeter. Came to the county in 1825. Married Samuel Holmes in 1836.

HOLMES, WILLIAM - Local - Apr 18, 1879 "Herald" Tuesday A.M. William Holmes jumped into the river near Hampshire Street took off his coat and hat and left a note to take them to his wife, 716 Maine Street. He was about 60 years old and made picture frames in this city. Body not found. Temporary insanity.

HOLSTINE, PETER – Neighborhood News – Aug 23, 1878 Terrible accident at Colchester Thursday A.M. Peter Holstine, a Swede, residing near Colchester had a accident at the coal mines there, was killed. "Macomb Eagle"

HONNOLD, MRS M.E.
    SEE: MOORE, MRS

HONNOLD, MRS MARY – A Card – Jun 8, 1877 Delay in payment of Mrs Mary Honnold's claim against Protection Life Insurance Co. on account of death of her husband, Robert Honnold.

HONNOLD, REV R. – Died – Jul 21 1876 Died on the 14th inst Rev R. Honnold, age 36 years of cancer.

HONNOLD, REV ROBERT – Aug 11, 1876 Rev Robert Honnold died in Camp Point July 14, 1876. Born in Lee County Iowa October 4, 1839. Moved with parents to Christian County Illinois when a child. He was a good husband and father. Leaves a wife and 4 children. From " Central Christian Advocate"

HONNOLD, ROBERT – Probate Notice – Sep 29, 1876 Robert Honnold 3rd Monday of November Mary E. Honnold, Ex.

HORN, A.E. – Mendon – Jan 29, 1880 Mr A.E. Horn lost a little daughter yesterday, age some 6 years.

HORN, ADAM – Local – Aug 17, 1882 Died, Adam Horn an old citizen of Fowler, Sunday.

HORNER, SARAH ALICE – Died – Jan 2, 1880 December 30th 1879, Sarah Alice, daughter of Albert L. and Maria E. Horner age 4 years 2 months 25 days.

HORNEY, SARAH
    SEE: BURKE, SARAH

HOUGH, SOPHIA – Clayton – May 18, 1882 Died, Miss Sophia Hough, daughter of R.G. Hough last Saturday the 6th.

HOUGHTON, JAS S. – Real Estate Transfer – Nov 24, 1881

Jas S. Houghton (deceased) by adm, to Frank Houghton, north 80 acres of the NE ¼ of section 4, Ursa twp $400.

HOWARD, ALANSON - State News - Oct 14 1880 Died, Alanson Howard, of Chenoa, died at Alexandria, Nebraska on the 9th inst, age 72 years.

HOWARD, MISS ALICE - Mendon - Apr 27, 1882 Died, Miss Alice Howard died of complaint Friday and buried Saturday at the Frazier cemetery in Ursa township.

HOWARD, WESLEY - Hash - Mar 8, 1878 Wesley Howard of Ripley township, Brown County shot and killed John Riggal Saturday P.M. surrendered himself and is in jail.

HOWDEN, LUCY
    SEE: WERTZ, MRS LUCY

HOWDEN, CAPT T.L.
    SEE: STEWART, MARTIN
    SEE: WERTZ, MRS LUCY

HOWELL, BARTON T. - Local - Feb 5, 1880 Died, Barton T. Howell of Mt Sterling committed suicide last Friday. Leaves a wife and 2 children.

HOWELL, D.J.
    SEE: STEWART, MRS SARAH

HOWELL, MRS DAVID
    SEE: STEWART, MRS MARTIN

HOWELL, J.B. - Neighborhood News - Jun 24, 1880 Died, Judge J.B. Howell died at his home in Keokuk last Thursday A.M. age 64 years.

HOWES, OLIVER - Supplement - Sep 1, 1876 Died since last years meeting of Old Settlers of Adams and Brown counties, Oliver Howes of Clayton.

HOYT, CALEB R. - Hash - Apr 24, 1874 We learn that Caleb R. Hoyt, formerly of Houston township died at his residence in Livingston County Missouri a few days since, of dropsy.

HUBBARD, REV. - Bowen - Sep 7, 1882 Died, Rev Hubbard who has been employed as minister of the Cong. Church was called home by the death of his wife in Vermont.

HUBER, MARY - Died - Sep 30, 1880 Died, September 24th of consumption, Mary, daughter of Solomon Huber, age 16 years.

HUBERT, MR - Hash - Jul 19, 1878 A farmer named Hubert, in Beverly township fell dead from heat.

HUDDLESTON, DAVID - Liberty - Dec 14, 1882 Buried, babe of David Huddleston's last Friday. Died of lung fever.

HUDSON, CYRUS H. - Railroad accident at Loraine - Jul 3, 1873 Cyrus H. Hudson residing 2 miles north of Loraine was run over by the train and killed (by engine #119).

HUFF, MRS - Keokuk Junction - Feb 5, 1880 Died, Mrs Huff of Basco, Hancock county, mother of F.M. Huff of the Junction. Died last Friday. Funeral Sunday.

HUFF, MRS - Junction - Jan 29, 1880 Mr F.M. Huff was called to Basco last week, his mother is not expected to live.

HUFF, MRS F.M. - Junction - Feb 5, 1880 Mrs F.M. Huff was called to Basco to attend the funeral of her mother in law.

HUFF, JOHN - Beverly - Sep 30, 1880 Died, John Huff Sr. an old farmer of this township died on the 22nd inst. A wife and 12 children survive him.

HUFF, MRS SUSAN - Junction - Jan 29, 1880 Mrs Susan Huff died, over 70 years old.

HUFNAGEL, MR - Columbus - Dec 7, 1882 Died, Old Mr Hufnagel, Thursday. Buried Saturday.

HUGHES, BEN - Neighborhood News - Apr 26, 1878 Body of Ben Hughes 16 years old was recovered from the river west of Quincy, Sunday. He was a nephew of J.D. Patton and was drowned about 3 weeks ago. "Whig"

HUGHES, BERRY - Neighborhood News - Mar 29, 1878 Died, Berry Hughes who boarded a boat at Keokuk fell overboard and drowned a short distance above La Grange. In his trunk was a card written at Clayton February 5, 1878 to Berry Hughes, Quincy and signed Jacob D. Hughes. Trunk was directed to Berry Hughes Milton, Iowa. He was 19 or 20 years old. From Keokuk Gate City paper.

HUGHES, MARY
    SEE: WYLE, JOHN

HUGHES, NATHAN - Probate Notice - Jan 27, 1881 Nathan Hughes, deceased 3rd Monday of March 1881 Nancy Hughes, ex.

HUGHES, NATHAN - Died - Dec 2, 1880 Died November 25th Nathan Hughes age 67 years. Born Clark County Indiana April 10, 1813. Came with parents to Adams county in 1832. Married Nancy Downing April 22, 1839. Wife and 8 grown children survive him.

HUGHES, VIRGINIA
    SEE: WILLARD, DAVID
    SEE: MARGARET A.

HUGHES, W.H.
    SEE: DOWNING, SARAH E.

HUGHES, MRS W.M. - Personal - May 11, 1877 Mrs W.M. Hughes is very low with consumption at the home of her father, E.C. Downing.

HUGHES, WM - Neighborhood News - Aug 2, 1878 A fatal accident Tuesday near Table Grove, Wm Hughes a farmer between 60 and 70 years of age. "Bushnell Gleaner"

HULL, MR - Clayton - Sep 12, 1879 Died, old man Hull the shoemaker died inside of 2 days with cholera morbus.

HULSE, MARTHA - Fowler - Apr 21, 1881 Died, March 29th of consumption, Miss Martha Hulse at her home near Cliola.

HULSE, SARAH - Beverly - Jan 29, 1880 Died, Mrs Sarah Hulse who lived a few miles SW of Beverly committed suicide January 18th.

HULSE, WM B. - Hash - Nov 26, 1875 Wm B. Hulse, of Ellington died at his residence Saturday night. Was a native of New York and settled in Adams County in 1840.

HUNSAKER, DANIEL - Livingston - Jul 7, 1881 Died, a child of Daniel Hunsaker's at George Kimmons last week.

HUNTER, JOHN - Hash - Feb 23, 1877 A little boy, son of John Hunter of McKee township was killed last Thursday by a falling tree. Buried Saturday.

HUSEMAN, HENRY - Fatally Shot - Dec 16, 1880 Friday Henry Huseman was fatally shot at Melrose township. Was a son of P. Huseman who lives in Section 8 in Melrose. "Accident" "News"

HUSTED, MARY
    SEE: GARLETTS, DAVID

HUTMACHER, FRANK - Local - Aug 4, 1881 Drowned, Friday evening Frank Hutmacher a small boy of Quincy fell from the ferry dock. Body not found yet. Saturday Albert Cornelius age 16 drowned near Bonnett and Duffy's stove foundry while bathing.

HYMAN, GEO. - Newtown - Apr 4, 1879 Mr Geo. Hyman living west of town is not expected to live.

HYMAN, GEO. - Newtown - Apr 11, 1879 Died, Mr Geo. Hyman, of this place died at his home last Monday. Buried at Payson. Leaves a wife and several children.

HYMERS, JESSE - Hash - Aug 4, 1876 Jesse Hymers was shot and killed by Henry Howerton and Robert Hymers was badly wounded by Charles Howerton near Hurdland, Knox county Missouri last Sunday.

IHNEN, ONKE - Keokuk Junction - Jul 1, 1880 A grandchild of Onke Ihnen, who lived somewhere in the county died Sunday.

IHNEN, ONKE - Local - Oct 31, 1879 A son of Onke Ihnen at Keokuk Junction was thrown from his horse Saturday, feared he won't live.

ILER, MRS - Junction - Jan 16, 1880 Died, Mrs Iler at 11 last night.

INGERSOLL, JOHN W. - Neighborhood News - Oct 19, 1877 Died, John W. Ingersoll an old resident of Canton died last Friday. Buried Monday.

INGERSOLL, MRS R.A.
    SEE: LIVINGSTON, MR

INGRAM, MISS LULU - Neighborhood News - Aug 2, 1878 Miss Lulu Ingram, living near Perry in Pike county committed suicide last Wednesday. Was engaged to be married.

IRONS, MISS JANE - Neighborhood News - Mar 1, 1878 Last Monday a 16 year old girl, Miss Jane Irons was going from Ellisville to her home when her blind horse fell on her, killing her. "Prairie City Herald"

IRWIN, SAMUEL - Neighborhood News - Sep 28, 1877 Died, Wednesday of last week a 4 year old daughter of Samuel Irwin who works at Chase's brick yard was scalded when she fell in a bucket of hot water. Died the next day. "Blandinsville Independent"

JACKSON, GEORGE W. - Trustee Sale - May 22, 1874 Trustee Sale of Real Estate, will of George W. Jackson and his wife Julia Ann Jackson dated Sep 16, 1869 recorded Adams County in Book 7 of Mortgages page 37 Benjamin A. Curry, trustee.

JACKSON, JAMES - Hash - Mar 22, 1878 James Jackson a section hand on the Carthage Division of the C.B. & Q was killed Saturday. Deceased was a Swede and had no relatives in this country. "Whig"

JACKSON, STEPHEN - Neighborhood News - Sep 28, 1877 Died, Stephen Jackson, an old resident of Warsaw, 88 years old. Died at the home of his son in law, George Boscow on the 10th inst.

JACOBS, E.N.
    SEE: PEARCE, ELLA J.

JACOBS, H.F.
    SEE: PEARCE, ELLA J.

JAMISON, MR
    SEE: KEENAN, MRS REBECCA ANN

JAMISON, SAMUEL - Local - Sep 21, 1882 Died, Col. Samuel Jamison, for 40 years a resident of Ellington died last week, age 82 years.

JANSEN, SARAH - Livingston - Apr 11, 1879 We regret the departure of our estimable young friend, Sarah Jansen, but hope that "true merit may ever meet a just reward.

JASPER, THOMAS
    SEE: TINDALL, MRS JOSEPH

JENKINS, MR - Mendon - Dec 27, 1878 Mr Jenkins an old and well known citizen formerly a miller died very suddenly yesterday A.M. at his home near Loraine.

JEWELL, CHARLES - Augusta Murder - Jul 18, 1879 Hancock Jail Enoch says he does not remember. Enoch J. (or S.) Jewell, 19 years old and lives with father in Birmingham, Illinois. Charles was 25 years old.

JEWELL, ENOCH - Local - Oct 31, 1879 Enoch Jewell who murdered his brother at Augusta July 4th while drunk was sentenced to 14 years in state prison.

JEWETT, CHARLES - Whiskey & Blood - Jul 11, 1879 The celebration of the 4th at Augusta drew a large crowd among them Charles and Enoch Jewett and _____ Slater. Started home and Enoch wanted to return for more whiskey, a fight and Enoch stabbed Charles who died with in a few minutes. Parents notified.

JIMISON, JAMES - Death List - Sep 7, 1877 Old settlers death list since last meeting: James Jimison, Liberty, age 60 years.

JIMISON, MRS MARY - Died - Nov 14, 1879 Died at her home in Adams County November 5th, Mrs Mary Jimison, wife of Edward Jimison in her 68th year. Leaves her husband and 6 children. Was a member of the Kingston Baptist Church.

JOHNS, CAROLINE
    SEE: KEENAN, JOSEPH

JOHNS, WILLIAM
    SEE: KEENAN, JOSEPH

JOHNSON, MRS A.
    SEE: STANSBERY, MRS SARAH

JOHNSON, CHARLES - Neighborhood News - Aug 9, 1878 Charles Johnson, colored, age 19 years, drowned last Monday while bathing in the C.B. & Q reservoir at Galesburg.

JOHNSON, FREDERICK G. - Local - Aug 19, 1880 Frederick G. Johnson of Melrose died last week in his 66th year. Mr Johnson was at one time county treasurer.

JOHNSON, JOHN - Local - Jul 11, 1879 John Johnson died suddenly Monday eve at his home in Coatsburg. Buried here Tuesday beside his wife who died last year.

JOHNSON, JOHN
　　SEE: GUTHRIE, MRS

JOHNSON, REBECCA - Died - Aug 4, 1881 Died at the home of Michael McGinley, York Neck, Adams County Illinois July 25, 1881 Rebecca Johnson. Aunt Rebecca had suffered for many years. Member of ME church 50 years.

JOHNSON, SARAH A. - Died - Jun 7, 1878 Died on the 4th inst of consumption, Mrs Sarah A., wife of John Johnson of Coatsburg and daughter of Jasper Asher, of this village, age 21 years.

JOHNSON, THOMAS - Neighborhood News - Jul 6, 1877 7 year old son of Thomas Johnson drowned in a creek.

JOHNSON, THOS. - Local - Mar 2, 1882 Body of Thos Johnson of Springfield was found near the town branch on the line of the Ohio and Mississippi Railroad where it had been washed by high water, age 43 years. Leaves a wife and 6 children.

JONAS, SAMUEL - Hash - Mar 29, 1878 Samuel Jonas an old citizen of Quincy died last Wednesday night. He was brother of the late Abraham Jonas and was for many years in business in Quincy, 71 years old.

JONES, MRS MARY - Obituary - May 20, 1880 Died at Milano, Milan county Texas, May 4th Mrs Mary, wife of P.W. Jones, late of Fowler, Illinois. Had been in Texas only a few months. Leaves 2 sisters in the north and an aged mother, loving husband and son.

JORDAN, JESSIE - 3 Children Burned - Oct 21, 1880 Tuesday night a log house about 1 mile south of town in the Macoupin bottom and occupied by Jessie Jordan (colored) burned. Three children found, oldest was Ettie age 12 or 13 years, boy Joshua age 10 and youngest Willie 5 or 6 years old. About 11 months ago Jordan buried his wife. "Carlinville Democrat"

JORDON, CALEB - Local - Dec 26, 1879 Caleb Jordon a citizen of Pike County, who resided below the Adams County line near New canton committed suicide Thursday. "Herald"

JOSLYN, JOHN - Died - Aug 26, 1880 Died in Camp Point August 16th, 1880 John Joslyn age 24 years. Born Kentucky and came to Illinois in 1871 with parents.

Married December 23, 1879 to Miss Mary E. Beckett. A wife and 2 children survive him.

JOYCE, - Feb 5, 1875 About 3 P.M. Tuesday, Joyce, who killed James McGuire cut his throat with a razor. Little hope for his recovery.

JOYCE, JOHN - Hash - Feb 12, 1875 John Joyce, the murderer of Jas McGuire cut his throat with a razor on the 2nd inst. Died on Thursday the 4th.

JOYCE, JOHN - Hash - Dec 25, 1874 The case of John Joyce for the murder of James McGuire has been continued to the February term of the circuit court.

JUDY, PARIS T. - Probate Notice - Jun 3, 1880 Paris T. Judy, deceased 3rd Monday of July 1880 Nancy Judy, adm.

JUDY, PARIS T. - Death of Paris T. Judy - May 6, 1880 Paris T. Judy an old citizen of Adams County died at his home in Gilmer township Thursday night. Lived Adams County 46 years. Was son of Winneford Judy. Born Clark County Kentucky December 11, 1811. Lived Kentucky until coming to Illinois in 1834. Married Miss Nancy Markwell of Kentucky, they had 1 son and 6 daughters: James M., Adelia A. (Mrs Wm Finlay), Rebecca E. (Mrs L.E. Finlay), Sarah N. (Mrs Wm Cresswell, Ida K. and Mandolia survive him. "Herald"

KASTNER, LOUIS - Hash - Apr 16, 1878 A man named Kastner committed suicide Saturday night by jumping in the river at Quincy, about 40 years old. His brother Louis Kastner keeps a grocery store on Maine Street near 10th.

KAY, LOIS - Died - Jan 28, 1876 Died, January 19, Lois, daughter of Chas. W. Kay, of Payson age 17 years.

KAY, ROBERT - Hash - May 18, 1877 Died, Robert Kay died at his home in Payson Saturday age 72 years. Was an old settler of this county.

KEENAN, HIRAM T. - Personal - Aug 14, 1874 Hiram T. Keenan arrived Monday A.M. to attend his father's funeral and returned Wednesday to St Louis.

KEENAN, JOSEPH - Died - Aug 14, 1874 Died on the 9th inst near this town Joseph Keenan, age nearly 86 years. Born in Bourbon county Kentucky Sept 27, 1788. At age

19 he moved with his fathers family to Warren county
Ohio where he lived 49 years and married 3 times. In
1858 he and his family moved near this town and he
stayed there until his death. Many years he was
considered the most wealthy man in Warren County Ohio.
He was unable to read or write. Buried by Benjamin
Lodge (Masonic) in Quincy on the 11th inst.

KEENAN, JOSEPH
   SEE: MCDONALD, MRS SALLIE KEENAN

KEENAN, JOSEPH - Hash - Sep 18, 1874 Thos. Bailey was
appointed adm. of the estate of Joseph Keenan, deceased.

KEENAN, JOSEPH - In Memoriam - Aug 14, 1874 Benjamin
lodge #297 AF & AM appointed to draft resolutions on the
death of Bro. Joseph Keenan who for more than 60 years
had practiced the principles of there beloved order.

KEENAN, JOSEPH - Legal Notice - Mar 6, 1875 Petition by
Thomas Bailey, adm of the estate of Joseph Keenan,
deceased vs Hiram T. Keenan, Wilson T. Keenan, Clara H.
Keenan, Morris W. Keenan, Zereida C. Danley, John S.
Danley, Sally McDonald, Samuel McDonald, Samantha
Patten, Eliza J. Keys, Caroline Johns, William Johns,
Melissa Keller, William B. Keller, Cyntha A. Galleher,
Carvel Galleher and William Bellew, defendants. S.
Patten, Eliza J. Keys, C. Johns, Wm Johns, Melissa
Keller, Wm Keller, Morris W. Keenan, Cyntha Galleher and
Carvel Galleher reside out of state.

KEENAN, MRS R.A. - Hash - Feb 5, 1875 Property of the
late Mrs R.A. Keenan will be sold at public sale
February 12th.

KEENAN, MRS REBECA A. - Personal - Feb 12, 1875 Samuel
Jamison has taken out letters of administration on the
estate of Mrs Rebeca A. Keenan.

KEENAN, MRS REBECCA ANN - Obituary - Feb 5, 1875 Died,
Mrs Rebecca Ann Keenan at her home in Camp Point January
31st, 68 years old. She was the daughter of Mr Jamison
who was a soldier in General Wayne's army from 1793 to
95. Her mother moved from Fort Pitt (now Pittsburg) to
Cincinnati decending the Ohio River to Fort Washington
November 2, 1795. Mrs Keenan was born Jun 16, 1807 in
Champaign County Ohio. She married Joseph Keenan and
they came to Illinois in 1856 and became residents of
Camp Point where Mr Keenan died August 1874. Of her

fathers family, but one Mr Samuel Jamison of Quincy, survives to mourn her loss.

KEENE, - Murder in Ursa - Apr 29, 1880 Body found in barn where Keene and wife lived. Keene left in a hurry some time ago for Iowa.

KEEP, E.B. - Death List - Sep 7, 1877 Old settlers death roll since last meeting: E.B. Keep, Brown County, age 62.

KELLER, ED - Neighborhood News - Apr 5, 1878 A young man named Ed Keller committed suicide Tuesday north of Lima. Didn't get along with wife and she went home to her parents.

KELLER, GEORGE - Local - May 5, 1881 Died, a boy named George Keller 8 years old was killed in the paper mills at Quincy Tuesday night when he became tangled up in a belt.

KELLER, MELISSA
    SEE: KEENA, JOSEPH

KELLER, P.C. - Hash - Jan 7, 1876 P.C. Keller, a prominent citizen of Ellington died suddenly in Quincy one day last week.

KELLER, WILLIAM B.
    SEE: KEENAN, JOSEPH

KELLEY, MR
    SEE: ROSS, JAMES

KELLEY, ELEANOR B. - Death's Doing - Dec 14, 1882 Died, Eleanor B. Kelly, wife of A.B. Kelley and only daughter of Thomas and Rebecca Bailey, Sunday night December 10, 1882 age 36 years. Services by a friend, Rev William Stewart of Quincy.

KELLEY, MILDRED
    SEE: ANDERS, JOHN

KELLOGG, DR - Exchange Notes - May 9, 1879 A little daughter of (3 years old) Dr Kellogg of Carthage was drowned last week by falling in an old well.

KELLY, MICHAEL - Liberty - Feb 22, 1878 Michael Kelly a citizen of McKee township and brother of Hon. Maurice

Kelly was buried yesterday.

KELLY, MICHAEL - Neighborhood News - Feb 22, 1878
Michael Kelly of McKee township died at his home Friday
A.M., 42 years old. Was a nephew of Capt Kelly of this
county who was killed during the Mexican War.

KEMP, MRS RHODA C. - Local - Nov 10, 1881   Died, Mrs
Rhoda C. Kemp Saturday P.M.

KEMP, MRS RHODA C. - Died - Nov 10, 1881   Died, November
5, 1881, Mrs Rhoda C. Kemp, 61 years old. Daughter of
Rev John Ham. Born Calloway County Missouri November
22, 1820. Came to Adams County when 10 years old with
parents settled near Columbus. Married June 24, 1843 to
Samuel Smith who died in 1850. Oct 7, 1857 she married
Matthew Kemp, a native of Ireland and lived 10 years
near Clayton then to Iowa where Mr Kemp died July 9,
1870. She and her 2 children stayed in Iowa until 1875
when they came to Camp Point. Father was a ME minister.
Leaves a son and daughter. Services at the Presbyterian
Church Sunday by Rev W.W. Whipple and Rev L.F. Walden
and Elder Lampton.

KEMP, RHODA C. - Probate Notice - Nov 17, 1881   Rhoda C.
Kemp, deceased 3rd Monday of January, 1882   Stephen H.
Kemp, adm.

KEMP, STEPHEN H. - Quincy - Dec 1, 1881   Stephen H. Kemp
has been appointed adm of his mothers estate.

KENDALL, MRS E.W. - Hash - Sep 7, 1877   Mrs E.W. Kendall
died in Quincy last Friday.

KENDALL, WM
    SEE: WOLF, MRS EMMA

KENDRICK, BENJAMIN - Personal - Jul 30, 1875   Benjamin
Kendrick, who settled in Brown County in 1831 died on
the 15th inst from a cancer on his cheek, 81 years old.

KENDRICK, MRS WM - Clayton - May 4, 1882   Mrs Wm
Kendrick died this A.M. from cancer. Mr Kendrick thinks
he will take his son Willie and go West.

KENNEDY, MR AND MRS DANIEL - Burton-Liberty - Mar 31,
1881   Died, two old persons of Columbus died last week,
Mr and Mrs Daniel Kennedy. Mrs Kennedy died on Monday
and Mr Kennedy on Wednesday. Mr Kennedy came to

Illinois in 1830 and was a resident of this county for over 40 years.

KENNEDY, GEORGE - Hash - Mar 1, 1878 George Kennedy, former resident of Columbus and Paloma was indicted last week by the grand jury of Lewis County Missouri for killing his son in law, Hendricks last fall.

KENNEDY, GEORGE B.
    SEE: HENDRICKS, RICHARD

KENNEY, MRS JERUSHA - Died - May 23, 1879 Died on Camp Point, Illinois on Thursday May 15th Mrs Jerusha Kenney, aged 67 years.

KENNEY, LEROY - Personal - May 23, 1879 Leroy Kenney, who is now a resident of Iowa, came down to attend his mother's funeral. Returned Wednesday.

KENT, HENRY - Local - Aug 15, 1879 Henry Kent, a well known citizen of Ellington died Wednesday age 82 years, resident of this county since 1838.

KERN, MARY E.
    SEE: STRICKLER, WILLIAM A.

KESPOHL, HENRY - Local - Aug 19, 1880 Died, Henry Kespohl of Quincy Sunday eve, age 67 years. Resident of this county since 1857.

KESTER, AUGUSTINE - Aug 23, 1878 Suicide in jail, Augustine Kester last Monday night. "Mt Sterling Message"

KESTER, FREDERICK - Nov 12, 1880 Frederick Kester on trial for wife murder at Danville has been sentenced to be hanged on the 21st of next January. (see Hester)

KETCHUM, WM - Murder of Wm Ketchum - Dec 12, 1879 William Ketchum, formerly a resident of Camp Point was murdered in Warren County last week. "Chicago Times" Monmouth, Ill. William Ketchum was killed while asleep by Henry Boyle whose real name was John Cox. 30 years old. Ketchum and wife had 3 children.

KETCHUM, WM P.
    SEE: BOYLE, HENRY

KETZLER, MRS A.
    SEE: ALLEN, EDDIE

KEYES, MRS C.W.
    SEE: COLLINS, FREDERICK

KEYS, ELIZA J.
    SEE: KEENAN, JOSEPH

KIMBLE, JAMES W. - Neighborhood News - Aug 31, 1877 Died, James W. Kimble age 74 years died at Galesburg last Saturday. He was one of John Brown's soldiers in the Kansas War for 3 years.

KIMMOND, GRANDMA - Burton-Liberty - Apr 7, 1881 Died, Grandma Kimmond's. Died March 28th age 90 years.

KIMMONS, LUKE - Livingston - Jan 2, 1880 Luke Kimmons lost his only remaining daughter Thursday, but it is all for the BEST.

KIMMONS, MRS REBECCA - Died - Apr 7, 1881 Died at the home of her oldest son, Ira Kimmons on Sunday eve March 27th, Mrs Rebecca Kimmons, widow of the late Thomas Kimmons of Liberty, age 90 years 15 days. Born Washington County Pennsylvania march 18, 1791. Married Thomas Kimmons October 1, 1811. Fall of 1835 he sold his farm in Washington County and they moved to Illinois. Arrived in Liberty November 2nd. Mr Kimmons died June 10, 1866. They had 11 children (4 still alive), 34 grandchildren (24 still living), 36 great grandchildren (21 still living).

KING, MRS CLINTON E.
    SEE: MORTON, NANCY

KING, O.H. - Memoriam - Jan 22, 1875 Memoriam of O.H. King who died December 20, 1874. Member of the Fowler Lodge #599 AF & AM.

KING, O.H.B. - Obituary - Jan 1, 1875 O.H.B. King member of Columbus Lodge #74 100F held December 22nd, 1874.

KING, ORVIL H. - In Memoriam - Jan 15, 1875 In memoriam of Orvil H. King member of Gilmer Grange #272. Leaves his widowed mother, brother and sisters.

KING, MRS WM - Mendon - Feb 21, 1879 Died, Mrs Wm King an old citizen living south of Ursa died a day or 2 ago.

KING, WM L. - Recent Deaths - Nov 21, 1879 Wm L. King of this county died at his home in Ursa township last week. Came to Quincy in 1830.

KINSELLA, JOHN F. - Local - Mar 24, 1881 Died, John F. Kinsella, Marysville, Missouri formerly of Columbus township. Died Sunday March 20th of consumption. Leaves a wife, the daughter of John E. Lowe of Camp Point.

KIRBY, THOMAS - Local - Jun 24, 1882 Drowned, Thomas Kirby, age 19 years living with Richard Nayler 2 miles east of Columbus, was drowned while bathing in a pond with several other boys.

KIRKPATRICK, A.B. - Personal - Mar 28, 1879 Rev T.J. Bryant of Paloma came up Wednesday to attend the funeral of Mr A.B. Kirkpatrick.

KIRKPATRICK, A.B. - Died - Mar 28, 1879 Died, March 25th, 1879 at his residence in Camp Point, Rev A.B. Kirkpatrick in his 79th year.

KIRKPATRICK, AUGUSTUS B. - Probate Notice - May 2, 1879 Augustus B. Kirkpatrick, deceased 3rd Monday of June 1879 (16th) J.H. Kirkpatrick, executor.

KIRKPATRICK, AUGUSTUS B. - Obituary - Apr 4, 1879 Rev Augustus B. Kirkpatrick, son of Rev John and Sarah Kirkpatrick born December 4, 1800 and died at his home in Camp Point March 25th, 1879 age 78 years 3 months 22 days. Born Georgia. When 2 years old moved to Edwardsville, Illinois. 1816 to Sangamon county. 1829 to Adams County.

KIRKPATRICK, J.H. - Personal - Mar 28, 1879 J.H. Kirkpatrick of Carthage was summoned this week of the bedside of his father.

KIRPATRICK, J. EDDY - Died - Mar 19, 1874 Died on the 14th inst, in the town of Carthage, J. Eddy, 3rd son of Mr and Mrs J.H. Kirpatrick, age 10 years 4 months 14 days.

KLEIN, ADOLPH - Local - Feb 17, 1881 Died, Adolph Klein age about 60 years living with Henry Zeiger in Columbus township died Monday.

KLINE, EDITH - Died - Dec 15, 1881 Died, December 1st at 10 before 8 A.M., Edith daughter of Jennie and F.E.

Kline of Cobden, Illinois of scarlet fever, age 9 years 7 days. Their little boy is also sick.

KNIGHT, LYDIA A.
    SEE: GAY, VIXEN P.

KOBEL, ISABEL - Died - Oct 23, 1874 Died, on the 19th of typhoid pneumonia, Isabel, daughter of Jacob Kobel and wife of <u>Brun</u> <u>Bruns</u>, age 30 years 2 months 5 days.

KOBEL, MRS JACOB - Hash - Sep 4, 1873 Mrs Jacob Kobel died very suddenly on Tuesday of heart disease.

KOBEL, MRS JANE - Obituary - Sep 11, 1873 Mrs Jane Kobel, wife of Jacob Kobel died 2nd inst at her home in Columbus township. Born in Roxburgh, Scotland April 11, 1821. Came with her mother when 7 years old to Canada then to state of Michigan where she married on October 12, 1841 to Jacob Kobel. In 1864 they moved to Columbus township. They had 13 children, 10 still living. Converted 22 years ago to the ME Church.

KOCH, ADAM - Obituary - Mar 12, 1875 Adam Koch deceased was member of West Union range #509 P. of H. Leaves a wife and children.

KOCHANOWSKI, VINCENT - "Capt Vincent Kochanowski" - Jan 3, 1879 Capt Vincent Kochanowski of Quincy died at the home of Adam Goerke 3 miles south of town Sunday A.M. age 51 years. Was born in Poland. Came to America sometime prior to the rebellion. Buried Camp Point Cemetery.

KOCK, CHAS K. - Local - Jul 11, 1879 Chas. K. Kock, committed suicide at his home in Quincy Sunday after digging his grave in the yard.

KOELLER, MARY - Died - Jan 29, 1875 Died, on the 22nd inst Mary, wife of Herman Koeller, age 40 years.

KONANTZ, MISS EMMA - Died - Dec 11, 1874 Died, Saturday eve at 10 at the home of her mother in Quincy, Miss Emma Konantz age 18 years.

KONANTZ, PAUL - Hash - Jan 26, 1877 Paul Konantz, an old citizen of Quincy died Monday eve age 66 years.

KYLE, J.B. - Personal - Jun 14, 1878 Dr J.B. Kyle a well known physician and formerly surgeon of the 84th

Ill. Infantry died on the 1st inst at his home in Macomb.

KYMES, WILLIAM - Quincy Items - Aug 15, 1879 Boiler explosion at Newcombs paper mill last Friday night. William Kymes the fireman was badly hurt, died that night.

LAFFERTY, MRS
    SEE: SWARTS, MRS LOU

LAMB, LOUIS - News - Nov 25, 1880 Mart Duggan a noted character of Leadville, killed Louis Lamb on the street Monday.

LAMB, M.H. - Personal - Oct 20, 1881 Died, a little daughter of Capt M.H. Lamb of Mt Sterling last week, aged about 4 years.

LAMOIX, W.H. - Richard Silk - Mar 1, 1878 People vs. Dr Wm H. Lamoix, murder, abortion caused the death of Mrs Fannie C. Price.

LAMPTON, EDDIE - Local - Aug 10, 1882 Elder James Stark of Augusta preached the funeral of Eddie Lampton, Monday.

LAMPTON, EDWIN - Died - Aug 10, 1882 Died of typhoid fever, Edwin, youngest son of Elder and Mrs E.J. Lampton age 7 years 1 month 9 days. Died August 5th. Services by Rev Stark of Augusta. Buried village cemetery.

LANCASTER, E.
    SEE: HICOX, MRS R.

LANCASTER, EDWARD - La Prairie - May 24, 1878 Died, Edward Lancaster Sr. an old citizen of Houston twp.

LANCASTER, EDWARD G. - Sale of Real Estate - Dec 6, 1878 Sale of real estate of Edward G. Lancaster, deceased complainant and Nicholas Lancaster and others were defendants, Saturday December 28th John C. Pearce, adm of Edward G. Lancaster, deceased.

LANCASTER, EDWARD G. - Probate Notice - Jun 7, 1878 Edward G. Lancaster, deceased 3rd Monday of July 1878 J.C. Pearce, adm.

LANCASTER, WM - Neighborhood News - Feb 22, 1878 Dead, the Carlinville "Democrat" tells of an insane man named

Wm Lancaster Jr who killed his father Wm Lancaster, son is 42 years old.

LANDERS, ABRAM
    SEE: ANDERS, JOHN

LANDIS, FELIX G.
    SEE: SHAFFER, MRS L.D.

LANDON, MRS REBECCA - Burton - Oct 10, 1879 Died, Mrs Rebecca Landon died at the home of her son, Dr W.M. Landon, in her 73rd year. Services by Rev S. Ollerenshaw. Born January 2, 1807 in Pickaway County Ohio. Married October 15, 1825 to Wm Landon. Mother of 9 (6 sons and 3 daughters) 8 are still alive. Died October 6th.

LANE, FRANK - Local - Dec 5, 1879 Frank Lane and Bill Smith were arrested for the lynching of Bill Young.

LANGDON, MRS A.L. - Death of Mrs A.L. Langdon - May 16, 1879 Died, Mrs Fone V. Langdon, wife of Add L. Langdon, editor of the "commercial Review". Died at her home in Quincy Monday A.M. daughter of Major H.V. Sullivan and in her 34th year.

LANGDON, JAMES JEWELL - Died - Feb 19, 1875 Died, James Jewell Langdon at his home in Quincy on the 11th inst. Born at Branford, Connecticut January 7, 1824 (51 years old). Came west to Chicago in 1840.

LANGLEY, JAMES - Neighboring News - Jul 15, 1880 The oldest ciitzen of Morgan county, Mr James Langley of Franklin died yesterday A.M. of old age, 95 years old.

LANING, EZEKIEL - Hash - Mar 23, 1877 Ezekiel Laning died in York Neck Wednesday of consumption. He is the 3rd victim of this dread disease in that family in 3 months.

LANOIX, DR - Trial of Dr Lanoix - May 31, 1878 Dr Lanoix charged with the murder of Mrs Fannie C. Price of Pittsfield who died and was buried in this city. Doctor not guilty. Martha Jackson (colored) nursed her, Martha Carey (colored) from Pittsfield was called by defense, also Mrs Brownell of St Louis, a sister of the deceased. Dr Lanoix son was put on the stand.

LASLEY, JOSEPH P.
    SEE: HAINES, GEORGE R.

LASLEY, MATTIE J. - Died - May 16, 1879 Died at Bayliss, Pike County Illinois April 28th, Mattie J. Lasley wife of Geo. R. Haines. She was born in Ohio August 31, 1850 and lost her parents soon after coming to Illinois. She became a member of Mr E.B. Curtis family and married November 17, 1870. Was a member of the Presbyterian Church.

LAUGHERY, MRS - Mendon - Nov 7, 1879 Mrs Laughery died Thursday A.M. and buried at Lima.

LAUGHLIN, FRANK - Hash - Aug 9, 1878 Frank Laughlin's babe, the has been sick several weeks, died Sunday. Taken to Clayton for burial.

LAUGHLIN, MRS - Mendon - Oct 3, 1879 Mrs Laughlin mentioned last week died Tuesday night. Funeral Thursday.

LAUGHLIN, GEO. - Supplement - Sep 1, 1876 Died since last years meeting of Old Settlers of Adams and Brown County, Geo. Laughlin of Clayton.

LAUGHLIN, MRS WM - Mendon - Sep 26, 1879 Mrs Wm Laughlin is very sick and not expected to live.

LAULE, ANNIE - Local - Aug 12, 1880 Annie Laule, age 19 was arrested at Quincy Sunday eve on the charge of throwning her infant child from the steamer Belle of La Crosse. The child was illegitimate and about 3 weeks old.

LAW, GEORGE - Neighborhood News - Dec 7, 1877 Died, George Law of La Harpe, Hancock County died.

LAWRENCE, WOODFORD - Death of an old Citizen - Jan 9, 1880 Woodford Lawrence one of the oldest citizens of Adams County died at his home in Payson township a few days ago, about 82 years old. Came to Adams County in 1824 before the county was organized and settled in what is now Payson township. Taught the first school in the township. Leaves several sons residing in this county and Missouri. "Herald"

LAWTON, CAPT W.H.H. - Obituary - Jun 22, 1882 Died, Capt W.H.H. Lawton of Griggsville a few days ago. Born at Hartland, Vermont Sept 12, 1832. Lived there until 16 years old. Went to Griggsville in 1856 (Pike County).

LEACH, MRS HARRIET - Died - Dec 19, 1879 Mrs Harriet Leach, widow of the late Portius F. Leach, died Saturday December 18th at the home of Joseph Aull, in her 67th year. Remains taken to Mendon for burial.

LEACH, P.F.
    SEE: DAILY, AMANDA

LEIGHTY, MR - Beverly - Jul 20, 1882 Died, on July 3rd, Mr Leighty, who was the oldest man in the township, 97 years old.

LESLIE, MARY - Fowler - Jan 26, 1877 Died, eve of January 9th at 9 p.m., Mary, wife of Chas. Leslie, railroad agent of this place of consumption. Buried at N. Stahl's Cemetery on January 11th. Leaves her husband.

LESMAN, MR - Keokuk Junction - Jul 22, 1880 Died, Thursday at his home near the Prairie Church east of town, Mr Lesman, age 72 years.

LESTER, RICHARD - Coatsburg - Aug 11, 1881 Richard Lester and lady, of Galesburg attended the funeral of Mrs Lester's father here Friday.

LEVI, MOSES - Died - Feb 16, 1877 Moses Levi, age 88 years, died in this city Thursday night. Came to Quincy 14 years ago. Funeral at 9:30 Sunday.   "Whig"

LEWIS, MRS - Mendon - Sep 20, 1878 Mrs Lewis, the mother of Mr John and Andrew McNay died last week at a quite advanced age.

LEWIS, ELIZABETH A.
    SEE: ANDERS, JOHN

LEWIS, HUGH - Local - Jan 9, 1880 Died, Hugh Lewis, formerly of Woodville, this county died January 5th at Canton, Missouri in his 86th year.

LEWIS, SAMUEL K.
    SEE: ANDERS, JOHN

LEWIS, W.H. - Accident - Aug 21, 1874 Monday eve W.H. Lewis of near Paloma was found bruised by the C.B. & Q tracks this side of Fowler. Died about 9 A.M. today. It is supposed he fell from the train. (Whig)

LIERLE, MRS DIANNA - Livingston - Dec 1, 1881 Died, at her home NW Liberty township on the 21st inst, Mrs Dianna Lierle. Services by Rev W.R. Lierle. Buried neighboring cemetery beside her husband, Wm Lierle whom she survived many years. Leaves 7 children and several grandchildren.

LIERLE, MART - Liberty - Nov 8, 1878 Mart Lierle buried his youngest child last week. A little girl 3 years old.

LIERLY, JAMES - Adm Sale - Feb 2, 1882 Adm Sale, James Lierly, deceased, in Columbus township 3-1/2 miles south of Columbus February 9th.

Lierly, James - Probate Notice - Feb 2, 1882 James Lierly deceased 1st Monday of March   Leuvina Lierly, adm.

LIERLY, JAMES - Livingston - Dec 29, 1881 Mrs Elmina Lierly, at the time of the funeral of her son James was very low with typhoid pneumonia but not without hope.

LIERLY, JAMES - Livingston - Dec 29, 1881 Died, James Lierly at his home in Columbus township December 21st of typhoid pneumonia in his 45th year. Services held at Union School by Rev A. Reinhart of Liberty. Leaves a wife and 5 children. Owned and lived on the homestead where he was born in 1837.

LIERLY, JAMES - Death of James Lierly - Dec 29, 1881 Died, James Lierly of Columbus, Thursday night of pneumonia. Born in Adams County in 1837. His father came to Adams County in 1827. James married Lovina Rowsey in 1861. Leaves 4 children. His father was the first man married in Columbus township.

LIERLY, JAMES - Liberty - Dec 29, 1881 Died, James Lierly of Columbus on the 22nd inst of lung fever.

LIMBAUGH, CATHERINE - Local - Apr 18, 1879 Died, Catherine Limbaugh, an aunt of David Wolf died at her home in Liberty township on the 8th inst, 93 years old. Born in Pennsylvania in 1786. In 1800 went with her father to Kentucky and in 1806 to Missouri where she married Michael Limbaugh. Lived Missouri till 1810.

Then to Boone County Illinois until 1829 when she came to Liberty township. Was a member of Dunkard Church.

LINDEMAN, LEOPOLD - Neighborhood News - Dec 21, 1877 died, Leopold Lindeman, a German living in Quincy died Thursday.

LING, AH - Local - Jan 6, 1881 Ah Ling, the Chinaman, killed in his laundry in Quincy some 3 years ago left $500.00. It was divided among relatives in China.

LING, JOHN - Murder in Quincy - Nov 8, 1878 John Ling, Chinaman, murdered in his laundry on Maine St. Quincy.

LINN, ALBERT - Obituary - Mar 19, 1875 Died at Abingdon, Ill. on the 11th inst of typhoid pneumonia, Prof. Albert Linn. Born Feb 25, 1810. Was 35 years 15 days at the time of his death. Was reared in Adams Co, principally in Columbus twp where he now lives. He was 1 of 11 children, all of whom survive him. He entered Abingdon College in spring of 1859 or 60 and graduated in June 1863 and was elected Prof. Of Mathematics. Was a member of the ME Church until 1868 when he joined the Christian Church and entered the ministry. Leaves a wife and 2 young boys. Funeral at Abingdon, Saturday.

LINN, DAVID - Personal - Nov 24, 1881 Dr David Linn of Frederick was called here last week for the funeral of his father. Visited his brother John F. also for a few days.

LINN, EMILY
    SEE: CURTIS, ELAM B.

LINN, JOHN - Obituary - Nov 24, 1881 Died, John Linn at his home in Columbus twp Nov 17, 1881 age 77 years 6 months 17 days. Father of 11 children, ten of whom followed his to the grave. Buried at Columbus Sat. Leaves 10 children, 31 grandchildren and 7 gr. grandchildren.

LINN, JOHN - Probate Notice - Jan 5, 1882 John Linn, deceased 3rd Monday of March 1882 (20th) A.J. Linn and Chas. W. Linn Ex.

LINN, MRS JOHN F.
    SEE: WARREN, MRS LYDIA

LINSCOMB, JOSEPH - Hash - Aug 11, 1876 Joseph Linscomb,

of Stone's Prairie fell dead while attempting to get in his buggy, last Monday, caused by disease of the heart.

LINTHICUM, JOSEPH - Supplement - Sep 1, 1876 Died since last years meeting of Old Settlers of Adams and Brown Counties, Joseph Linthicum of Clayton.

LISCO, WILLIE - Died - Jul 20, 1882 Died at Galesburg, Ill July 15th Willie, son of the late George and Mary Lisco age 1 year 8 months 7 days. Buried Pleasant View Cemetery on Sunday.

LITTLE, JOHN - Clayton - Jul 15, 1880 Mr and Mrs John Little buried their little babe Monday which they had adopted some time since.

LITTLE, SQUIRE - Hash - Aug 27, 1875 An infant child of Squire Little died Tuesday eve.

LIVINGSTON, MR - Mendon Matters - Sep 27, 1878 A lady named Livingston, a relative of Mrs R.A. Ingersoll of our vicinity died at that lady's residence Saturday last.

LIVINGSTON, JAMES - Local - Mar 30, 1882 Died, a little girl of James Livingston. Died of scarlet fever Saturday night.

LIVINGSTON, JOHN - Hash - Oct 30, 1873 John Livingston and family arrived from Chicago Monday with their dead child which was interred in our cemetery Tuesday afternoon.

LIVINGSTON, JOHN - Personal - Aug 8, 1879 John Livingston and wife of Bushness came down Monday to attend the funeral of John's father.

LIVINGSTON, KEZIAH - Died - Mar 31, 1876 Died, on the 28th inst at Bushnell, Illinois Keziah Livingston age 69 years.

LIVINGSTON, THOMAS - Died - Aug 8, 1879 Died at Bardolph on the 2nd inst, Thomas Livingston, age 74 years. Buried in Camp Point Cemetery. Died at the home of his son near Bardolph.

LOCKE, MRS D.
    SEE: NORRIS, MRS

LOCKE, G. - Hash - May 10, 1878 Dr G. Locke, of Huntsville, Schuyler County dropped dead at the home of Mr Logan on Lone Tree Prairie last week. Heart disease.

LOGUE, MARIA - Clayton - Mar 28, 1879 Funeral of Miss Maria Logue was from the Presbyterian Church last Friday. (corrected on April 4th to read Maria Loyd)

LOHRMAN, MRS F.
    SEE: GITTER, MRS

LOOS, GEORGE - Columbus - Jan 12, 1882 Died, at the home of their father in Columbus of scarlet fever January 2nd, George, about 8 years old and on January 6th Eddie. Both children of Henry Loos. Mother died a few months ago.

LOOSE, LENA - Columbus - Oct 26, 1882 Died, Lena Loose October 18th and buried following day. Services by Rev Bryant. Buried in our cemetery.

LOWARY, D.P. - Mendon - Dec 16, 1880 Died, last Wednesday Mr D.P. Lowary of Loraine. Leaves a wife and I think 3 children. (as per paper)

LOWARY, DANIEL P. - Local - Dec 16, 1880 Died, Daniel P. Lowary died at Loraine last Wednesday, 35 years old.

LOWE, JOHN E.
    SEE: KINSELLA, JOHN F.

LOYD, MARIA - Clayton - Apr 4, 1879 The notice of Miss Maria Loyd's death last week, read by mistake Maria Logue.

LUCKEL, JACOB - Hash - Aug 10, 1877 Died, child of Jacob Luckel died Saturday night and on Monday night his wife died (typhoid fever).

LUSK, LEVI - "Levi Lusk" - Aug 3, 1877 Died, Levi Lusk died at Mt Sterling on the 25th ult. Born New York May 10, 1795. Settled in Newport, Kentucky in 1818 and moved to Illinois in 1835 stopping in Rushville. Moved to Mt Sterling in 1866. Funeral on the 26th ult. Services by Sir Knight D.R. Lucas. Belonged to Masons.

LUSK, NELLIE - Died - May 9, 1879 Died, Tuesday May 6th, Nellie, infant daughter of J.J. and Mary E. Luck, age 17 months. Buried Woodland Cemetery, Quincy, Wednesday.

LYLE, SAMUEL M. - Died - Sep 25, 1873 Died, Friday September 19th Samuel M., son of James Lyle, of cerebro spinal meningitis.

LYMAN, ANSON - Neighborhood News - Dec 28, 1877 Anson Lyman died at Winchester, Illinois Tuesday of last week, was a heavy drinker.

LYON, CURTIS J.
    SEE: CURTIS, ELAM B.

LYON, ELIZA - Died - Sep 10, 1875 Died on the 3rd inst, of heart disease, Mrs Eliza Lyon in her 72nd year.

LYON, WILLIE JO - Died - Jul 24, 1874 Died, Tuesday July 21st of cholera infantum, Willie Jo infant son of T.A. and Clarissa Lyon age 5 months 5 days.

MAERTZ, EMMA A.
    SEE: CYRUS, JOHN M.

MAGIN, PETER - Exchange Notes - Jan 10, 1879 At Taylorville, Illinois on the 1st, Peter Magin, an old resident was killed in a sleigh accident.

MALDEN, ELIJAH - Liberty - Feb 5, 1880 Elijah Malden passed over that dark river on Thursday to that beautiful land from whence but few return.

MALINSON, T. - Fowler - Mar 23, 1882 Killed, one week ago Friday news received that T. Malinson had perished in the fire at the Elmore House at Trenton, Missouri where he had gone to look for work. He had been painting at the hotel. Remains brought here Thursday. Funeral Sunday at ME Church. Leaves a wife.

MALOAN, RACHAEL - Newtown - Jan 3, 1879 Rachael, daughter of Anson and Mary Maloan died Thursday between 6 & 7 A.M.

MALONE, JOHN
    SEE: SCHWARTZ, DANIEL

MANARD, DELILAH - Died - Sep 29, 1876 Died on the 13th inst at the home of James Moore Esq. of paralysis, Mrs Delilah Manard, age 95 years.

MANARD, WILLIAM - William Manard Killed - Feb 12, 1880 Body found Saturday morn after his horse probably fell,

throwning him and falling on him. Had been a resident
of this township about 35 years. Manard family all
grown and live near, 2 or 3 still at home. Mrs Manard
was shot while camping 10 or 12 years ago on Alstyne's
prairie at Quincy. William's brother, Abednego Manard
was killed several years ago by being thrown from buggy.

MANARD, WM G. - Legal Notes - Jan 1, 1875 Wm G. Manard,
Joseph Van Dyke, Eliza Stonaker, Wm T. Crafton and
Daniel Manard   vs. Martha Manard, Hariet Smith, Isiah
Smith, James L. Manard and Abednego Manard. Bill to set
aside will.

MANARD, WM G. - Nov 26, 1875 The case of Wm G. Manard
et al vs Martha Manard et al was tried in the circuit
court last week and decided in favor of the defendant.
The suit was to set aside the will of the late Abednego
Manard.

MANARD, WM M. - Local - May 26, 1881 A farm of 72 acres
belonging to the estate of Wm M. Manard known as the
Moore place was sold at a adm sale Saturday.

MANN, ELLIS H. - Adm Sale - Jul 24, 1874 Adm sale of
real estate of Ellis H., deceased, against Sarah E.
Mann. Henry Motter, adm W.H. Keath, Sol't for adm.

MARKWELL, NANCY
    SEE: JUDY, PARIS T.

MARRETT, MRS CATHERINE - Clayton - Nov 7, 1879 Mrs
Catherine Marrett an old lady with large family
connection died at her daughters, Mrs Z.F. Bennett a few
days ago.

MARSH, HENRY C.
    SEE: WARD, MELINDA C.

MARSH, NANCY C.
    SEE: WARD, MELINDA C.

MARSH, SARAH FRANCIS - Died - May 4, 1882 Died, Sarah
Francis, daughter of Elijah and Martha J. Marsh of
scarlet fever April 21st, age 2 years 8 months.

MARSH, WM
    SEE: CRAWFORD, MRS ABIGAL S.

MARSHALL, WILLIAM - Probate Notice - Oct 13, 1876

William Marshall   3rd Monday of December   Thos. Marshall, adm.

MARTIN, ARTHUR – Columbus – May 18, 1882 Died, Arthur Martin, formerly of this place, at Washington, Missouri this week.

MARTIN, ED – Local – Aug 15, 1879 Ed Martin's little babe died this week.

MARTIN, GALE – Local – Jan 20, 1881 Gale Martin, father of E.G. Martin died Tuesday night age 71 years.

MARTIN, GALE – Personal – Jan 13, 1881 Gale Martin is ill at the home of his son, E.G. Martin.

MARTIN, MRS GALE – Local – Oct 7, 1880 Died, Mrs Gale Martin died Monday age 71 years. Buried in the village cemetery Tuesday.

MARTIN, LAURETTA – Died – Jan 29, 1875 Died on the 22nd ult of pneumonia, Miss Lauretta Martin age 16 years. Leaving a mother the last member of the family to mourn her loss.

MARVIL, IDA – Bowen – Sep 21, 1882 Died, Miss Ida Marvil, Tuesday September 5th. Services at Presbyterian Church in Chili.

MAY, HENRY – Supplement – Sep 1, 1876 Died since last years meeting of Old Settlers of Adams and Brown Counties, Henry May of Versailles.

MAYNARD, REBECCA
    SEE: BAILEY, JAMES

MEACHUM, S.S. – Death List – Sep 7, 1877 Old settlers death list since last meeting: S.S. Meachum, Burton.

MEAD, C.N. – Neighborhood News – Aug 10, 1877 Died, Mrs C.N. Mead, mother of Chas. W. Mead. Died in Quincy last Thursday age 85 years.

MEAD, C.W. – Hash – Nov 20, 1873 The funeral of the late Mrs C.W. Mead took place Sunday in Quincy from the St John's Episcopal Church. Services by Rev Sidney Corbet, D.D.

MEAD, S.B. – Augusta – Nov 25, 1880 Died, Dr S.B. Mead,

one of the first settlers of Augusta died at his home at this place last week. Funeral last Saturday.

MEANS, SAM B. - Neighborhood News - Mar 29, 1878 An old man, Sam B. Means who lives 2 miles south of Center in Ralls County was killed Friday. "Whig"

MECKLE, JACOB - Accident at Augusta - Aug 7, 1873 Jacob Meckle age about 40 years a farmer who lives ½ mile north of Augusta was struck by his rearing horse and killed. Mrs Meckle and child survive the buggy accident.

MEGINNIS, S.S. - Neighborhood News - Aug 9, 1878 News was received Saturday of the death at Winchester, Illinois of the Rev S.S. Meginnis of the ME Church. Born in Indiana in 1837.

MELVIN, HENRY S. - Local - Jun 16, 1881 Died, Henry S. Melvin a brother of our Tho. A. died at Bushnell last week.

MERCER, HENRY - Neighborhood News - Aug 30, 1878 Henry Mercer, 24 years old drowned in a pond at Liberty last Saturday. Funeral Sunday.

MERCER, HENRY - Livingston - Aug 30, 1878 Henry Mercer was drowned Saturday eve in a pond near Liberty.

METEERS, GEO. W. - Hash - Aug 17, 1877 Geo. W. Meteers of Brown County was drowned Sunday in Lake Erie by falling overboard from a steamer. Body not recovered.

METZ, WM - Hash - May 1, 1873 Wm Metz, well known through out the country to the drug trade, died Monday in Quincy.

MEYER, GUSTAV - Hash - Jan 5, 1877 Gustav Meyer, who was assaulted by some unknown person in Quincy December 23rd died Saturday night.

MEYERS, GEORGE - Local - May 11, 1882 Died, Mr George Meyers of Buckhorn called "Old Blackhawk". Born in state of Pennsylvania in 1781. Came to this state in 1800. Died April 28th. Leaves of wife who is almost 90 and 6 children. Was father of 18. Mt Sterling Democrat

MILBY, MRS WILLIAM - Clayton - Mar 10, 1881 Mrs William Milby died here Monday age 72.

MILES, JAS - Neighborhood News - Aug 24, 1877 A young man named Jas. Miles, of Knox County was recently drowned while bathing in Spoon River.

MILLER, ANNA - Local - Sep 9, 1880 Anna Miller, a girl about 14 years old was burned to death in Quincy Sunday by her clothing catching fire from the stove.

MILLER, D.W. - Local - Dec 30, 1880 D.W. Miller of Quincy died last week.

MILLER, MAUD - Young Lady Shot - Nov 5, 1880 Thursday eve Maud Miller was shot in the breast while riding in a buggy with Chas. Waldo just east of the Tremont House on Hampshire Street. It is not known who shot her. "Herald"

MILLER, NATHAN - Suicide of Nathan Miller - Nov 9, 1877 Friday, Nathan Miller hung himself south of his residence in Camp Point. Was a resident about 20 years. Was 63 years old and a native of Ohio.

MILLER, NATHAN - Adm Sale - Nov 21, 1877 Adm sale Dec 14, 1877 by W.L. Oliver adm estate Nathan Miller   Lew Strickler, adm.

MILLER, NATHAN - Probate Notice - Nov 21, 1877 Nathan Miller, deceased 2nd Monday of January 1878 Wm L. Oliver, adm.

MILLER, NATHAN - Settle Up - Feb 21, 1879 P.S. the Nathan Miller estate notes being past due, call and settle up with the estate. W.L. Oliver, adm

MILLER, RUFUS L. - Local - Jul 14, 1881 Died, Col Rufus L. Miller at his home in Quincy Sunday from the heat on the 4th. Born Maryland and was 54 years old. Funeral Tuesday.

MINNES, FRED - Murder at Marblehead - Mar 17, 1881 Marblehead a station on the Louisiana branch of the C.B. & Q a few miles south of Quincy was the scene of a murder Tuesday of last week. Fred Minnes was killed by Jesse Hall. Minnes was 26 years old. Hall was from S.W. Missouri.

MINTON, MR - Houston - Dec 28, 1882 Died, Mr Minton of the western part of the township was buried at Ebenezer Friday December 15th.

MITCHELL, MRS
    SEE: HANNA, COL.

MITCHELL, DAVID - Jul 27, 1877 Died, David Mitchell of Prairie City, Illinois body was found in the river at Warsaw by F.W. Roberts, Monday. He had been missing some time. Foul play.

MITCHELL, JACOB - Neighborhood News - Jul 1, 1880 Jacob Mitchell who was recently killed while attempting to escape jail at Springfield. Was a member of a highly respected family at Champaign.

MITCHELL, JOS - Died - Jun 22, 1882 Died of lung fever and paralysis June 14th at 3 P.M. Jos. Mitchell age 18 years 4 months 20 days. Leaves mother and brothers.

MITCHELL, JOSEPH - Local - Jun 22, 1882 Died, Joseph Mitchell of consumption last Wednesday. Remains were not brought home.

MITCHELL, JULIA E. - Memorial Tribute - Jan 20, 1881 Memorial tribute to the friends, relatives and school mates of Julia E. Mitchell. By Stella and Laura E.

MITTS, MRS <u>ALL</u> - Richfield - Mar 31, 1881 Died, Mrs <u>All</u> Mitts from consumption.

MOLDEN, MR - Livingston - Oct 4, 1878 Mr Molden is no more, his life was but a burden for many years.

MONTGOMERY, ROBERT - Hash - Nov 13, 1874 A number of masons went to Clayton Tuesday to assist in the funeral ceremonies of Robert Montgomery.

MOON, MISS ELIZA - Hash - Sep 7, 1877 Miss Eliza Moon of Loraine, age 16 years committed suicide last Friday by hanging herself.

MOORE, MRS - Personal - Jul 21, 1881 Mrs M.E. Honnold was summoned to Columbus Sunday by the death of a child of her sister, Mrs Moore of Atchison.

MOORE, CAROLINE
    SEE: EDWARDS, MARGARET

MOORE, MRS DORCAS - Died - Feb 2, 1877 Died, on the 20th inst at the residence of James Moore Esq. of pneumonia, Mrs Dorcas Moore, age 62 years.

MOORE, MRS DORCAS - Hash - Jan 26, 1877 The remains of Mrs Dorcas Moore who died Sunday, were taken to Brookfield, Missouri for interment.

MOORE, FRANCIS O. - Died - Feb 12, 1874 Died, Francis O. Moore one of the old settlers of Quincy, died at Omaha Sunday night, age 77 years. Buried in Quincy.

MOORE, JAMES L. - Mendon - May 27, 1880 James L. Moore lost his little girl some 3 years of age last week.

MOORE, JAMES P. - Death of Jas. P. Moore - Oct 14, 1880 (St Joseph, Missouri Gazette of September 26th) James P. Moore of St Joseph was kicked by a horse in the face, 35 years old. Born in Columbus, Illinois June 25, 1845. Came here about 15 years ago. 3 years ago he married in Atchinson the daughter of Mr John Seaton of that place.

MOORE, DR JOHN - Local - Mar 25, 1880 Dr John Moore died Monday at his home in Quincy in his 65th year.

MOORE, JOHN S. - Quincy - Aug 22, 1879 John S. Moore, of Topeka, Kansas, a brother in law of John P. Cadogan of the Herald died at the latters home Sunday, age 40 years.

MOORE, MRS RILEY - Clayton - Aug 22, 1879 Mrs Riley Moore of Concord was buried here Sunday.

MOORE, S.G. - March Circuit Court - Apr 17, 1873 The case of Peter R. Moore adm of the estate of S.G. Moore vs Amos Reynolds was taken up for trial by a jury.

MOORE, SMITH G. - Feb 26, 1875 To whom it may concern: I, Peter R. Moore adm of the estate of Smith G. Moore, deceased will on March 12th make application to sell for the heirs and creditors. Peter R. Moore, adm.

MOORE, THOS. - Paloma - Jul 28, 1881 Infant daughter of Mr and Mrs Thos. Moore Columbus died Sunday. Buried Monday P.M. Services by Rev T.J. Bryant.

MOORES, RACHAEL - Obituary - Oct 10, 1879 Rachael Moores died September 30th age 81 years. Born March 9, 1798 in Hardin County Ohio.

MOREHOUSE, CHARLEY - Exchange Notes - Nov 8, 1878 Charley Morehouse, whose family live at Hannibal was run over and killed by a train at Milford, Illinois a few days ago.

MORELY, ARTHUR - Died - Oct 19, 1882 Died, October 14th of cerebro spinal meningitis, Arthur, son of William and Ellen Morely, age 6 years 6 months 22 days.

MOREY, S.J. - Clayton - Aug 17, 1882 E. Hartman has been appointed school treasurer for this township to fill the vacancy caused by the death of S.J. Morey.

MOREY, SETH J. - Death of Seth J. Morey - Jul 27, 1882 Died, Seth J. Morey at his home in Clayton Friday A.M. Born in Columbia County New York January 23, 1815 and came to Illinois in 1838 where he taught several years. Married Jane A. Wallace in 1843. Services Saturday.

MORGAN, MRS - Riceville - Jul 21, 1881 Died, a Mrs Morgan of Richfield died Friday.

MORGAN, JAMES M. - Suicide - Mar 31, 1876 James M. Morgan, alias James Ross who committed suicide at La Prairie. He came from Champaign to get away from associations which seemed adverse to reformation. Services by the pastors of Methodist and Presbyterian Churches and taken to the cemetery for burial. His brother is Mr Wm H. Morgan of Tolono. He came to La Prairie and claimed his brother we knew as James Ross to be James M. Morgan and son of Mr Woodson Morgan of Tolono.

MORGAN, JOHN - Exchange Notes - Mar 14, 1879 Died, John Morgan, a bridge carpenter on the C.B. & Q died at his home in Stillwell a few days ago. "Warsaw Bulletin"

MOROE, SARAH - Neighborhood News - Sep 20, 1878 Miss Sarah Moroe about 17 years old died Wed. "Augusta Herald"

MORRILL, JAKE
    SEE: HEITZMAN, MR

MORRIS, DR - Exchange Notes - Feb 14, 1879 Dr Morris, of Fall Creek was buried by the Knights of Beauscant Commandery this week.

MORRIS, EDGAR R. - Local - Jun 17, 1880 Judge Edgar R. Morris of Seymour, Texas son of the late I.N. Morris was shot and killed by a saloon keeper named W.A. Taylor.

MORRIS, GEORGE - Exchange Notes - Feb 14, 1879 The burial of Dr George Morris took place in Fall Creek township Sunday.

MORRIS, I.N. - Local - Nov 7, 1879 Funeral services of Hon. I.N. Morris was Friday at his home in Quincy. Buried Woodland Cemetery.

MORRIS, I.N.
    SEE: WARREN, CALVIN A.

MORRISON, H.H. - Riceville - Nov 17, 1881 Died, H.H. Morrison, a well to do farmer of Richfield township at his residence Tuesday night from typhoid fever. Born in Sangamon county in 1824. Married in 1845 to Miss Cynthia Chapman and they had 12 children (3 dead).

MORTON, C.H. - Personal - Jul 26, 1878 Col. C.H. Morton is lying seriously ill at his residence in Quincy from aphasia.

MORTON, C.H. - Suicide of Col. Morton - Jun 3, 1880 Col. C.H. Morton, better known as "Charley Morton" committed suicide at his home in Quincy Wednesday A.M. He came to Quincy with his father in 1835 when he was 9 years old. Joined army in 1862 and was in the 84th Illinois. Remains buried Friday afternoon in Woodland Cemetery.

MORTON, NANCY - Newtown - Apr 22, 1880 Died, at the residence of her daughter Mrs Clinton E. King, Friday April 23rd Mrs Nancy Morton, wife of Charles M. Morton deceased. Mrs Morton was born March 16, 1804 in North Carolina. Came to Quincy in 1829 and married Mr Morton in 1835. Mr Morton died July 6, 1874. Buried in family cemetery near the old homestead. Services by Rev Huntly of Payson assisted by Rev Hawker in the Baptist Church in Newtown Saturday April 24th.

MORTON, NANCY - Probate Notice - Oct 14, 1880 Nancy Morton, deceased 3rd Monday of December 1880 Geo. R. Stewart, adm.

MOSES, MR - Liberty - May 9, 1879 A child of Mr Moses, near Kingston last week drowned in a kettle of slop.

MOTTER, H.R.
    SEE: TANSILL, FANNY OTIS

MOYER, MARTIN - Columbus - Nov 9, 1882 Infant child of Martin Moyer was buried at Coatsburg Friday.

MOYEY, DOROTHY LINDON
    SEE: STRAUB, JOHN

MULLER, MRS HENRY - Local - Nov 16, 1882 Word received of death of Mrs Henry Muller at Eureka Springs, Arkansas.

MULLER, MRS HENRY - Local - Nov 16, 1882 Died, Mrs Henry Muller Saturday at Eureka Springs, Arkansas. Remains arrived at Golden Monday eve. Buried in family cemetery Tuesday.

MULLER, M.M. - News - Jan 6, 1881 The wife and infant child of M.M. Muller lately a resident of Chicago were suffocated by the burning of the old Thompson Hotel at Madison, Wisconsin.

MUNROE, THADDEUS - Death of an old Citizen - Feb 5, 1874 Thaddeus Munroe, one of the oldest settlers of Quincy died Sunday eve at the home of his son in Mendon. He came to Quincy in 1835 and started the first cabinet makers establishment. He as elected coroner several years.

MUNSON, BRYON P. - Bryon P. Munson - Dec 14, 1877 Died, Thursday eve, Bryon P. Munson of Quincy. Lived Camp Point several years before moving to Quincy. Born in Vermont August 1837. Leaves a wife and adopted daughter.

MUNSON, MRS MARY B. - Died - Nov 24, 1876 Died on the 18th inst, Mary B. Munson, aged 41 years, wife of Byron P. Munson of Quincy. Remains taken to Vermont for burial leaving Quincy Sunday eve on the Wabash.

MUNSON, W.G. - Local Hash - Jan 31, 1879 W.G. Munson, a brother of T.L. and the late Bryon T. died last week at Beloit, Kansas. Remains were buried at Quincy Sunday.

MURPHY, ELMIRA - Local - Nov 28, 1879 Died, Mrs Elmira Murphy, nee Easum who was well known here died September 30th of cancer.

MURRAH, JOHN - Real Estate - Feb 27, 1873 The heirs of the late John Murrah sold Wm Semon 85 acres in Honey Creek township for $1500.00

MUSSER, THOS H. - Hash - Sep 14, 1877 Died, Thos H. Musser a well known saddler of Quincy, died Monday, age 58.

MYERS, MAGGIE - Livingston - Aug 4, 1881 Died, Maggie, daughter of Mr and Mrs Pierson Myers of Gilmer (some 4 years old) last Friday from the effects of the mumps.

MCADAMS, MRS E. - Death List - Sep 7, 1877 Old settlers death list since last meeting: Mrs E. McAdams, Ursa.

MCAFEE, JOHN - Local - Apr 1, 1880 John McAfee of Quincy died Saturday A.M. age 21 years.

MCANULTY, MRS LUCINDA - Local - Dec 29, 1881 Died, Mrs Lucinda McAnulty, wife of Samuel McAnulty Tuesday eve in her 73rd year.

MCANULTY, SALATHIEL - Hash - Jul 27, 1877 Died, Samuel McAnulty received a letter from his nephew, John W. McAnulty, dated Lyons, Kansas July 15th says his son Salathiel G. committed suicide after his wife died on the 6th (sons wife). She was buried on the 7th and Salathiel shot himself on the 8th.

MCANULTY, MRS SAMUEL - Personal - Nov 29, 1878 Mrs Samuel McAnulty is attending her sick sister at Versailles who is not expected to live.

MCBRATNEY, MRS - Clayton - Apr 6, 1882 Died, Mrs McBratney lately.

MCCANN, MAT - Neighborhood News - Jun 21, 1878 A accident in which Mat McCann son of Barney McCann and Mr B. Lewis on 12th and Broadway Sunday. McCann will probably not recover. "Herald"

MCCANN, SALLIE E. - Died - Dec 28, 1882 Died in Stanberry, Missouri of typhoid fever and malaria, Sallie E., daughter of Thos. J. and Amanda McCann, 18 years old.

MCCARTY, MRS C.A. - Local - Mar 2, 1882 Died, Mrs C.A. McCarty at her home in Newton County Indiana February 19 in her 23rd year. Was the daughter of William McFarland, Golden. Leaves a husband and 2 little boys.

MCCARTY, GEORGE - Clayton - Oct 7, 1880 Mr George McCarty buried a little daughter Tuesday.

MCCLAIN, ROBERT - Clayton - Jul 18, 1879 Robert McClain, a miserable old man, hung himself a few days since.

MCCLEARY, MRS SOPHRONIA - Hash - Jul 28, 1876 Mrs Sophronia McCleary, the oldest sister of Joseph Smith, the Morman prophet, died at Colchester, McDonough County Illinois in the 75th year of her age.

MCCLINTOCK, DAVID S. - Death's Doings - Dec 14, 1882 Died, at his home near Golden on the 8th inst, David S. McClintock, age 34 years. Leaves a wife and 3 children.

MCCLINTOCK, DAVID S. - Probate Notice - Dec 28, 1882 David S. McClintock 3rd Monday of March William A. Downing, adm.

MCCLINTOCK, JAMES
    SEE: CLARK, MRS MARY ELLA

MCCLINTOCK, MRS MARY - Local - Mar 17, 1881 Died, Mrs Mary McClintock a long time resident of this vicinity died last Saturday. Buried Hebron Cemetery Sunday. She was a sister of James Sharp.

MCCLINTOCK, MRS MARY ANN - Golden - Mar 17, 1881 Died, Mrs Mary Ann McClintock. Leaves many relatives.

MCCLINTOCK, MARY ELLA
    SEE: CLARK, MRS MARY ELLA

MCCLINTOCK, MRS THOMAS
    SEE: PORTER, JOHN

MCCLINTOCK, WILLIAM - Local - Nov 10, 1881 Died, William McClintock an old resident of Camp Point township Sunday eve in his 85th year. Had been blind last few years. Was a native of Ireland. Lived on the farm where he died 40 years.

MCCLINTOCK, WILLIAM - Died - Nov 10, 1881 Died, Sunday eve November 6th William McClintock age 84 years 8 months 24 days. Born Ireland February 12, 1797. Came to U.S. about 1830 and located in Ohio in 1832 where he married Margaret Sharp in 1839. Came to Adams County in 1842. Services at Hebron Church by Rev L.F. Walden.

MCCLINTOCK, WM - Probate Notice - Dec 29, 1881 Wm McClintock, deceased 3rd Monday of March 1882 (20th)

Rezin H. Downing, adm.

MCCORMICK, DR A.Y. – Fowler – Oct 27, 1876 Dr A.Y. McCormick has just buried his little daughter about 15 months old, who died Saturday eve.

MCCORMICK, FLORENCE – Fowler – Oct 27, 1876 Little Florence, infant daughter of Dr and Mrs A.Y. McCormick died Saturday eve the 21st. She was an only child.

MCCORMICK, MICHAEL – Trial of McCormick – Jan 29, 1880 Trial of Michael McCormick for the murder of Elijah Clair last July 4th. Jury returned verdict of guilty of manslaughter, 7 years in penitentiary.

MCCORMICK, WILLIAM – Hash – Dec 28, 1877 William McCormick living near Ursa fell thru the railroad bridge over Rock Creek breaking his back. Death is momentarily expected.

MCCOY, JAMES – Clayton – Nov 12, 1875 Last Friday James McCoy an old citizen whose occupation is mail carrier and teamster was riding a young colt and hurt very badly, will probably not recover.

MCCREARY, SAMUEL – Local – Sep 21, 1882 Died, Samuel McCreary of Rushville on the 11th age 66 years. Served 36 years as a J.P.

MCDAVITT, DORY T. – Obituary – Nov 21, 1877 Died, Dory T. McDavitt of Chatten November 14th. Was an only son, 21 years old.

MCDAVITT, DORY – La Prairie – Dec 7, 1877 Died, Dory McDavitt of Chatten, Houston township. Died at the home of his parents November 15th.

MCDONALD, MRS SALLIE KEENAN – Local – Aug 29, 1879 Died, Mrs Sallie Keenan McDonald, eldest daughter of the late Joseph Keenan, died on the 7th inst at Payson, age 66 years.

MCDONALD, SALLY
    SEE: KEENAN, JOSEPH

MCDONALD, SAMUEL
    SEE: KEENAN, JOSEPH

MCDONALD, THOMAS – Thomas McDonald Shot by Zach Wilson

Aug 18, 1876 Zach Wilson shot Thomas McDonald. Zach had been seeing McDonald's daughter and brought disgrace on the family. Miss McDonald is about 18 years old and about 2 weeks ago she gave birth to a child. Newton McDonald brother of deceased. Jim Wilson brother of Zach. Thomas McDonald was 60 years old and lived on a leased farm ½ mile from Plymouth and came from Kentucky several years ago. Zach is about 28 years old and son of Col. Sam Wilson of McDonough County.

MCDONALD, THOMAS
    SEE: WILSON, ZACHORIAH T.

MCDONALD, THOS
    SEE: WILSON, JAMES
    SEE: WILSON, JIM

MCDOWAL, DR R.R. - Various Squibs - Aug 3, 1877 Died, Dr R.R. McDowal of Fulton county. Died at his home in Lewiston Wednesday of last week, 63 years old.

MCELROY, MR - Clayton - Apr 18, 1879 Mr McElroy a retired old man and member of the Presbyterian Church died last Friday. Wife found him.

MCELROY, JOHN - Probate Notice - May 2, 1879 John McElroy, deceased 3rd Monday of June 1879 (16th) David W. McElroy and Jno. A. McElroy, executors.

MCFADEN, SAMUEL - Criminal Court - Feb 21, 1879 People vs Samuel McFaden, murder of Winfield Scott in Ursa township last Christmas eve.

MCFARLAND, ADAM - Mendon - Feb 16, 1882 Died, Adam McFarland last night. Leaves a wife and 4 children.

MCFARLAND, D.B. - Died - Jan 11, 1878 Died at the residence of D.G. McFarland on the 6th inst of consumption, D.B. McFarland. Born Greene County Ohio April 6, 1825. Came with parents to Adams County fall of 1832. In 1869 moved to Chariton county Missouri for 6 years. Then back to Illinois with family. Leaves a wife, 8 children (1 son in Missouri) Services at Hebron January 7th.

MCFARLAND, MRS ELIZA - Deaths Doings - Dec 14, 1882 Died, December 8th at the family home in Houston township, Mrs Eliza McFarland, wife of Wm M. McFarland in her 69th year. Born Greene County Ohio February 3,

1814. Married Mr McFarland November 30th, 1837 and came to Adams County in spring of "38". 1839 joined ME Church at meeting held on the farm of James Willard under the ministry of Smith McMurray and William Rutledge. Baptised next spring in the branch north of Hebron. T.J. Bryant.

MCFARLAND, ELIZA - Local - Dec 7, 1882 Died, Eliza McFarland, wife of William M. McFarland of Houston, Monday 68 years old. Leaves husband.

MCFARLAND, LEWIS - Golden - Jun 30, 1881 Died, Lewis McFarland living 3-1/2 miles west of Golden last Saturday A.M. Leaves a wife well advanced in age and 1 daughter. Funeral at Hebron by Rev W.A. Crawford of Augusta.

MCFARLAND, LEWIS - Death of Lewis McFarland - Jun 30, 1881 Died, Lewis McFarland one of the earliest settlers of Camp Point Saturday A.M. June 25th. Born in Kentucky in 1806, went to Ohio with parents. Stayed until 1831 when he came to Illinois. Returned to Ohio to marry Miss Jane Dunlap who died in 1834. In 1837 he married Margaret Sanson who survives him, also 1 daughter Mrs M.L. Stewart survives him. Buried in Hebron Cemetery. Services by Rev W.A. Crawford.

MCFARLAND, WILLIAM
    SEE: MCCARTY, MRS C.A.

MCGAUGHEY, CAROLINE - Died - May 25, 1877 Died at her home in Camp Point on the 20th inst Caroline, wife of Woodford H. McGaughey Esq. age 52 years.

MCGINLEY, ROBERT
    SEE: BARGER, CYRUS

MCGINLEY, ROBERT - Homicide - Nov 27, 1874 Robert McGinley was killed while in a fight with Cyrus Barger. Barger cut him very badly. McGinley died within a few minutes. It occurred on the 21st inst at Reuben Strickler's singing school at Union Church in Big Neck. Both men were about 21. Robert McGinley was about 22 years old and the oldest son of Michael McGinley an old citizen of York neck. Cyrus Barger is about 21 years old and is the son of Christ Barger, living 2 miles south of Woodville in the Texas settlement. McGinley was buried in the family cemetery on the Thompson farm 2 miles west of Camp Point Monday.

MCGINNIS, SMITH - Local - May 26, 1881 Smith McGinnis one of the old settlers of Houston township died last week at the home of Dr V. McDavitt, Quincy, lived in Missouri since the war.

MCGINNIS, WM - Local - Mar 25, 1880 Died, Wm McGinnis former resident of Houston and North East township died at Meadville, Missouri on the 17th inst. Leaves 8 children.

MCGRAW, MRS J.C. - Local - Apr 18, 1879 Mrs J.C. McGraw, wife of the chief of Police of Quincy died Thursday A.M. age 38 years.

MCGUIRE, JAMES
    SEE: JOYCE

MCGUIRE, JAS
    SEE: JOYCE, JOHN

MCGUIRE, JAS. - Murder - Dec 11, 1874 About 10 Wednesday Jas. McGuire was killed by a man named Joyce in McGuire's saloon on Hampshire Street, Quincy. In the saloon was McGuire, his son James who was behind the bar and a man named John McGinnis. Joyce is an Irishman about 45 years old and boarded with McGuire. McGuire is Irish and lived in Quincy 18 years, 43 years old and leaves a wife and 7 children.

MCKEE, ALBERT - Supplement - Sep 1, 1876 Died since last years meeting of Old Settlers of Adams and Brown Counties: Albert McKee of Ellington.

MCKNIGHT, PERMELIA
    SEE: WOLFE, DAVID

MCLAIN, ROBERT - Local - Jul 18, 1879 Robert McLain living in Clayton committed suicide Sunday eve July 7th. Had been seperated from wife 3 years on account of adultery on her part.

MCMULLEN, OLD LADY - Clayton - Oct 21, 1880 The old lady McMullen was buried here Tuesday.

MCMULLEN, JOHN - Neighborhood News - Dec 7, 1877 Died, John McMullen a young man residing in Good Hope, Henderson County committed suicide last week.

MCMURRAY, GEORGE - Death List - Sep 7, 1877 Old

settlers death list since last meeting: George McMurray, Clayton, age 74.

MCNAY, ANDREW
    SEE: LEWIS, MRS

MCNAY, JOHN
    SEE: LEWIS, MRS

MCNEAL, A.B. - Obituary - Jun 24, 1880 Dr A.B. McNeal died at his home in Columbus Wednesday A.M. June 16th, 1880. Services by Rev T.J. Bryant in the ME Church Columbus Friday. Born March 8, 1810 in Clearmount County Ohio. Came to Illinois in 1842. Buried in Columbus Cemetery Friday June 18th. Leaves a widow and 7 children (most all are grown). "Herald"

MCNEAL, A.B. - Paloma - Jun 24, 1880 Died, Dr A.B. McNeal died Wednesday A.M. June 16th. Lived Columbus. Services by Rev T.J. Bryant Friday A.M. June 18th. Born March 8, 1810 in Lancaster, Pennsylvania. Came to Illinois in 1842. Leaves a widow and several children. Buried Columbus Cemetery.

MCNEAL, ABRAHAM B. - Probate Notice - Aug 26, 1880 Abraham B. McNeal, deceased   3rd Monday of October, 1880 Brazillia Earel, adm.

MCNEAL, ABRAHAM B. - Probate Notice - Sep 16, 1880 Abraham B. McNeal, deceased   3rd Monday of October, 1880 Barzillia Earel, adm.

MCNEAL, CENTENNEALLA - Columbus - May 25, 1882 Died at her home in Columbus , Centennealla McNeal Wednesday May __, 1882. Nella was the youngest daughter of Mrs Dr McNeal and was born July 4, 1876. Leaves her mother.

MCNEAL, EDWIN - Hash - Apr 28, 1876 Edwin McNeal who was struck by the coal train near Eubanks last week died from his injuries. 73 years old and an old resident of this county.

MCNEALL, ABRAHAM B. - Public Sale of Desperate Claims - Oct 19, 1882 Sale by adm of the estate of Abraham B. McNeall, deceased Saturday November 4th at the P.O. in Columbus. Barzillia Earel, adm.

MCPHERSON, WILLIAM - Hash - Apr 9, 1874 William McPherson, a painter well known in the vicinity of Camp

Point, died at the county poor house last week. William's love of alcohol hastened his departure.

MCREA, MRS W.F. - Liberty - Oct 27, 1881 Died, Mrs W.F. McRea died of consumption at her home near Newtown Sunday 23rd. Leaves 2 children and a husband.

MCVAY, HERSCHEL - Mendon - Jan 19, 1882 Died-News Sunday of the death of Herschel McVay who left here a few months ago for California (a young man).

NANCE, A.M. - Clayton - Feb 15, 1878 Mr A.M. Nance, one of our oldest citizens is lying very low.

NANCE, A.M. - Clayton - Apr 5, 1878 A.M. Nance, of this place, died at the home of her father in law at Rushville Sunday. Remains brought here for burial.

NANCE, A.M. - Hash - Apr 5, 1878 A.M. Nance, Clayton, died at Rushville and his remains were brought home Monday for burial.

NANCE, CLEMENT - Hash - Feb 15, 1878 Died, Clement Nance died Saturday at his home in Quincy, age 70 years. Came to Illinois from Indiana in spring of 1837 and settled in Columbus until 1855 when he moved to Quincy.

NASH, LUCIUS - Local - Aug 15, 1879 Lucius Nash, father of the Nash brothers at Bowen died on the 5th inst. His remains taken to Massachusetts for burial.

NATIONS, JESSIE - Died - Sep 21, 1882 September 14th of typhoid fever, Jessie, only daughter of David and Susan Nations age 21 years 11 months 13 days.

NATIONS, JOHN - Liberty - Jul 22, 1880 Died, Old Uncle John Nations, Monday July 12th at his daughter's, Mrs Polly Taylor's in Columbus. Was in his 80th year. Born February A.D. 1801. Was an old settler of Adams county.

NAYLOR, GEO. - Local - Mar 14, 1879 Geo. Naylor, at one time deputy circuit clerk, died in Quincy last week.

NELSON, BASIL - Sudden Death - Oct 26, 1882 Died last Thursday forenoon, Basil Nelson of Houston township living near Big Neck Post Office was found dead in his barn. Was an early settler of the township. Leaves a wife. Cause of death unknown.

NELSON, BAZEL – Probate Notice – Nov 9, 1882   Bazel Nelson, deceased   3rd Monday of January 1883   Mary Nelson and George W. Nelson adm's.

NELSON, MRS MARTHA KOBEL – Died – Nov 2, 1882   Died at Little Walnut, Kansas on the 24th ult of consumption, Mrs Martha Kobel Nelson.   Lived many year at Camp Point and taught at Maplewood.   Married about a year ago and has for several years lived in Kansas.   Leaves husband, father, brothers and sisters.

NEUMAN, XAVER – Local – Mar 2, 1882   Died, Xaver Neuman, a brother of Jacob Neuman of this place died in Quincy last week, age 56 years.   Leaves a large family and several brothers and sisters residents of this county.

NEVINS, JAMES – Neighborhood News – Jul 20, 1877   Died, James Nevins, a harvest hand was run over by the CB & Q train at Bushnell Thursday and killed.

NEVINS, JOHNNIE – Obituary – Jul 8, 1880   Died in Gilmer township June 25th little Johnnie youngest son of Thomas and Kate Nevins age 1 year 6 months 18 days.

NEWHOUSE, MRS – Clayton – Feb 12, 1875   Mrs Newhouse who has been ill for some time died Sunday night at 9.   Funeral Tuesday at the ME church.   Services by Mr Pilcher.   She was a devoted wife and mother.

NEWTON, M.W. – Local – Feb 28, 1879   Died, M.W. Newton, a well known premoter of secret societies, died in Quincy last Friday.   Buried by Knights Templar Sunday.

NEWTON, ORIN – Clayton – Oct 3, 1879   Orin Newton of Ft Wayne formerly of this place buried a child here last week.

NILES, DR ADDISON – Personal – Apr 9, 1875   Died, Dr Addison Niles, of Quincy died Monday.   He had been a doctor of that city for a number of years.

NORRIS, MRS - Local – Jul 14, 1881   Small pox deaths at Hulls: Mrs Norris on Sunday, Phillips, the first victim and 2 children, Wm Coffey, Mrs Dr Locke and 2 unknown children.   Barry Adage.

NORTON, CHARLIE – Local – Nov 14, 1879   Charlie Norton, a nephew of Miss E. Norton and Mrs John Wyle died at Memphis October 24th of yellow fever.   He formerly resided here and attended school.

OAXS, H.
    SEE: WINE S.

OBLANDER, GEORGE - Neighborhood News - Dec 7, 1877
Died, George Oblander of <u>Bushness</u> died last week.

O'CONNOR, MICHAEL - Neighborhood News - Jul 19, 1878
Michael O'Connor of Galesburg went out with a young
woman named Robinson, Mrs O'Connor followed shot and
killed her husband and then herself.

ODEAR, R.M. - Local - Mar 23, 1882   Died, R.M. Odear in
the lower end of York Neck last week.   Buried Saturday
by Columbus lodge of Masons.

ODELL, SILAS G. - Local - Dec 29, 1881   Died, a babe of
Silas G. Odell last week of pneumonia.

OGLE, FRANKLIN E. - A Sad Affliction - Dec 1, 1881
Died, a baby of Franklin E. Ogle Sunday night.   Funeral
Tuesday.   Tuesday, Hattie, 7 years old died same disease
buried same grave at Fowler.   Then little Eddie, 3 years
old died.

OGLE, MARY L.
    SEE: FISHER, WM V.

O'HARRA, WILLIAM - Local - Jul 25, 1879   William O'Harra
a citizen of Camp Point township many years died Sunday
at his home in Bowensburg, age 70 years.

OHNEMUS, PETER - Hash - Oct 8, 1875   Peter Ohnemus,
prop. of a feed store on Maine Street, Quincy, committed
suicide by drowning.   His remains were found near the
mouth of "Big Slough".

OLIVER, JOHN D. - Hash - Jan 12, 1877   John D. Oliver
was found dead in his bed Wednesday morn.   Casco Mils
are draped in mourning.   John Donkey Oliver, farewell.

OLIVER, WM L.
    SEE: DOWNING, ALMA EMMA

OLIVER, Z.E.
    SEE: DOWNING, ALMA EMMA

OLLENCOTTE, WM - Local - Jun 27, 1879   A man named Wm

Ollencotte, age 60 years, fell dead from heart disease while working in a harvest field 2 miles east of Quincy.

OLLERENSHAW, REV - Burton - Aug 15, 1879 During the past 2 weeks in Burton, died August 3rd little Birdie, an adopted daughter of Rev Ollerenshaw. Funeral by Rev Ollerenshaw himself.

OMER, DANIEL - Hash - Dec 18, 1873 Daniel Omer started for Kentucky Thursday night. He received a dispatch from Louisville that his father was dead.

OMER, GEO. W. - Local - Mar 30, 1882 Died, Geo. W. Omer's little boy Friday night of typhoid fever.

OMER, JACOB - Clayton - Aug 30, 1878 Jacob Omer and James Campbell had a fight, over the effects of a deceased daughter of Mr Omer's that had married a son of Mr Campbell.

OMER, MRS JACOB - Clayton - Jul 22, 1880 Mrs Jacob Omer died Saturday A.M. in her 58th year. Buried from the ME Church Sunday.

OMER, MRS MARY
    SEE: BROWN, MRS JOSIAH

OMER, MRS SARAH A. - Died - Aug 18, 1876 Died at her home near Clayton Friday August 4th, 1876, Mrs Sarah A. Omer wife of Peter Omer, age 40 years 5 months. Leaves a large family. Services by Rev J.C. Sargent at the home. Quite a large concourse of friends followed the remains to its last resting place.

OMER, WM H. - Local - Mar 2, 1882 Died, a 3 year old daughter of Wm H. Omer last week.

O'NEIL, MARY - Fowler - Mar 21, 1879 Died, at Lampa Santa Barbara, California, February 27th Mary O'Neil, wife of John O'Neil, formerly of Cliola. Was in her 35th year. Born near Cliola and was married and lived on the home farm until October 1877 when they went to California. Leaves husband and 5 children.

ORR, WILLIE - Neighborhood News - Oct 11, 1878 "Barry" Willie Orr, son of Elder Orr of the ME district died a few days ago of poison. "News"

OWEN, MR - Columbus - Jan 19, 1882 Died, a little step

daughter of Mr Owen about 6 years old died on Thursday of scarlet fever.

OWEN, MRS - Columbus - Jan 19, 1882 Died, Mrs Owen after an illness of 3 days on Wednesday January 11th.

OWEN, MRS D.C. - La Prairie - Sep 20, 1878 Died Monday, Mrs D.C. Owen.

OWEN, MRS D.C. - La Prairie - Sep 20, 1878 Died this week, Mrs D.C. Owen on Monday.

OWEN, STEPHEN - Drowned - Apr 17, 1873 Stephen Owen, living near Chili was drowned while attempting to cross the north fork of Bear Creek on Sunday April 6th. Body was recovered about 150 yards below the place where he drowned.

OWENS, ROSE - Neighborhood News - Oct 5, 1877 Died, Rose Owens, daughter of Frank Owens died in this city Tuesday. She took poison. "Carthage Gazette"

PAGE, GRACIE - Died - Jan 19, 1882 Died in Big Neck January 10th little Gracie, age 8 months 16 days, daughter of E.C. and Margaret Page.

PARKER, MISS EMILY - Clayton - Nov 30, 1882 Died, Miss Emily Parker at Kansas City. Remains brought home for burial.

PARKER, MRS FRANK
    SEE: EWING, MRS

PARKER, JOSEPH A. - Died - Dec 20, 1878 Died at Fowler on the 14th inst, Joseph A. Parker age 85 years. Mr Parker came from New York and settled in Adams County more than 40 years ago and lived Fowler the past 10 years. His first wife and 6 children died before him. His 2nd wife survives him.

PARKER, MISS MARY - Clayton - Oct 3, 1879 Miss Mary Parker of Rushville who has visited here often died at that place last week.

PARKER, MISS P. - Columbus - Jan 19, 1882 Died at the home of John Nichols January 7th, Miss P. Parker of consumption.

PARKINS, MRS MARY - Local - Apr 1, 1880 The Macomb

Journal says the Mrs Mary Parkins who was a resident of Camp Point during the war, whose husband lost his life in the service has finally succeeded in getting her pension allowed. Just payment $2,000.00 and $96.00 a year hereafter.

PARN, HENRY - Local - Sep 30, 1880 Henry Parn, a German farmer living south of town a few miles died Sunday with typhoid fever.

PARN, HENRY - Probate Notice - Dec 2, 1880 Henry Parn, deceased 3rd Monday of January 1881 Mary Parn, adm.

PARVIN, WM - Local - Nov 3, 1881 Died, Wm Parvin who lived about 4 miles east of Liberty committed suicide last week by hanging.

PARVIN, WM - Liberty - Nov 3, 1881 Died, Wm Parvin, one of the oldest settlers of McKee township committed suicide last Wednesday by hanging himself. Wife found him in the barn. Funeral Thursday at his home in McKee.

PATH, MRS - Local - Jun 30, 1881 Died, Mrs Path of Quincy committed suicide Sunday. Mr Path went to cellar and found her.

PATTEN, SAMANTHA
    SEE: KEENAN, JOSEPH

PATTON, J.D.
    SEE: HUGHES, BEN

PAULLIN, DANIEL - Local - Apr 14, 1881 Died - A dispatch to the Chicago Tribune from Dubuque the 7th states that Daniel Paullin of Quincy died in that city on Wednesday (consumption). Leaves 3 sons and 2 daughters.

PEABODY, MRS JOHN L.
    SEE: WILKS, CORDELIA

PEARCE, BESSIE - Obituary - Dec 31, 1875 Little Bessie, only daughter of Mr and Mrs Wm J. Pearce died December 18th.

PEARCE, ELLA J. - Died - Nov 2, 1882 Died at her home near Chatten October 30th, Ella J., wife of Jackson R. Pearce and daughter of H.F. and E.N. Jacobs age 21 years 2 months 5 days. Services by Rev T.J. Bryant.

PEARSON, MR - Mendon - Aug 25, 1881 Died, father Pearson one of our oldest citizens Sunday, at the home of his sister, Mrs Whittlesy, 4 miles north of Mendon at the age of 81 years.

PEARSON, ALBIAN - Local - Aug 3, 1882 Drowned, a man named Albian Pearson in the river near Bonnett, Duffy and Co. foundry, Quincy, last Wednesday.

PEARSON, J.C. - Local - Oct 26, 1882 Died, Dr J.C. Pearson of Ursa Monday age 58 years.

PEART, THOMAS - Probate Notice - Jan 19, 1877 Thomas Peart 3rd Monday of March Howard Ogle, adm.

PEASE, ALBERT N. - Local - Sep 19, 1879 Fireman, Albert N. Pease was killed in a train accident at Eubanks station going into Quincy Monday night.

PEASE, JOHN - Died - Jul 8, 1880 Died, John Pease on a Missouri Pacific train last Monday eve. John Pease and wife of Barry, Illinois had been to Kansas to visit a son and were on their way home. After the train passed Warrenburg the old man became ill, age 77 years. Remains taken off at Sedalia and sent on to Barry. Monroe City, News (Missouri).

PEASE, LUCIUS - Neighborhood News - Nov 30, 1877 Lucius Pease an old resident of Kirkwood was ran over and killed by a train Wednesday.

PEEBLES, A.B. - Local - Oct 24, 1879 A.B. Peebles, coroner of Pike county died last week.

PENCE, JOHN
    SEE: BOWLES, WM

PENFIELD, MRS - Fowler - Nov 12, 1880 Died, Mrs Penfield. She was at one time a resident of Fowler.

PENFIELD, SYLVESTER G. - Local - Jul 11, 1879 Sylvester G. Penfield died in Coatsburg Monday eve. Was bookeeper at Casco Mills moving from here to Fowler to keep books of the Alden Fruit Preserving Co. Leaves an aged mother.

PENNEY, SAMUEL - Hash - Jan 29, 1875 The remains of Samuel Penney were brought here from Quincy last Tuesday and buried in the Camp Point Cemetery. He was a brother of Mrs J.T. Hagerty and was a native of Rushville.

PENNY, GEORGIANA
    SEE: HAGERTY, JOHN T.

PEPPLE, JOHN - Mendon - Nov 28, 1879 A little child of Mr John Pepple died this A.M.

PEPPLE, MRS WM - Mendon - Apr 25, 1879 Mrs Wm Pepple of this village died Sunday afternoon. Funeral Monday P.M. Lived Mendon 25 years.

PERRIN, OLIVER - Local - Dec 2, 1880 Died, Oliver Perrin, Pres, of the 3rd National Bank of Cincinnati. Died Monday the 29th of heart disease. Was a relative of Mrs L. Dewey and had a number of relatives here.

PERRY, MATTHEW - Clayton - Sep 2, 1880 Matthew Perry killed in a wagon accident.

PERRY, ROBERT - Neighborhood News - Aug 23, 1878 Accident in Montezuma last Wednesday, Robert Perry, son of Henry Perry, age about 14 years, accidently discharged his own gun, died. He and brother were getting ready to go hunting. "Pittsfield Democrat"

PETERSON, JAMES - Local - Apr 28, 1881 Died, John Redick cracked the skull of his brother in law, James Peterson and fled. In this county nearly opposite Hannibal.

PETERSON, JAMES - Local - Nov 11, 1881 George Redick of Pike county has been sentenced to 15 years for the murder of James Peterson.

PETERSON, TUCKSON - Neighborhood News - Jul 5, 1878 Mr Tuckson Peterson, a native of Denmark, employed by Mr Wm Wood shot himself accidently. 35 years old, had been in this vicinity 2 years. Leaves a wife. "Bushnell Record"

PETITT, MR - Obituary - Apr 7, 1881 Died, Old Mr Petitt who had lived Kingston nearly 40 years. Died March 20th.

PEVEHOUSE, GRANNY - Clayton - Dec 16, 1880 Died, Granny Pevehouse Saturday.

PEYTON, J.M. - State News - Aug 5, 1880 Died, Mrs J.M. Peyton of Elgin on the 1st inst, 85 years old.

PEYTON, JOHN - Local - Jan 12, 1882 Died, John Peyton, who was a medical student at Keokuk Medical School. Contracted small pox and died at Clayton Friday night. Body buried 2 Saturday morning.

PFEIFFER, MATTHIAS - Hash - Apr 16, 1878 Matthias Pfeiffer, a boy 11 years old was drowned in Melrose township on Sunday.

PHIPPS, THOS J. - Hash - May 25, 1877 Died, Thos. J. Phipps formerly a resident of Big Neck, died in Nodaway County Missouri May 12th.

PICKETT, RACHEL - Marblehead - Dec 28, 1882 Died, at her home Monday December 18th Rachel Pickett, age 22 years of consumption.

PICKINS, HELEN - Aug 3, 1882 Died, at Augusta, Illinois July 28th Helen, daughter of G.W. and Sarah Pickins age 14 years 8 month. Baptized by Rev Curtis Powell and joined ME Church at Pulaski in 1878.

PICKLER, RICHARD B. - Probate Notice - Oct 29, 1875 Richard B. Pickler 3rd Monday of December 1875 David Curl, adm.

PIERCE, WILLIAM - Died - March 4, 1880 William Pierce of Camp Point township died Wednesday A.M.

PIERCE, WILLIAM - Probate Notice - Mar 18, 1880 William Pierce, deceased   3rd Monday of May E.B. Pierce, adm.

PIERSON, DR - Dec 13, 1878 "Herald" Augusta, Illinois, Dr Pierson murdered two weeks ago Saturday night had lived in Augusta 37 years and 58 years old.

PIERSON, DR - Local Hash - Nov 29, 1878 The murder of Dr Pierson of Augusta has been the exciting topic this week.

PIERSON, DR
    SEE: FERGUSON, ED

PIERSON, DR DANIEL
    SEE: HETRICK, MARION

PIERSON, DR DANIEL - Horrible Homicide - Nov 29, 1878 Augusta, Illinois November 24, The victim was Dr Daniel Pierson of this place.

PIERSON, DR DANIEL – A Mystery Cleared Up – Mar 7, 1879 "St Paul Pioneer Press" On last November 23rd Dr Daniel Pierson of Augusta, Illinois was murdered. Two colored men arrested in Minnesota, Geo. McWilliams and Edwin Ferguson. Both confessed. Marion Hettrick also involved, he stuck the doctor to death.

PILCHER, MRS ADELAIDE – Local – Aug 17, 1882 Died, Mrs Adelaide Pilcher, wife of Rev A.M. Pilcher at Rochelle, Ogle County on the 5th. Remains taken to Jacksonville the home of her youth for burial.

PILE, DANIEL – Mar 19, 1875 Daniel Pile, deceased February 1875 settlement, will sell to the highest bidders the following claims—Henry R. Motter, Ex.

PITTMAN, J.M. – Death of J.M. Pittman – Apr 4, 1879 Died, J.M. Pittman former citizen of Quincy died at Santa Clara County California on February 24th. Born in Missouri in 1813. Came to Quincy when 22 years old. "Whig"

PLEW, JAMES W. – Probate Notice – Mar 25, 1880 James W. Plew, deceased 3rd Monday of May 1880 Edw. H. Buckley, adm.

PLEW, MRS JAMES – Clayton – Aug 17, 1877 Died Mrs James Plew who has suffered so much for the last year. Died Monday A.M. Buried in Mt Pleasant Cemetery.

PLOWMAN, ADA – Died – Aug 14, 1873 Died August 1st, 1873, Ada Plowman age 9 months.

PLOWMAN, WALTER N. – Obituary – Oct 9, 1873 Died October 1, 1873 of diptheria, Walter N., eldest son of James and Jennie Plowman age 4 years and 6 months. Leaves father and mother, brother and sister.

POLING, MRS – Mendon – Jun 2, 1881 Died, Mrs Poling, one of our oldest settlers. Died Friday at the home of her daughter, Mrs H.C. Walker in this village.

POLING, MRS C.D. – Mendon – Dec 16, 1880 Died, Mrs C.D. Poling of our village. Died last Sunday A.M. Leaves a husband and 2 children.

POLING, EDWIN – Mendon – Jul 1, 1880 Edwin Poling. Late of this city, but now of Coatsburg buried his youngest child here last week.

PORTER, JOHN - Local - Oct 17, 1879 John Porter, of Springfield, son of Mrs Thomas McClintock died in that city Tuesday.

PORTER, SAM - Local - Dec 29, 1881 A colored ruffian, Sam Porter was killed in Quincy Sunday by a boy about 12 named Ben Summers.

POTTER, MRS - Newtown - Nov 22, 1878 A Mrs Potter formerly of Missouri, but lately living with her stepmother in Payson township was buried in our cemetery Thursday.

POTTER, URIAH - Local - Jun 8, 1882 Thomas Marshall appointed conservator of the estate of Uriah Potter. Mr Potter has a fine farm in Liberty township.

POWELL, MRS J.S. - Fowler - Nov 2, 1882 Mr W. Chase and Lettie attended the funeral of their cousin, Mrs J.S. Powell at Columbus last Monday.

POWELL, JOHN - Local - Mar 10, 1881 Died, John Powell of Ellington Monday, age 79 years. Came to county in 1832.

POWELL, MARY WADDELL - Obituary - Oct 26, 1882 Died, near West Point, Hancock County Illinois October 22, Mary Waddell Powell, daughter of J.O. and L. Waddell. Born December 11, 1857. Joined ME Church when 13 years old at Mt Pleasant. Married last February 22nd to J.S. Powell and moved to Hancock County. Services Monday by Rev A.M. Danely and Rev T.J. Bryant.

PRATHER, WM S. - Public Notice - Jun 24, 1875 Wm S. Prather, deceased 2nd Monday of 1875 August Thomas C. Prather, John Prather and Wm Lancaster, Executors.

PRATT, MRS SARAH - Obituary - Feb 26, 1880 Died, at the home of her son, Z.S. Pratt, Mrs Sarah Pratt, age 70 years. Had been a resident of Camp Point, living with her son the past 4 years.

PRATT, MRS SARAH - Obituary - Feb 26, 1880 Died on February 18th Mrs Sarah Pratt at the home of her son Mr Z.S. Pratt in Camp Point, Illinois. Born in New York March 1, 1810. Moved to Illinois in 1856. Buried Friday in Woodland Cemetery, Quincy by the side of a son, the only one that preceded her. Remaining 3 were present at the burial.

PRATT, MRS Z.S.
    SEE: CHATTEN, WILLIAM
    SEE: WHITE, MRS FRANK

PREBBLE, MRS AMANDA – Hash – Oct 13, 1876 Mrs Amanda Prebble who was formerly a resident of Camp Point died at Bayliss, Pike County Sunday.

PRENTISS, MRS ALWILDA – Local – Sep 26, 1879 Died, Mrs Alwilda Prentiss, daughter of Dr John Torrence died at the home of her father about 12 Saturday night from dropsy, 34 years old. Buried in public cemetery near this city. "Barry Adage"

PRICE, MRS – The Quincy Mystery – Jan 18, 1878 Mrs Price of Pittsfield died in Dr Park's office in Quincy. Abortion??

PRICE, MRS FANNIE C.
    SEE: LAMOIX, W.H.
    SEE: LANOIX, DR

PRICE, MRS FANNY – Hash – Apr 12, 1878 Capt McGraw returned to Quincy last Saturday from San Francisco with Dr Lanoix for the abortion case of Mrs Fanny Price of Pittsfield.

PROBST, J.H. – Hash – May 22, 1873 J.H. Probst, of Lafayette, Indiana suicided at Chilicothe, Missouri on last Thursday night. He did it with his little razor and did it artistically.

PROCTOR, EMMA – Newtown – Oct 18, 1878 Died, Emma Proctor age 16 of this place. Leaves her parents.

PULLMAN, HOWARD – Burton-Liberty – Apr 14, 1881 Died, a little child of Howard Pullman's died Saturday April 2.

PULMAN, ARTHUR J. – May 12, 1881 Died, of pneumonia April 2nd Arthur J. son of Howard and Ann S. Pulman age 1 year 7 days.

PULMAN, FANNIE – Livingston – Feb 16, 1882 Died, Miss Fannie Pulman at H.J. Vicker's, Burton township, February 9th, age 27 years. Services at Pleasant Grove Church by Rev A.M. Danely. Leaves her mother.

PURMAN, MRS WILLIAM – Neighborhood News – May 17, 1878 Death of Mrs Wm Purman of Bardolph caused from fright by the storm Tuesday night. Leaves husband and children.

QUAIL, ED - Local - Jul 11, 1879 Ed Quail was drowned while bathing in the river at Millville Sunday.

RAANE, WILLIAM - Probate Notice - May 18, 1882 William Raane, deceased 3rd Monday of July, 1882 (17th) Mary Raane, adm.

RAILEY, SAMUEL - Liberty - Aug 11, 1881 Died, Samuel Railey, one of the pioneers of this county died last week in his 74th year. Leaves a large family.

RALSTON, DR J.N. - Supplement - Sep 1, 1876 Died since last years meeting of Old Settlers of Adams and Brown Counties, Dr J.N. Ralston of Quincy.

RALSTON, DR JOSEPH N. - Died - Jun 30, 1876 Died-Dr Joseph N. Ralston, one of the oldest citizens of Quincy died at his home on York Street Sunday afternoon. Born in Bourbon County Kentucky in January 1801. Studied medicine in Lexington. Came to Quincy in 1832. Buried with Masonic honors. "Whig"

RANDOLPH, JAS. - Mendon - Mar 18, 1880 The drowning of Jas. Randolph in the slough this side of Canton last week (probably bad whiskey).

RANDOLPH, JOHN - Local - Mar 11, 1880 The body of John Randolph the man who left home last week and was not heard from for many days was found in Lima Lake. It is supposed he was intoxicated and accidently drowned.

RANDOLPH, WALTER E. - Local - Jun 27, 1879 Walter E. Randolph of Carthage was killed by the cars at Ft. Madison last Monday.

RANKIN, CHARLEY - Personal - Jan 17, 1879 Charley Rankin has returned to Maplewood, having been absent since the death of his father.

RANKIN, ROBERT - Local Hash - Dec 20, 1878 Robert Rankin, of Fall Creek died Wednesday night of last week.

RATCLIFF, JOSEPH - Clayton - Jan 29, 1880 Joseph Ratcliff's wife was buried at the Mounds Tuesday.

RAY, WM H. - Local - Feb 3, 1881 Died, Hon. Wm H. Ray died at his home in Rushville Thursday of last week.

Was an early settler of Schuyler County came to
Rushville in 1834.

RAYMOND, CHAS. - Neighborhood News - May 10, 1878 Chas.
Raymond prop. of the Canton distillery was found dead in
a Peoria saloon Sunday A.M.

REA, MINNIE - Junction - Mar 11, 1880 Died, Minnie Rea,
daughter of Dr Rea of Meredosia. They lived at the
Junction some 4 years ago.

READ, JOSIAH - Newtown - May 18, 1882 H.W. Read of Knox
College attended the funeral of his father, Josiah Read.

REAUGH, JANE
    SEE: WILKES, DANIEL

REAUGH, SAMUEL - Local - Jun 16, 1881 Died, Samuel
Reaugh died June 7th of heart disease, age 69 years at
his home in Novelty, Missouri. He was an old settler of
Adams County residing many years near Columbus.

REDICK, JOHN
    SEE: PETERSON, ED

REDMOND, THOMAS - Exchange Notes - Dec 27, 1878 Thomas
Redmond of Quincy died last Friday night age 74 years.
Was mayor of Quincy several times. Came from Ireland
when 16 years old.

REECE, S.S. - Neighborhood News - Aug 3, 1877 Died,
S.S. Reece, of Keene township, Adams County. Died at
his home Monday A.M.

REED, - Mendon - Jul 25, 1879 A lady named Reed died on
Sunday at the home of her brother in law, Mr W. Halsey,
of Keene township, age 81 years.

REED, J.I. - State News - Aug 5, 1880 Died, J.I. Reed
age 56 years an old resident of Joliet dropped dead
Saturday last.

REED, JOSIAH - Death of an old Citizen - May 11, 1882
Died, Tuesday May 2nd Josiah Reed of Newtown. Came here
from New York. Was a native of Vermont. Married twice,
first to Amy Roe, second to Caroline Strong. One son a
mute by the former marriage. Son is an instructor at
Jacksonville. Four children by the latter. Mrs Reed is
left only with an adopted daughter, but 2 sons live in

the immediate vicinity.

REEDER, JOHN J. - Local - Feb 26, 1880 Died, John J. Reeder and Jacob Wagner citizens of Melrose township died this week. Mr Reeder came to the county at an early day and Mr Wagner in 1840.

REES, MRS WM - Mendon - Jul 25, 1879 Mrs Wm Rees, daughter of Mrs Battell of our village was buried here yesterday afternoon.

REESE, S.S. - Death List - Sep 7, 1877 Old settlers death list since last meeting: S.S. Reese, Keene age 35.

REID, CORNELIUS M. - Obituary - Feb 12, 1875 Died on the 2nd inst, of consumption, at his residence at Vance's Station, Alabama, Cornelius M. Reid, age 47 years. Leaves a wife and 6 children in a helpless condition.

REINECKER, HERMAN - Local - Jul 22, 1880 Herman Reinecker was drowned in the river at Quincy last Wednesday body not recovered.

RENNACKER, GEO. - Death List - Sep 7, 1877 Old settlers death roll since last meeting: Geo. Rennacker, Concord, age 80 years.

RENSCHEL, MR - Coatsburg - Dec 29, 1881 Died, a child of Mr Renschel last Friday. Funeral Sunday afternoon.

REYNOLD, EFFIE SEATON
    SEE: SEATON, JOHN T.

REYNOLDS, ALICE E. - Local - Oct 14, 1880 A note from Rev J. Campbell of Cawker City, Kansas tells of the death of Alice E., daughter of Henry M. Reynolds of abcess of the liver.

REYNOLDS, AMOS
    SEE: MOORE, S.G.
    SEE: SEATON, JOHN T.
    SEE: SLONAKER, ADAM W.

REYNOLDS, FRANK - Local - Jul 14, 1881 Died, Frank Reynolds of this county died Monday.

REYNOLDS, MINNIE - Neighborhood News - Aug 2, 1878 Minnie Reynolds, a young girl 17 years old living near Plymouth committed suicide Saturday.

REYNOLDS, WALTER - Local - Nov 28, 1879 Walter Reynolds of Quincy, but recently living with his nephew George R. Reynolds of this township died suddenly Sunday A.M.

RHEA, LON - Local - Oct 6, 1881 Died, the babe of Mr and Mrs Lon Rhea Thursday A.M.

RHODES, JACOB - Riceville - Feb 23, 1882 Died, a little boy of Jacob Rhodes age 4 years Friday night with diptheria.

RHODES, WILLIAM - Murder - Jan 26, 1877 A photographer killed in his studio in Quincy William Rhodes who occupied the rear rooms on the 3rd floor of George A. Miller's building on the corner of 6th and Hampshire.

RICE, JACOB - Mendon - Nov 14, 1879 A little child of Jacob Rice aged some 4 years died Thursday morning last.

RICE, JAMES M. - Local - Dec 12, 1879 Died, Major James M. Rice, formerly of Quincy died at Trinidad, Colorado last Friday.

RICE, JESSE D. - Local - Aug 15, 1879 Jesse D. Rice of Richfield died on the 6th at the home of his son age 85 years.

RICHARD, FRANK MADISON - Bowen - Sep 7, 1882 Died, Mr and Mrs Richards of Wisconsin arrived here Saturday the 17th to see their son, Frank Madison who died Friday the 24th. Buried at Providence graveyard 8 miles north of town.

RICHARDS, AUSTIN J. - Died - Dec 15, 1881 Died December 7th Austin J. son of the late John W. and Margaret Richards age 7 years 9 months.

RICHARDS, MRS J.W.
    SEE: STOLTE, HENRY

RICHARDS, JAS - Hash - Feb 8, 1878 Daniel H. Conner received word from Bardolph Wednesday A.M. of the death of his brother in law, Jas Richards, who resided in McDonough County, New Philadelphia. Mr Richards formerly lived in this county.

RICHARDS, JOHN - Burton Liberty - Apr 28, 1881 Died, John Richards an old citizen died Friday A.M.

RICHARDS, WILLIS - Mendon - Jun 9, 1881 Willis Richards who lives 3-1/2 miles NW of this village died Saturday eve. Leaves a wife and two children.

RICHARDSON, MRS CHARLES H. - Local - Jul 15, 1880 Died, Mrs Charles H. Richardson, formerly of Quincy died recently at Tensas Parish, Louisiana, was a sister of Wm E. Avise of Quincy.

RICHARDSON, Col. - Hash - Dec 31, 1875 The funeral of Col. Richardson took place in Quincy Tuesday afternoon.

RICHARDSON, ELVIN - Obituary - Mar 3, 1881 Died, Elvin Richardson, age 12 years, only child of Mrs Jennie Richardson died on the 21st.

RICHARDSON, GEO. J. - Hash - May 5, 1876 Judge Sibley has appointed Wm A. Richardson master in chancery to fill the vacancy caused by the death of his brother Geo. J. Richardson.

RICHARDSON, GEORGE J. - Death - Apr 28, 1876 Hon. George J. Richardson died at his home in Quincy Thursday eve. He was son of the late Wm A. Richardson. He was born in 1846 and nearly 30 years old. Appointed to West Point in 1862.

RICHARDSON, W.A. - Obituary - Dec 31, 1875 Col W.A. Richardson, of Quincy, died at his home December 27th age 60 years. Born in Kentucky. Came to Illinois in 1831. He was a volunteer in the Blackhawk War.

RICHARDSON, WM A. - Supplement - Sep 1, 1876 Died since last years meeting of old settlers of Adams and Brown Counties held in Clayton: Wm A. Richardson of Quincy.

RIGGAL, JOHN
    SEE: HOWARD, WESLEY

RILEY, FREDDIE C. - Died - Jul 14, 1876 Died, on Saturday morn little Freddie C. Riley almost 3 years old. He was an only child. Services by D.H. Johnson. (July 1, 1876 was the date of the article)

RIPLEY, DAVID - Local - Nov 28, 1879 Died, David Ripley, city marshall of Barry died last Friday very suddenly.

RIPPEL, MRS CHRIS - Concord - Jun 16, 1881 Mrs Chris

Rippel died Friday eve.

RIPPENKRAGER, WILLIAM - Murder - Apr 14, 1876 Report of shooting in Quincy of a hotel runner named William Rippenkrager by a stranger named John B. Atterberry. Mr Atterberry lived in Menard County and was on his way to the Black Hills.

RITCHEY, JAMES S. - Drowned - Nov 17, 1881 Died, James S. Ritchey and wife who live 1 mile west of Mt Sterling were drowned in a slough near Ripley, Brown County about 2 P.M. Saturday.

ROBBINS, ELIZABETH - Death List - Sep 7, 1877 Old settlers death list since last meeting: Elizabeth Robbins, North East, age 82 years.

ROBBINS, MRS ELIZABETH - Died - Feb 23, 1877 Died, February 19th Mrs Elizabeth Robbins, age 82 years. Born in the state of North Carolina Feb 9, 1798. Came to Illinois with her husband and children in 1836. Member of ME Church. Leaves a large number of relatives.

ROBBINS, HARRIETT
    SEE: WARREN, CALVIN A.

ROBBINS, JARED - La Prairie - Dec 20, 1878 Mr Jared Robbins died at his fathers on Sunday A.M.

ROBBINS, MRS JOSEPH - Hash - Mar 24, 1876 Mrs Robbins, wife of Joseph Robbins was buried in Quincy Monday. She was a native of Massachusetts and came to Quincy about 12 years ago.

ROBERTS, ANNIE W.
    SEE: WEBSTER, JOHN K.

ROBERTS, CHARLES - Fatal Accident - Nov 27, 1873 We are informed that a young man named Charles Roberts, 19 years old, son of Wm Roberts of Ursa township was shot thru the heart and killed while hunting. He had set his gun by the fence on the farm of Mr Ben Smith and leaned his breast against the nozzle.

ROBERTS, ESPA - Neighborhood News - Dec 14, 1877 Died, Espa Roberts, a young man, fell from a canoe into the Illinois River near Liverpool and drowned.

ROBERTS, RICHARD - Neighborhood News - Jan 25, 1878

Richard Roberts was killed in a coal shaft at Colchester Monday eve.

ROBERTS, RICHARD T. – Personal – Oct 17, 1879 A little daughter of Richard T. Roberts died Sunday.

ROBERTS, MRS SUSIE F. – Local – Aug 18, 1881 Died, Mrs Susie F. Roberts, youngest daughter of Capt. C.J. Wood a former townsmen died at her fathers home in Aurora Monday eve the 8th inst of fatty degeneration, 25 years old.

ROBERTSON, MRS – Mendon – Jul 29, 1880 Died, Mrs Robertson, an old resident of our town Sunday afternoon. Was a sister of the late Edward Tyndall of Ursa.

ROBERTSON, JOHN B. – Obituary – Sep 28, 1882 Died, at Beverly on Sunday A.M. September 24th John B. Robertson age 92 years 3 months 4 days. Born in New York June 10, 1790. Came to Illinois in 1834 where he located on the farm where he died. Was first postmaster of Beverly and kept the job for nearly 40 years. Married in 1814 to Kate Courey who survives him. Had 11 children, 8 living, 6 sons and 2 daughters, 35 grandchildren and 8 great grandchildren. Services by Rev Norris at the home.

ROBINSON, JESSE – Clayton – Jul 11, 1879 Jesse Robinson was buried last Monday. Was 78 years old.

ROBISON, JESSE – Probate Notice – Aug 15, 1879 Jesse Robison   1st Monday of October   Lucinda Robison, adm.

ROCKINFIELD, GEORGE – Local – Aug 4, 1881 Died, George Rockinfield an old resident of Columbus township last week.

ROE, AMY
   SEE: REED, JOSIAH

ROE, LUTHER – Death of Luther Roe – Jan 26, 1882 Died, Luther Roe at Sparta, Illinois on January 17th. Born at Newburg, New York December 28th, 1847, 35 years old. Came with parents to Newtown when quite young. At 16 years he enlisted as a member of the 50th Reg. Served until his father died and he was discharged to support his mother and 3 young children. Four years ago he got the job of brakeman on the St Louis and Cairo Railroad. Died before his mother could get there. Services Saturday from his mothers home and Baptist Church. Service by Rev King.

ROE, M.L. - Riceville - Feb 2, 1882 Died, M.L. Roe.

ROGERS, EDWARD - Hash - Jun 29, 1877 Died, Edward Rogers, the painter who fell from the dome of the court house. Died Wednesday.

ROGERS, H.A. - Local - Jan 5, 1882 Died, H.A. Rogers a druggist of Quincy Monday. Connected with Rogers and Malone and later, Rogers and Montgomery.

ROGERS, JAMES W. - Died - Mar 4, 1880 Died, March 2, 1880, James W. Rogers age 38 years. Mr Rogers came from Indiana about a year ago. Left a wife and boy.

ROGERS, JAMES W. - Local - Jul 4, 1879 A little son of James W. Rogers died suddenly Tuesday afternoon.

ROGERS, SAMUEL W. - Hash - Apr 19, 1878 Died, Dr Samuel W. Rogers an old physician of Quincy died Wednesday at Charleston, New Hampshire in his 74th year.

ROGERS, TIMOTHY - Hash - Dec 10, 1875 Timothy Rogers has erected a family vault in Woodland Cemetery, Quincy at a cost of $13,000.

ROGERS, WILLIAM T. - Funeral of Wm T. Rogers - Apr 22, 1880 William T. Rogers, mayor of Quincy died at his home in Quincy Sunday A.M. April 11th. Was the eldest son of Timothy Rogers. Brother of E.A. Rogers. Buried Quincy on the 14th. Services at the Vermont Street Baptist Church. Remains were placed in the private vault recently completed by Timothy Rogers.

ROSE, JENNIE - Coatsburg - May 4, 1882 Died, near Coatsburg April 14th Jennie Rose, age 24 years. Funeral by Rev H.C. Coats.

ROSEBERRY, WILLIAM - Public Sale - Sep 11, 1873 Public sale of real estate, the farm of William Roseberry, deceased ½ mile east of Columbus at public sale October 2, 1873. M.G. Roseberry, agent for the estate.

ROSS, BERNETTA - Died - Sep 3, 1875 Died on Tuesday the 24th inst at home in Camp Point, Bernetta Ross, wife of Elder Jas. R. Ross age 50 years 5 months. Leaves her aged husband.

ROSS, CHARLEY - Charley Ross Shot - Aug 29, 1879
Charley Ross a Quincy bartender who at one time lived in
Camp Point was shot and killed by James A. Frink
Saturday.

ROSS, DORA - Died - Dec 2, 1880 Died November 25th of
diptheria, Dora, youngest daughter of Mrs M.C. and the
late William C. Ross age 2 years 6 months.

ROSS, JAMES - La Prairie - Mar 3, 1876 The suicide of
James Ross was on the 16th inst instead of the 14th as
reported. Some thinks his name was not Ross but Kelley,
some have no idea what it was. Been in this community
about 11 months and had many sincere friends.

ROSS, JAMES
    SEE: MORGAN, JAMES M.

ROSS, JAMES - Suicide - Feb 25, 1876 On Monday the 14th
inst a young man named James Ross committed suicide at
La Prairie by jumping into a well. He has resided at La
Prairie only a short time and nothing is known of his
previous history.

ROSS, JENNIE - Hash - Nov 26, 1875 Miss Jennie Ross who
has been a victim of consumption for several years died
Monday A.M. at 1. Buried in York Neck Cemetery Tuesday.

ROSS, JEROME - Died - May 8, 1873 Died, Jerome Ross,
son of R.H. Ross of this place, at Mt Sterling Saturday
eve the 3rd inst of consumption. He was buried with
Masonic honors Monday.

ROSS, WILLIAM C. - Died - Feb 19, 1874 Died, on the 11th
inst, of cerebro spinal meningitis, infant daughter of
William C. and M.C. Ross.

ROSS, WILLIAM C. - Obituary Notice - Dec 12, 1879
William C. Ross died at the home of John Gault, Houston
township, December 5th, age 42 years 9 months. Resident
of the county more than 20 years. Enlisted as a private
in Co. E 50th Reg. in Illinois Infantry. Farmed in Wythe
township Hancock County until about a year ago. Married
November 1864 to Miss Clemmie Cyrus of Houston, whom he
leaves with 5 children. Buried Sunday in York Neck
Cemetery.

ROSSBACH, ADAM - Local - Nov 12, 1880 Died, Adam
Rossbach, living near the old Cramer distillery north of

the city committed suicide Wednesday by taking poison.
Leaves a wife and family. "Whig"

ROTH, MRS A.
    SEE: SCHELL, GEORGE

ROTH, JOHN A. - Hash - Sep 29, 1876 Mrs A. Roth has commenced suit against Mutual Life Ins. Co. to recover $1,100 in insurance on the life of her husband, John A. Roth.

ROTH, JOHN A. - Obituary - Oct 8, 1875 Died, John A. Roth, on the 1st inst. He was a native of Kirweiler, Bavaria, born April 11, 1815. Came to America in 1837 and settled in Quincy where he married and lived until 1855 when he came to this town. Went to California during the gold rush for 3 years. Member of the Masonic and Knights Templar.

ROTH, JOHN A. - Personal - Oct 1, 1875 John A. Roth was prostrated by apoplexy Wednesday A.M., no hopes are entertained for his recovery.

ROTH, JOHN A. - Probate Notice - Oct 22, 1875 John A. Roth 3rd Monday of December 1875 Apalonia Roth, adm.

ROTH, MARGARET A. - Died - Nov 20, 1874 Died on the 12th inst on consumption, Margaret A., wife of Joseph Roth, age 30 years.

ROUNDS, C.S. - Exchange Notes - Mar 14, 1879 C.S. Rounds of Griggsville, partner of Robert Allen, producer and stock dealer was killed by the train in East St Louis Saturday. Leaves a wife and 5 children. "Barry Unicorn"

ROUTT, THEODORE
    SEE: HAYES, JOHN

ROWSEY, LOVINA
    SEE: LIERLY, JAMES

RUMP, F. - Burton - Oct 28, 1880 A little child of F. Rump, age 5 months died last Wednesday.

RUNNION, MRS WM - Jottings - Apr 29, 1880 Died, Mrs William Runnion of consumption last Thursday. Buried Friday. Was one of the early settlers of York Neck. Leaves a number of relatives.

RUPP, JOSEPH - Neighborhood News - Jul 13, 1877 Joseph Rupp about 20 years old was drowned in the river at Quincy Sunday eve. His body has not been recovered.

RUSSELL, CATHERINE - Died - Jul 21, 1876 Died, in Gilmer on the 12th inst Catherine, wife of Wakefield Russell age 48 years.

RUTHERFORD, JAMES - Neighborhood News - Jun 14, 1878 Mr James Rutherford living about 4 miles north of Perry was struck by lightning and killed last week. "Pittsfield Democrat" Leaves a wife and 4 children.

RYAN, WILLIAM - Neighborhood News - Jul 27, 1877 Died, William Ryan, of Chicago was found dead in bed at the Occidental Hotel Friday A.M. He was about 80 years old.

SACKETT, ASA - Suicide at Richfield - Jun 17, 1880 "Barry Adage" An old man named Asa Sackett died near Richfield Tuesday last and buried at Philadelphia on Wednesday.

SALISBURY - Hancock County Murder - Sep 2, 1880 Thomas Duff found guilty of murdering Salisbury at Fountain Green, Hancock County last week.

SALISBURY, A. - Local - Aug 26, 1880 A man named Duff is under arrest at Carthage for killing a man named A. Salisbury at Fountain Green, a small village near the T.P. and W. road in the northeast part of Hancock County Saturday night.

SALMON, ISAIAH H. - Local - Nov 12, 1880 Died, Isaiah H. Salmon died Saturday eve. Was printer for the Whig many years.

SAMMONS, ELVY
    SEE: ANDERS, JOHN

SAMMONS, WESLEY
    SEE: ANDERS, JOHN

SAMUELS, MR
    SEE: FAIRFAX, MRS HENRY

SANDERS, MR - Neighborhood News - Oct 19, 1877 A man named Sanders living 5 miles west of Walnut Grove took arsenic Monday. Died Tuesday.

SANSON, MARGARET
    SEE: MCFARLAND, LEWIS

SARTORUS, HERMAN
    SEE: BLOCK, MRS MAGGIE

SASSENBERG, EDWARD - Mendon - Jul 29, 1880 Edward Sassenberg, a miller at the Pearl Mills lost a child yesterday morning from congestion of the spine.

SAUNDERS, GEO. N. - Neighborhood News - Oct 12, 1877 Geo. N. Saunders an old citizen of Walnut Grove township, McDonough County committed suicide last Monday, 40 to 50 years old. Leaves a family.

SAVAGE, C.A. - Hash - May 1, 1873 C.A. Savage, of Quincy was struck with paralysis Friday night and died Tuesday.

SAWTELL, W.H. - Bowen - Sep 7, 1882 Died, W.H. Sawtell at home in Bowen on the 18th inst. Had lived Bowen many years.

SAWYER, E.E.B. - Trustee's Sale - Jun 26, 1873 Trustee's Sale of real estate, August 26, 1873, of E.E.B. Sawyer's and Esther Sawyer, his wife dated February 22, 1872 and recorded in the office of the recorder of Adams County in the state of Illinois in Book 12 of mortgages at page 48. By John Downing

SAWYER, MRS E.E.B. - Personal - Aug 2, 1878 Isaac Bailey of Griggsville was in town Sunday attending the funeral of Mrs E.E.B. Sawyer.

SAWYER, MRS ESTHER - Obituary - Aug 2, 1878 Died, Saturday A.M. July 27th Esther, wife of E.E.B. Sawyer and daughter of Levi and Nabby Bailey, age 45 years 5 months 23 days. Born Poland, ME. February 4, 1833 married Ephriam E.B. Sawyer and came west in 1861. Leaves husband and children.

SCARBOROUGH, MRS ELECTRA - Local - May 23, 1879 Died, Mrs Electra Scarborough, one of the first settlers of Adams County died at Payson May 8th.

SCHAFER, ADAM - Liberty - Aug 18, 1881 Died, Adam Schafer buried his babe Friday. Died Wednesday night.

SCHAFER, G.J. - Burton - Jan 29, 1880 G.J. Schafer was

called last week to Morris, Ill. to attend the funeral of his sister in law.

SCHAFFER, GEORGE - Hash - Nov 26, 1875   George Schaffer, age 21 was accidently shot in Quincy last Thursday. He died the next day.

SCHANDON, JACOB - Local - May 9, 1879   Andy Steinbach and Jacob Schandon were drowned in the river at Quincy Sun. Steinbach's body was found and other one wasn't.

SCHEDELL, MRS - Death List - Sep 7, 1877   Old Settlers death list since last meeting: Mrs Schedell, Ellington, age 73.

SCHEIFERDECKER, LOUIS - Probate Notice - Nov 8, 1878   Louis Scheiferdecker   3rd Monday of December 1878   Fredericka Scheiferdecker, adm.

SCHELL, GEORGE - Local - Aug 19, 1880   Died, George Schell of Quincy Sunday A.M. on the 8th inst. He was a brother of Mrs A. Roth of this place.

SCHELL, JOHN - Hash - Dec 29, 1876   John Schell, an old citizen of Quincy of German birth died Tuesday. The deceased was 55 years old and has resided in Quincy since 1834.

SCHELL, JOHN - Death List - Sep 7, 1877   Old settlers death list since last meeting: John Schell, Quincy age 65 years.

SCHOFIELD, BRYANT T. - Death of B.T. Schofield - Mar 24, 1881   Died, Bryant T. Schofield at his home in Carthage Saturday A.M. Born Pennsylvania and a brother of congressman Schofield of that state.

SCHOTT, JOHN B. - Neighborhood News - Mar 15, 1878   The body of John B. Schott, the Warsaw brewer who disappeared some time ago was found in the river near La Grange a few days since. Buried Monday.

SCHOTT, JOHN - Neighborhood News - Jan 25, 1878   John Schott of Warsaw mysteriously disappeared Tuesday of last week. His mind gave way 2 years since, caused by the death of his brother and business trouble, since has taken to drink.

SCHWARTZ, D.F. - Liberty - Jul 29, 1880   Died, the wife

of D.F. Schwartz died last Saturday.

SCHWARTZ, DANIEL – Local – Sep 28, 1882 The circuit court Friday found Daniel and Joseph Schwartz guilty of manslaughter in killing John Malone in Liberty township last spring and gave each 1 year on penitentiary.

SCHWARTZ, ELIZABETH
    SEE: DISMORE, ROBERT

SCHWARZ, HENRY – Oct 22, 1875 Legal notice for all claims and demands against Henry Schwarz, deceased 3rd Monday of December 1875 Christina Schwarz, Ex.

SCOFIELD, GLENNI – Hash – Mar 29, 1878 Glenni W. Scofield of Pennsylvania who has been appointed register of the treasury, Vice Allison, deceased is a brother of B.T. Scofield of Carthage.

SCOTT, JAMES – Exchange Notes – Apr 25, 1879 A young man named James Scott living a few miles east of Denver was killed last week. "Carthage Gazette"

SCOTT, WINFIELD
    SEE: MCFADEN, SAMUEL

SCRANTON, AMOS – Exchange Notes – Feb 14, 1879 Amos Scranton was killed in a wagon accident. Lived one mile east of Mendon. His son William was with him. "Mendon Dispatch"

SCRANTON, AMOS – Mendon – Feb 14, 1879 Died, Mr Amos Scranton one of our oldest citizens fell from a load of hay and was killed Wednesday. Funeral on Saturday.

SCRANTON, EDWARD – Local – Jan 6, 1881 The Kansas City "Mail" says of Scranton, formerly of Mendon. The remains of Edward Scranton arrived here this A.M. from Conejoo, Colorado. His leg was amputated, from the effects of which he died. Remains will be forwarded to Quincy, Illinois.

SCRANTON, PHEBE
    SEE: HENDRICKSON, MRS PHEBE

SEATON, HATTIE M. – Died – Oct 19, 1877 Died, on the 18th inst of croup, Hattie M. daughter of Richard and Ellen Seaton age 1 year 3 months 15 days.

SEATON, JOHN
    SEE: MOORE, JAMES P.

SEATON, JOHN T. - Local - Feb 21, 1879 Amos Reynolds has been appointed guardian of John T. Seaton and Effie Seaton Reynolds.

SEATON, RICHARD - Legal - Nov 20, 1873 Ex. Sale of desperate and doubtful claims, notes on H.M. Sears bearing date of April 20, 1868 for $52.40. W.M. Glover bearing date of Nov 5, 1863 for $200.00. Silas Bailey dated Aug 16, 1870 for $400, E.E.B. Sawyer dated Dec 6, 1872 for $500. John S. Seaton, Ex of the last will of Richard Seaton, deceased.

SEATON, RICHARD - To Whom It May Concern - Sep 18, 1873 Ex. of estate of Richard Seaton claims and debts to estate are: Nov 3, 1863 William Glover $200, Sep 20, 1868 Henry M. Sears $50.84, Aug 16, 1870 Silas Bailey $486 also Aug 31, 1871, Nov 6, 1871 and Jan 30, 1873. Jan 20, 1873 E.E.B. Sawyer $533.33 also Dec 19, 1873 and Dec 6, 1873 also 8 shares in Camp Point Mfg will sold. John S. Seatmn, Executor   Sept 17, 1873

SEATON, RICHARD - Notice of Final Settlement - May 7, 1875 Notice of Final Settlement for the estate of Richard Seaton, deceased to John S. Seaton, Richard Seaton, Rebecca P. Bailey, the heirs at law of Margaret W. Wallace, deceased, the heirs at law of Kenner Seaton deceased and all others concerned. 3rd Monday of May John S. Seaton Executor.

SEATON, MRS RICHARD
    SEE: CURRY, MRS THOMAS

SEATON, RICHARD
    SEE: SLONAKER, ADAM W.

SEATON, RICHARD - Obituary - Apr 24, 1873 Richard Seaton died Mon the 21st inst at the home of his son Richard Seaton Jr. He was born about 7 miles from Louisville, KY Jan. 10, 1790 being the youngest son of Kenner Seaton. He and his father settled on Floyds Fork some 10 miles east where he lived until 1835 when he and his family and the late Peter B. Garrett and others moved to Ill and settled about 1 mile east of this town, where he improved a large farm. In 1856 his son took the farm and he moved into town where he resided after the death of his wife with his daughter, Mrs Bailey, until their house burned last Sept. He served 6 or 8 months in the War of 1812 for which he received a pension under the Act of 1871. Was a member of the Christian Church.

SEAVER, IRA A. - Hash - Jul 19, 1878   Ira A. Seaver, died in Quincy from sun stroke last Monday.

SECRESE, ANDREW J. - Local - Jun 9, 1881   Died, Andrew J. Secrese of Bowen was killed by being crushed between 2 cars at Clayton Thursday, former resident of Columbus.

SECREST, A.J. - Liberty - Feb 12, 1880   Died, A.J. Secrest's wife died Sunday, buried Monday.

SEEHORN, ELI - Death List - Sep 7, 1877   Old settlers death list since last meeting: Eli Seehorn, Fall Creek, age 70.

SEEHORN, OFFICER
    SEE: DISSLER, HENRY

SEEHORN, T.J. - Policeman Murdered - Aug 23, 1878   Henry Dissler, a blacksmith and living near Fairweather, this county, knifed T.J. Seehorn who died when officer Seehorn was trying to run him in for being drunk. Mr Dissler had a large family. "News" 20th

SEELIG, MRS RHODA - Died - Sep 21, 1877   Died, at her home in Camp Point on September 17th, 1877 Mrs Rhoda Seelig Esq. age 43 years. Leaves husband, daughter and an infant son.

SEGER, SAMUEL E. - Local - Mar 23, 1882   Died, Samuel E. Seger well known grocery merchant of Quincy at Mendota Tuesday afternoon while on his way to Freeport, 56 years old.

SELBY, MRS JAMES - Hash - Sep 13, 1878   The funeral sermon of Mrs James Selby deceased will be at the ME church Keokuk Junction next Sunday at 11 A.M. by Rev G.S. Weaver of Galesburg.

SELBY, THOMPSON - Died - Dec 28, 1882   Died December 30th at the home of his son in law, Scott Taylor in Houston township, Thompson Selby in his 65th year. Born Athens County Ohio April 25, 1818. Came to Adams County with family in fall of "43" settled York Neck. Services at Hebron by Rev T.H. Tabor and buried Hebron.

SELBY, WILLIAM - Neighborhood News - Feb 15, 1878 Died, last Thursday a 5 year old son of William Selby of Lima fell backwards in a tub of hot water. Died about 24 hours later.

SEWARD, MISS KEZIAH - Mendon - Feb 7, 1879 Died, Miss Keziah Seward, daughter of Abijah Seward, died on Monday eve.

SEWARD, WM H. - Local - Sep 7, 1882 Killed, Wm H. Seward of Augusta at the mill of Dewey and Seward, Friday, 57 years and was father of one of the partners who was in Springfield. Mr Seward was taking his place at the mill.

SEYMOUR, ARTHUR B.
    SEE: CURTIS, ELAM B.

SEYMOUR, HATTIE - Obituary - Aug 15, 1879 Died, August 10, 1879 at the home of John H. Francis Camp Point, Miss Hattie Seymour age 18 years daughter of Frank and L.K. Seymour born August 14, 1861. When 9 years old she lost both parents and then made her home with Mr Francis.

SHAFFER, MRS - Hash - Jan 11, 1878 Mrs Shaffer whose disappearance and murder was reported last week was found Wednesday A.M. at the house of F. Hutnagel about 4 miles from her house. She had tried to commit suicide.

SHAFFER, MRS L.D. - A Woman Missing - Jan 4, 1878 Mrs L.D. Shaffer murdered, suspect is Mr Shaffer. She was his second wife and the daughter of Felix G. Landis, about 35 years old. Shaffer's lived about 3 miles south of Columbus.

SHAMBAUGH, MRS EMMA - Mendon - Oct 7, 1880 Died, Mrs Emma Shambaugh wife of D.P. Shambaugh died last night of consumption.

SHANAMAN, ULTMAN - Hash - Aug 24, 1877 Ultman Shanaman living near the German Lutheran Church, Clayton township, fell out of a wagon. Feared he cannot recover.

SHANE, WILLIAM OSCAR - Died - Nov 23 1882 Died at Paloma, Adams County Illinois on Saturday November 18th William Oscar infant son of William F. and Elizabeth J. Shane age 3 weeks 4 days. Funeral at ME Church on Sunday afternoon by Rev A.M. Danely.

SHARP, EDWARD - Died - Jul 24, 1874 Died, in Concord township, this county on the 17th inst, Edward Sharp age about 65 years. Was an old resident of this part of county having lived on his farm over 30 years and was a extensive fruit grower. Death caused by an injury received to one of his feet getting cut up in a mower.

SHARP, JAMES
    SEE: MCCLINTOCK, MRS MARY

SHARP, MARGARET
    SEE: MCCLINTOCK, WILLIAM

SHARP, MRS PERMELIA - Local - Jul 27, 1882 Died, Mrs Permelia, wife of James Sharp, living 1-1/2 miles west of Camp Point Tuesday of typhoid fever.

SHARP, MRS PERMELIA JANE - Obituary - Aug 3, 1882 Died, Mrs Permelia Jane Sharp, daughter of Rev J.H. and Nancy Bates. Born October 11, 1834. Married James Sharp April 21, 1864 and died July 25, 1882 age 47 years 9 months 14 days.

SHARP, MRS THOMAS C. - Local - Oct 17, 1879 The wife of Judge Thomas C. Sharp editor of the Carthage "Gazette" died on the 3rd, 60 years old.

SHEER, MRS DAVID S. - Burton - Oct 7, 1880 Died, Mrs Sheer, wife of David S., of Melrose died Tuesday night.

SHEER, JOHN - State Items - Apr 24, 1874 John Sheer, about 16 years, of Burton township accidently shot himself Saturday. It is feared the wound will be fatal.

SHEFFIELD, DAVID M. - Personal - Feb 26, 1874 David M. Sheffield is lying very low with consumption.

SHEFFIELD, DAVID M. - Died - Mar 16, 1874 Died on Sunday March 15th of consumption, David M. Sheffield.

SHELTON, WILLIE
    SEE: HAYES, JOHN

SHEPHERD, M. - Local - Mar 11, 1880 Died, Dr M. Shepherd, an old physician of Payson died Monday.

SHEPHERD, MONROE - Mendon - Jul 29, 1880 Died, Monroe Shepherd of Loraine this A.M.

SHERMAN, MRS
        SEE: TAYLOR, MRS MARGARET

SHERMAN, SETH C. - Death of Seth C. Sherman - Jan 17, 1879 Seth C. Sherman died at his home in Quincy Saturday A.M. Born in Vermont and came to Vandalia, Illinois early in life. Moved to Quincy in 1833. 73 years old. Leaves a wife and 2 children (Mrs Jeptha Dudley of this city and F. Sherman of Omaha). The following article was on the other side: Mrs Elizabeth Sherman,(wife of Seth C. Sherman) died at 1 yesterday. Mr Sherman died Saturday. Funeral of husband and wife will be at the Cathedral at 3 Wednesday P.M. Both buried in 1 grave at Woodland. "Herald"

SHERRICK, MRS DARRAH - Hash - Jul 19, 1878 Mrs Darrah Sherrick, of Big Neck, died Saturday of inflamation of the bowels. She was a daughter of Wm Brown of Chatten.

SHERRICK, MARTIN - Probate Notice - Jan 22, 1875 Martin Sherrick 3rd Monday of March 1875 John W. Sherrick, adm.

SHERRICK, MARTIN - Obituary - Jan 22, 1875 Martin Sherrick, deceased. Member of Houston Grange #1273 P. of H.

SHERRICK, MARTIN - Personal - Jan 22, 1875 John Sherrick has been appointed adm of the estate of Martin Sherrick, deceased.

SHERRICK, MARTIN - Died - Jan 15, 1875 Died on the 10th inst at Keokuk, Iowa of hemorrhage of the bowels, Martin Sherrick age ___ years. (sic) He came to Illinois from Pennsylvania in 1842 and settled in what is now Big Neck, Houston township. Member of Methodist Church there and had gone to Keokuk 3 weeks ago for medical treatment. He leaves a wife, 2 sons and 1 daughter.

SHIELDS, DR. - Clayton - Oct 14, 1880 Old doctor Shields of Mt Sterling was buried at that place Monday.

SHIELDS, WM - Local - Oct 14, 1880 Died, Dr Wm Shields of Mt Sterling died Saturday, age 65 years.

SHOEMAKER, CHARLIE - Mendon - Feb 12, 1880 Died, Uncle Charlie Shoemaker one of our oldest citizens died last Friday night nearly 90 years old.

SHORTNESS, CHARLES - Local - Aug 19, 1880 A boy named Charles Shortness was drowned at Quincy while bathing. Did not recover the body.

SHRIVER, FANNY - Died - May 16, 1879 Died of pneumonia May 9th Fanny, daughter of B.F. and Malinda Shriver age 14 years.

SHUHARDT, MR - Local - May 2, 1879 Died, a small son of Mr Shuhardt who moved on the Bates farm this spring.

SHUMAN, HENRIETTA E. - Died - Jul 23, 1875 Died on the 21st inst, Henrietta E., wife of L.W. Shuman age 27 years.

SIEBERS, THEODORE
    SEE: ANDERS, JOHN

SIMMOND, JAMES W.
    SEE: ALLEN, ISAAC

SIMMONDS, MR - Died - Sep 1, 1881 Died, Mr Simmonds, prop. of the Clayton House last week.

SIMMONDS, EUNICE ELVINA - Died - Jul 11, 1879 Died on the 5th inst, Eunice Elvina, daughter of James W. and Lucy A. Simmonds age 19 months.

SIMMONDS, JAMES W. - Local - May 4, 1882 Died, James W. Simmonds who formerly lived here died at Vernon, Iowa last week. Leaves a wife and large family of children.

SIMMONS, JOHN - Clayton - Oct 25, 1878 John Simmons of Keokuk Junction buried his little boy at Pleasant View Church last Sunday. They have lost both of their children with membranous croup.

SIMMONS, JOHN W. - Local - Sep 1, 1881 Post mortem was held on the body of John W. Simmons who died last week (disease was cancer of the stomach).

SIMMONS, MAUD - Clayton - Mar 6, 1875 Died, February 25th of membranous croup Maud Simmons, age about 3 years, daughter of John and Malinda Simmons. Funeral at ME Church. Buried in Pleasant View Cemetery.

SIMPKINS, ELIAS - Local - Oct 28, 1880 A man named Baker at Pittsfield shot and killed a policeman named Elias Simpkins.

SIMPKINS, GEORGE - Clayton - Aug 1, 1879 George
Simpkins an old citizen of these parts died here Sunday.

SIMPSON, BEN - Neighborhood News - Jun 14, 1878 Ben
Simpson an old citizen of Industry township, whose
family resides on the Burton property in Macomb
committed suicide Monday, about 40 years old. Leaves a
wife and 3 children living here. "Macomb Eagle"

SIMPSON, MRS JOHN - Local Hash - Jan 31, 1879 Mrs John
Simpson of Houston township died last Friday. Her
husband died a few years ago and was one of the early
settlers of this county.

SKAATS, JAMES H. - Death of James H. Skaats - Jan 31,
1879 James H. Skaats died at his home in Camp Point
Monday eve January 27th age 60 years. Born Dearborn
County Indiana January 13, 1819. Moved to Cincinnati
with parents when 6 years old. When 19 years went to St
Louis and one year later to Columbus, Adams County.
While living in Columbus he married Miss Mary Viar and
returned to Cincinnati for 17 year. Moved to Camp Point
in 1865. They had 13 children. Leaves a wife of nearly
40 years and an adopted daughter. Was a member of Odd
Fellows and buried at Pleasant View Cemetery Wednesday
A.M.

SKAATS, JAMES H. - Notice of Settlement - Feb 14, 1879
All persons indebted to the estate of James H. Skaats,
deceased are requested to come and settle. F.H. Bates
at Eagle Mills

SKINNER, MRS O.
    SEE: BROWNING, O.H.

SKINNER, O.C. - Death List - Sep 7, 1877 Old settlers
death list since last meeting: O.C. Skinner, Quincy age
60.

SKINNER, ONIAS C. - Died - Feb 9, 1877 Judge Onias C.
Skinner died at his home in Quincy Sunday A.M. February
4th age 62 years. Born in Oneida county New York. Came
to Peoria at age 15 years.

SLACK, MRS B.F.
    SEE: WALKER, MRS

SLACK, LEWIS - Death List - Sep 7, 1877 Old settlers
death list since last meeting: Lewis Slack, Ursa, age

77 years.

SLAGEL - Hash - Nov 13, 1874 James Stinson who murdered Slagel in Brown County a few days ago was arrested at the Cleaveland farm, 3 miles from Quincy last Thursday.

SLOAN, MR - Coatsburg - Mar 2, 1882 Died, little Willie, 4 months and 29 days, only child of Mr and Mrs Sloan. Funeral at U.B. Church last Sunday by Rev Coats.

SLOAN, C. - Clayton - Dec 23, 1880 A little son of C. Sloan of Concord is not expected to recover from a peculiar affection of one of his eyes for which doctors seem to have no precedent. The bone casing back of the eye has decayed and an accumulation gathered that pressed the eyeball completely out of the socket.

SLOCUM - Local - Sep 1, 1881 Slocum the bigamist is dead. He died at Elmira, N.Y. of delirium tremens.

SLOCUM, J.C. - Slocum Dead - Feb 21, 1879 Word received that J.C. Slocum, the husband of an injured and neglected wife. The husband of 3 illegal wives including one in Hannibal is dead. Mr Slocum died in jail in Ohio where he was taken by the Bryon County Sheriff. "News"

SLONAKER, ADAM W. - Adm Sale of Real Estate - Feb 3, 1881 Estate of Adam W. Slonaker against Richard Seaton, Martha Slonaker, Amos Reynolds, Dora Slonaker, Samuel Slonaker, George E. Slonaker and Martha Slonaker, guardian of Dora Slonaker and Samuel Slonaker. George R. Reynolds, adm.

SLONAKER, ADAM W. - Probate Notice - Nov 9, 1877 Adam W. Slonaker 3rd Monday of December 1877 George R. Reynolds, adm.

SLONEKER, ADAM W. - Oct 26, 1877 Died, on October 12th Adam W. Sloneker, of consumption. Born August 8, 1829 in Westmoreland County Pennsylvania. Came to Illinois with parents in 1835 on to Iowa in 1836 and 1849 on to California 2 years. Back to Illinois where he purchased the Irving estate. Married 1854 to Miss Martha Walters who with 4 children survive him. Member of ME Church since 1854.

SLONEKER, ANELIA - Died - May 9, 1879 Died Saturday, May 3rd, Anelia, daughter of Mrs Martha S. Sloneker, age

4 years 4 months.

SLONEKER, ELLA - Died - Apr 14, 1876 Died, Ella Sloneker of consumption at the residence of her parents in York Neck (18 years of age), Sunday A.M. April 9th. Sick 3 months.

SMART, MRS S.E.
    SEE: BOYLE, MRS JOHN

SMITH, MR - Liberty - Aug 10, 1882 Died, Mr Smith, one of the oldest residents of Liberty township died at his home 2 miles northwest of Liberty of cancer.

SMITH, BEN - Clayton - Oct 24, 1879 Ben Smith buried a little son last week, about 7 years old.

SMITH, HARIET
    SEE: MANARD, WM G.

SMITH, IDA - Clayton - Mar 21, 1879 Miss Ida Smith has been called to the funeral of her father at Carrolton.

SMITH, ISIAH
    SEE: MANARD, WM G.

SMITH, J.K. - Clayton - Feb 26, 1880 William Smith of Carthage, son of J.K. Smith has been here since his father died. Will is in the drug business there and doing well.

SMITH, JEANETTE CASEY - Obituary - Nov 2, 1882 Died in Dallas County Iowa October 20th Mrs Jeanette Casey smith age 49 years 9 months 29 days. Born Shelby County Kentucky December 21, 1832 and in 1849 went to Scott County Indiana. Married August 8, 1850 to Joseph Smith and came to Adams County Illinois in 1856 where they lived 10 years and on to Dallas County Iowa in 1866. Mother of 10 children, 8 survive her. Member of ME Church 37 years.

SMITH, JOHN K. - Clayton - Feb 19, 1880 Mr John K. Smith, an old prominent citizen of this place with his wife were visiting Mr Henry Hopper Tuesday and started for home. Mr Smith let the lines fall and Mrs Smith seeing something was wrong took the lines when he fell back in the seat, before she could drive back to the house he was dead.

SMITH, JOHN K. - Clayton - Mar 4, 1880 B.A. Curry has administered on the estate of John K. Smith and will sell the personal effects the 20th.

SMITH, JOHN K. - Obituary - Feb 26, 1880 John K. Smith died near Clayton, Illinois February 17, 1880. Born in Jefferson County Kentucky October 11, 1822 was 57 years 4 months 6 days old. Was youngest of 4 children-2 brothers and 1 sister survive him and living in this vicinity. Parents were George and Isabella Smith. They came to Adams County in 1836 and settled in Columbus township. He married Susan Curry June 20, 1847 and moved to Clayton township. Was baptised in 1873. Buried Pleasant View Cemetery February 19th. Leaves wife and 2 sons.

SMITH, JOHN W. - Local - Aug 18, 1881 Died, John W. Smith a C.B. & Q. switchman at Burlington was killed by cars Thursday night.

SMITH, JOSEPH - Hash - May 8, 1873 Joseph Smith, an Englishman, suicided at Sciota, McDonough county last Friday week, with a razor.

SMITH, JOSEPH
    SEE: BIDAMON, MRS EMMA
    SEE: MCCLEARY, MRS SOPHRONIA

SMITH, MRS LETITIA - Died - May 9, 1879 Died at Adrain, Illinois Tuesday may 6th of consumption, Letitia, widow of Jacob Smith and daughter of William Bellew, age 37 years. Buried Camp Point Wednesday.

SMITH, MARY - Probate Notice - Dec 22, 1881 Mary Smith, deceased 3rd Monday of March 1882 (20th) John C. Smith, adm.

SMITH, MARY - Probate Notice - Jan 5, 1882 Mary Smith, deceased 3rd Monday of March 1882 (20th) John C. Smith, adm.

SMITH, PETER - Death of Peter Smith - Jul 5, 1878 Died, Peter Smith of Quincy died at his home 624 Jersey Street Sunday A.M. Born Chester, Massachusetts in 1880 and lived there until after his marriage to Mary E. Topliff in 1832. Went to Amherst, Massachusetts for 2 years and to Sharon, Ohio in 1834 till fall of 1836 and settled in Quincy.

SMITH, R.T. - Death List - Sep 7, 1877 Old settlers death list since last meeting: R.T. Smith, Clayton, age 72 years.

SMITH, REUBEN T. - Clayton - Dec 15, 1876 Mr Reuben T. Smith fell down while feeding stock and died very suddenly at his farm near this place on Tuesday A.M. of this week. He was a member of the Baptist Church.

SMITH, RUFUS - Local - Apr 6, 1882 Died. Rufus Smith of Golden was brought home last week from Joplin, Missouri and died at his mothers home soon after his arrival last week.

SMITH, SAMUEL
    SEE: KEMP, MRS RHODA C.

SMITH, THOMPSON - Clayton - Jan 29, 1880 Thompson Smith died and was buried Sunday.

SMITH, WILLIAM G. - Local - Sep 28, 1882 Died, William G. Smith a well known blacksmith died of neuralgia of the heart Wednesday A.M.

SMITH, WM G.
    SEE: BOWERS, MRS ADA

SMYTH, THOMAS - Burton - Aug 1, 1879 Died, Mr Thomas Smyth an old citizen of the county. Died July 23rd. Native of Ireland, born in county of Donegal in 1811. Came to America in 1840. Married Marie Gray in 1855. Leaves 6 sons and 2 daughters. Lived in Philadelphia, Pennsylvania as short time and 16 years in Melrose township Adams County and then to his late home in Burton township.

SNODGRASS, CHARLES - Fatal Accident - Nov 27, 1874 About 4 P.M. Tuesday, Charles Snodgrass age 25 years, residing in Mt Sterling was killed by the bumper of a hay press falling on his head killing him instantly.

SNYDER, MRS HIRAM - Local - Jul 25, 1879 Mrs Hiram Snyder died Wednesday forenoon. Had been an invalid for several months.

SOVERN, MRS ABEL - Clayton - Oct 3, 1879 Mrs Abel Sovern, north of town died last week.

SPANGLER, HARRY - Neighborhood News - Jul 20, 1877

Monday afternoon Harry Spangler age 14 years and son of Joe Spangler Sr of this city took poison, question of whether he will live. "Carthage Gazette"

SPENCER, REV G.M. – Fowler – Feb 14, 1879 Died, Rev G.M. Spencer at his home in Lima Monday February 3rd. Leaves a wife.

SPICER, CHARLES – Mendon – Jan 24, 1879 Mr Charles Spicer, near Loraine, died very suddenly last Thursday night.

SPILKER, AUGUST – Neighborhood News – Sep 21, 1877 August Spilker a boy about 11 or 12 years old drowned last Saturday. Father works for F.W. Jansen and Son's Furniture Works.

SPINKER, HENRY – Mendon – Aug 12, 1880 Two children of Henry Spinker, who lives 4 miles northwest of town died last week.

STABLER, MRS – Columbus – Aug 24, 1882 Died, Mrs Stabler.

STABLER, LYDIA – Obituary – Aug 24, 1882 Died, Lydia Stump August 17th. Born in Baltimore County Maryland June 6, 1814. Married Wm Stabler at Shrewsburg, York County Pennsylvania August 2, 1836 stayed there until fall of "55" when they moved to Columbus, Illinois, age 68 years 2 months 11 days. Buried Columbus Cemetery. Services by Rev A.M. Danely of the ME Church. Had 13 children. Leaves her husband, 4 sons and 3 daughters all of mature age.

STABLER, LYDIA S. – Columbus – Aug 24, 1882 Died, Lydia S. Stabler on August 17th age 68 years 2 months. Services by Bro. Danely.

STAHL, MRS N. – Fowler – Nov 3, 1881 Mrs N. Stahl, who has been a great sufferer for years, now lies at the point of death at her home near Fowler.

STANBACH, JAMES – Hash – Jul 28, 1876 James Stanbach of Mendon, Chariton County Missouri was shot and killed at that place a few days ago. Mr Stanbach was a former resident of this county having moved to Missouri about 3 years ago.

STANSBERY, MRS SARAH – Coatsburg – Nov 8, 1878 Mrs

Sarah Stansbery of Lima, daughter of Mrs A. Johnson was buried at the Coatsburg graveyard on the 4th inst.

STARR, MRS - Mendon - Nov 28, 1879 Died, Mrs Starr, the mother of R.B. Starr died today.

STEEL, CHARLES
    SEE: WILLARD, MARGARET A.

STEINBACH, ANDY - Local - May 9, 1879 Andy Steinbach and Jacob Schandon were drowned in the river at Quincy Sunday. Steinbach's body was found, other one wasn't.

STEPHENSON, MRS SARAH - Neighborhood News - Mar 22, 1878 Died, Mrs Sarah Stephenson, a widow died in Haw Creek township, Knox county recently, age 100 years 6 months 17 days. Born in Maryland in 1778. Resident of Illinois 50 years. Galesburg "Plaindeler"

STEVENS, MRS - Death List - Sep 7, 1877 Old settlers death list since last meeting: Mrs Stevens, McKee, age 64 years.

STEVENS, AMZI - Mendon - Apr 27, 1882 Died, Amzi Stevens a former resident of this village, but for many years of Hancock County died Saturday and will be buried here today, 68 years old.

STEVENS, BENJAMIN - Death List - Sep 7, 1877 Old settlers death list since last meeting: Benjamin Stevens, McKee, age 68 years.

STEVENS, DEWITT C. - Died - Aug 3, 1877 Died, at the residence of R.J. Stevens, Quincy, July 31st, Dewitt C. Stevens, son of G.G. Stevens of Greenwood County Kansas, 22 years old. Native of Eldridge, Onondago County New York. He was nearly blind.

STEVENS, DUDLEY - Local - May 5, 1881 Died, Dudley Stevens of near La Prairie was killed Sunday A.M. by a freight train (drunk and laid down on track). Son of a wealthy farmer in the neighborhood.

STEVENS, MRS HENRY - Local - Jan 20, 1881 The Quincy papers report the death of Mrs Henry Stevens.

STEVENS, MARY
    SEE: CURTIS, ELAM B.

STEVENS, MRS SOLON - Mendon - Apr 22, 1880   Died, Mrs Solon Stevens from storm injuries.

STEWART, MRS J.H.
    SEE: COLLINS, FREDERICK

STEWART, JOHN
    SEE: DAVIS, MRS ELVA L.

STEWART, MRS M.L.
    SEE: MCFARLAND, LEWIS

STEWART, MRS MARTIN - Local - May 6, 1880   Mrs Martin Stewart died last Friday at the home of her daughter, Mrs David Howell, Maryville, Missouri.

STEWART, MARTIN - Obituary Notices - Dec 12, 1879   Died, Martin Stewart November 25th at the home of his son in law, Capt T.L. Howden, Nodaway County Missouri age 76 years 3 months 11 days. Born in Athens County Ohio August 15, 1803 and married September 14, 1823 to Miss Sarah Thompson who survives him. Came to Adams County in 1832. They had 14 children, 8 still living (4 sons and 5 daughters) sons all live Adams County and the daughters all live west of the Mississippi. Joined the ME Church in 1840.

STEWART, MRS SARAH - Obituary - May 20, 1880   Died, at the home of her son in law at Maryville, Missouri April 30, 1880 Mrs Sarah Stewart, relic of Martin Stewart deceased, age 74 years 3 months 24 days. Born in Athens County Ohio January 6, 1806. Maiden name was Sarah Thompson. Married Martin Stewart September 14, 1823 and they came to Adams County Illinois in 1832. She and husband left Camp Point last fall to visit children in Nodaway County Missouri. On November 25 the remains of her companion of 56 years were laid to rest in Bur Oak Cemetery and she left to go to the home of Mr D.J. Howell at Maryville on April 20th where she died on the 30th. Was the mother of 14 children, 8 still living. Buried beside her husband. Services by Rev J.D. James.

STEWART, WILLIAM - Hash - Nov 17, 1876   William Stewart, a young man 19 years old employed as night switchman in the C.B. & Q yards was killed Saturday A.M. by being run over by a freight train.

STILES, MR - Hash - Oct 2, 1874   A man named Stiles moving back from the neighborhood of Atchison, Kansas to

Coles County Illinois died in his wagon in town Tuesday A.M. He was buried in the cemetery and the family all sick but one wended on their sorrowful way.

STINER, W.A. - Clayton - Jan 5, 1877 W.A. Stiner was an intelligent youth just arrived at manhood and had many warm friends here. His body was taken to Mt Sterling for interment.

STOCKWELL, W.W. - Local - Jul 28, 1881 Died, W.W. Stockwell and old citizen of Quincy for the past 35 years died Saturday A.M. at Excelsior Springs in Clay County Missouri. Born in Vermont about 62 years ago. Remains arrived here this A.M. on the train. "Herald"

STOLTE, HENRY - Burton - Dec 15, 1881 Died, Henry Stolte and the son of Mrs J.W. Richards. Henry Stolte had been sick 2 years. Died at his parents home in Burton. Services Thursday at Presbyterian Church. Was 24 years old. Leaves father and mother and brothers and sisters.

STONAKER, ELIZA
    SEE: MANARD, WM G.

STONE, MRS - Died - May 22 1873 Died, Mrs Stone, daughter of Mr J.B. Christie of this place died at her home in Michigan last Monday and her remains were brought here and interred yesterday.

STONE, MRS MICAJAH - Mendon - Feb 9, 1882 Died, Mrs Micajah Stone Saturday A.M. Funeral Sunday. 58 years old. Leaves a husband and 3 daughters.

STONE, MRS MIRRANDA - Supplement - Sep 1, 1876 Died since last years meeting of Old Settlers of Adams and Brown Counties, Mrs Mirranda Stone of Brown County.

STORMER, LEWIS - La Prairie - Jun 29, 1882 Death of Lewis Stormer on the 22nd, 22 years old. Leaves parents.

STORMER, LOUIS - Local - Jun 29, 1882 Louis Stormer, son of John W. Stormer, formerly of La Prairie, but now of Hancock County was found dead in the watering trough at his father's house last week. Cause of death was apolexy, about 23 years old.

STOUT, MRS B.F.
    SEE: WALKER, MR

STOUTZ, JACOB - Sep 27, 1878 Jacob Stoutz, a citizen of Bloomington, committed suicide Tuesday.

STOW, MRS FANNIE M. - Died - Dec 26, 1879 Died near Buttersville, Arkansas December 16th, 1879, Fannie M., wife of H.H. Stow age 38 years 9 days. Joined Me Church at 12 years of age.

STRATHMAN, HENRY - Burton - Feb 12, 1880 Died, on Thursday afternoon while hauling straw, Henry Strathman age 14 years. Was killed when his load slipped.

STRAUB, JOHN - Fowler - Jan 24, 1879 Died, John Straub Sr. Sunday eve January 12th at 7:30 P.M. Born Carbon County Pennsylvania June 12, 1807. Married Dorothy Lindon Moyey January 6, 1827. Moved to Illinois in 1837, resident of Adams County 42 years. Was father of 11 children, 1 died in infancy, raised 5 sons and 5 daughters. One son died in battle of Antieltam, Maryland in 1862. Leaves 9 children, 46 grandchildren and 5 great grandchildren. Was 71 years old. Leaves a wife. (Article dated January 21, 1879 Fowler, Illinois)

STREETER, JOSHUA
    SEE: HOLMES, MRS SAMUEL

STRICKLER, MRS ANNA - Died - Jan 1, 1881 Died, December 29th at Augusta of pneumonia, Mrs Anna Strickler, relict of the late David Strickler, age 77 years. Mr Strickler died 13 years ago. Her funeral services by Rev T.D. Davis at York Neck.

STRICKLER, ANNA - Probate Notice - Mar 17, 1881 Anna Strickler, deceased 3rd Monday of May (16th) George W. Cyrus, adm.

STRICKLER, MRS ANNIE - Died - Dec 30, 1880 Died, December 29th at Augusta, Illinois of pneumonia Mrs Annie Strickler, relict of the late David Strickler, age 77 years. Funeral at the York Neck Church today at 2 P.M.

STRICKLER, CATHERINE - Died - Mar 19, 1874 Died on Monday the 16th inst, Catherine, wife of Stewart Strickler, age 45 years of consumption.

STRICKLER, DAVID
    SEE: THOMAS, MRS ELIZABETH

STRICKLER, JOHN - Died - Jan 13, 1881 Died January 5,

1881, of typhoid fever, John Strickler in his 39th year. Born Houston township, lived there until 1872 when he moved to Camp Point. Leaves a wife and 2 children.

STRICKLER, LEWIS L. - Mendon - Nov 28, 1879 Lewis L. Strickler died at his home 3-1/2 miles northwest of Mendon Sunday. Burial tomorrow, age 58 years.

STRICKLER, LEWIS - Mendon - Nov 28, 1879 Lewis Strickler is not expected to live.

STRICKLER, MRS MAGGIE B. - Died - Aug 25, 1881 Died at the home of Robert Elliott, 1 mile west of La Prairie, Adams County, August 18, 1881, Mrs Maggie B. Strickler. Was daughter of Robert and Sarah L. Elliott. Born in Baltimore County Maryland December 19, 1860. Married Lewis A. Strickler June 1, 1881.

STRICKLER, STEWART
    SEE: WOODS, MRS MARTHA A.

STRICKLER, STEWART - Died - Apr 27, 1877 Died on the 23rd inst of typhoid fever Stewart Strickler, age 57 years. Born in Pennsylvania. Came to Illinois with his parents to Adams County in 1837 (Houston township). Married Miss Catherine Witt in 1846, she died 2 years ago. Leaves 4 children. Buried in York Neck Cemetery on Tuesday.

STRICKLER, STEWART - Hash - Aug 24, 1877 The personal property of Stewart Strickler, deceased, will be sold at public auction Thursday September 13th.

STRICKLER, STEWART - Probate Notice - Jun 29, 1877 Stewart Strickler 3rd Monday of September 1877 Wesley Strickler, adm.

STRICKLER, WILLIAM A. - Supplement - Apr 20, 1882 Probate Notice William A. Strickler, deceased 1st Monday of June 1882 (5th) A.P. Gay, adm.

STRICKLER, WILLIAM A. - Probate Notice - Apr 6, 1882 William A. Strickler, deceased 1st Monday of March 1882 A.P. Gay, adm.

STRICKLER, WILLIAM A. - Death of William A. Strickler Mar 30, 1882 Died, at Golden, Illinois March 26th William A. Strickler, 67 years 9 months 2 days old. Born Fayette County Pennsylvania May 28, 1814. Came to

York Neck 1839. June 1841 he married Mary E. Kern. Moved to Golden in February 1875 and ran the American House. Funeral Tuesday at York Neck Church. Services by Rev T.J. Bryant of La Prairie and a short one by Rev L.F. Walden.

STRONG, CAROLINE
    SEE: REED, JOSIAH

STUMP, LYDIA
    SEE: STABLER, LYDIA

STUMP, LYDIA - Obituary - Aug 24, 1882 Died, Lydia Stump August 17th. Born in Baltimore County Maryland June 6, 1814. Married Wm Stabler at Shrewsburg, York County Pennsylvania August 2, 1836 stayed there until fall of "55" when they moved to Columbus, Illinois, age 68 years 2 months 11 days. Buried Columbus Cemetery. Services by Rev A.M. Danely of the ME Church. Had 13 children. Leaves her husband, 4 sons and 3 daughters all of mature age.

SUDDETH, JAMES - Suicide of James Suddeth - Sep 14, 1882 Died, Thursday eve James Suddeth and near J.M. McGill's. Had parted from his wife lately and had seen her with another man, about 22 years old and a farmer.

SUDDETH, JAMES - Neighborhood News - Mar 29, 1878 James Suddeth, son of Mr Wm Suddeth in Bainbridge township was badly hurt. Recovery is doubtful. Rushville "Citizen"

SULLIVAN, H.V.
    SEE: LANGDON, MRS A.L.

SULLIVAN, JOHN - Clayton - Oct 17, 1879 John Sullivan buried a child this week.

SUMMERS, NATHANIEL - Local - Jul 1, 1880 Died, Nathaniel Summers of Melrose township at his home Sunday eve, 76 years old. Born in Sussex County Delaware in 1804. In 1812 went to Kentucky with parents. In 1828 he came to Quincy. Was father of 11 children, 6 survive him.

SWAIN, MRS RACHEL - Personal - Jun 30, 1881 Died, Mrs Rachel Swain, an elder sister of Samuel Curless was buried in Keene township Saturday.

SWAN, DORA B. - Death of Dora B. Swan - Aug 17, 1882

Died, Dora Belle Swan on the 8th at the home of her sister, Mrs H.S. Hahn in her 20th year.

SWAN, DORA BELLE - Died - Aug 10, 1882 Died on August 8th of typhoid fever, Miss Dora Belle Swan at the home of her sister, Mrs H.S. Hahn age 19 years 6 months 5 days.

SWANK, MRS - Liberty - Aug 31, 1882 Died, Mrs Swank of flux at her sisters in Missouri on 23rd inst. Buried Missouri. Leaves a husband and large family (was visiting her sister since the 10th).

SWARTS, MRS LOU - Clayton - Aug 15, 1879 Mrs Lou Swarts, daughter of Mrs Lafferty died in Nebraska last week.

SWISEGOOD, MR
    SEE: WILSON, JAS

SYKES, JAMES
    SEE: CUNNINGHAM, GEORGE

SYLVESTER, PHILLIP A. - Hash - Aug 25, 1876 Phillip A. Sylvester, formerly of Quincy committed suicide in St Louis last Friday.

TANNER, FRANCIS
    SEE: FELT, MRS ALEY

TANSILL, FANNIE - Clayton - Dec 19, 1879 Robert W. Tansill, of Chicago lost his daughter, Fannie with diptheria.

TANSILL, FANNY OTIS - Died - Dec 4, 1879 Died in Chicago, the 26th inst, Fanny Otis Tansill of diptheria, age 13 years. She and her brother spent most of last summer with their grandparents, Mr and Mrs H.R. Motter.

TARR, WM R. - Mendon - Dec 13, 1878 Mr Wm R. Tarr one of our oldest citizens died yesterday at 10 A.M. Funeral tomorrow with Masonic honors at 10 A.M.

TAYLOR, MRS MARGARET - Camp Point - Jun 16, 1881 Mrs Margaret Taylor, mother of Mrs Sherman was buried last Saturday.

TAYLOR, MRS POLLY
    SEE: NATIONS, JOHN

TAYLOR, SCOTT
    SEE: SELBY, THOMPSON

TELLY, MR - Local - Mar 25, 1880 Died, a brakeman named Telly, of Bardolph was run over and killed by a train at Biggsville one day last week.

TENNIS, MRS - Burton - Apr 15, 1880 Died-Mrs Tennis died Sunday A.M. Funeral Monday at 2 P.M.

TENNY, DANIEL - Neighboring News - Jul 15, 1880 Daniel Tenny of McLean was buried on Sunday.

TERRILL, G.F. - Recent Deaths - Nov 21, 1879 G.F. Terrill of Burton township near Newtown was found dead in bed Monday A.M. Born Orange County Virginia 1818 came to Adams County 1849, had 9 children (7 living). "Herald"

TERRILL, GEORGE F. - Death of George F. Terrill - Nov 28, 1879 Died, Monday morn, Mr G.F. Terrill an old citizen of this place died at his home the night before. Buried in the family graveyard at Mr Morton's Tuesday. Leaves a wife and several children. (Newtown November 18th).

TERRILL, GEORGE F. - In Memoriam - Jan 9, 1880 Died, at Newtown, Adams County November 17th, 1879, George F. Terrill age 61 years. Born Orange county Virginia 1818.

TERRILL, HENRY - Hash - May 3, 1878 Henry Terrill was drowned in Crooked Creek in Hancock County last Monday.

THEMAN, FRANK - Local - Aug 10, 1882 Drowned, a cigar man named Frank Theman was drowned in the river while bathing, about 25 years old. Leaves a wife and 3 children.

THOMAS, MR - Junction - Jan 29, 1880 Died, daughter of Mr Thomas died Wednesday eve. Funeral from the German Lutheran Church.

THOMAS, MRS ELIZABETH - Died - Sep 29, 1881 Died, September 24, 1881 at her home near Knox City, Missouri Elizabeth Thomas, wife of Jacob Thomas and eldest daughter of the late David Strickler of this county. Leaves husband and 3 grown sons and a little adopted daughter.

THOMAS, HENRY - Local - May 13, 1880 Henry Thomas was killed by lightning at New Canton Saturday A.M.

THOMAS, MRS JOHN - Hash - May 8, 1874 We learn that Mrs John Thomas of Columbus died very suddenly Monday afternoon. He dropped dead on the road as she was returning from the neighbors, cause not known.

THOMAS, JOHN - Neighborhood News - May 27, 1880 A 13 year old son of John Thomas of Chambersburg was drowned in McGee' Creek on last Thursday while bathing. 'Barry Adage"

THOMAS, JOHN - Probate Notice - Apr 14, 1876 John Thomas 3rd Monday of June Presley F. Thomas, adm.

THOMAS, LAF - Local - Oct 5, 1882 Died, little boy of La Thomas Sunday A.M. from diptheria. Buried York Neck Cemetery.

THOMAS, MICHAEL - Local - Sep 12, 1879 Michael Thomas a former resident of this county was killed at Louisiana, Missouri last week by the caving in of a gravel bank which crushed him so seriously that he died in a few hours.

THOMAS, PETER - Death of Peter Thomas - Mar 7, 1879 Died, at his home in Augusta Feb 25, Peter Thomas in his 84th year. Born Virginia December 17, 1795. Moved with parents to Ohio when 12 years old. Married Sarah Weilder in 1817. They had 10 children, 7 sons and 3 daughters. Settled in Camp Point in 1845. Moved to Augusta in 1871 where several children lived. Leaves 2 brothers, nine children and numerous grandchildren.

THOMAS, MRS WM - From La Prairie - May 11, 1877 Died, Mrs Wm Thomas died on Monday afternoon.

THOMAS, MRS WM R. - Hash - May 11, 1877 Died, Mrs Wm R. Thomas of La Prairie, daughter of Joseph S. Beckett died Monday.

THOMPSON, ANDREW - Hash - Jul 19, 1878 Andrew Thompson, Quincy died Saturday night from the effects of a sun stroke.

THOMPSON, CARL S. - May 13, 1880 Mr Carl S. Thompson a young man formerly of Augusta and while here connected with the "Herald" died at his home in Abingdon last

Saturday. "Augusta Mail"

THOMPSON, MRS ELIZABETH PURVES - Local - Mar 10, 1881 Died, Mrs Elizabeth Purves Thompson died at New Orleans, age 85 years. Came to Adams County 40 years ago. Went to New Orleans about a year ago for her health.

THOMPSON, MARGARET - Carthage - Mar 9, 1882 Died, Miss Margaret Thompson on February 1st, was an elderly lady. Was a teacher of painting and wax work in the city.

THOMPSON, MARVIN - Local - Apr 20, 1882 Word received from California on the 18th of the death of Marvin Thompson. No particulars yet.

THOMPSON, MRS ROBERT - Chatten - Jun 1, 1882 Died on the 23rd of this month, Mrs Robert Thompson. Mr Thompson and his mother also, both died last week. They leave several small children.

THOMPSON, SARAH
    SEE: STEWART, MARTIN

THOMPSON, SCOTT - Clayton - Feb 8, 1878 Died, in this city Monday last of consumption, Scott Thompson 21 years old.

THOMPSON, WILLIAM - Local - Apr 1, 1880 An old man named William Thompson of Adams County fell down his cellar stairway, near Payson, one night last week. Was over 90 years old and had been blind over 27 years. "Barry Adage"

THOMPSON, MRS WM - Mendon - Mar 14, 1879 Mrs Wm Thompson is very sick.

THOMPSON, MRS WM - Mendon - Mar 28, 1879 Mrs Thompson, wife of Wm Thompson died on Sunday last, funeral yesterday.

THORNTON, PET - La Prairie - Oct 27, 1876 Died, "Pet" Thornton age 7 years 9 months and 13 days.

THORPE, CHARLES - Neighborhood News - Jul 19, 1878 Charles Thorpe was hit by a train and died, from a good family of Canton.

TINDALL, MRS JOSEPH - Neighborhood News - Oct 5, 1877 Mrs Joseph Tindall was kicked by a colt, feared she can not recover, daughter of Mr James Frasier of Ellington and niece of Mr Thomas Jasper of this city. "Whig"

TIPPET, WM - Mendon - Feb 21, 1879 Died, a young child of Wm Tippet, late of Bushnell died here last night.

TIPPETT, MRS HATTIE - Mendon - Feb 12, 1880 Died, Mrs Hattie Tippett died last Tuesday afternoon.

TOBIN, THEODORE - Local - Jul 14, 1881 Theodore Tobin, a saloon keeper died from sunstroke.

TOBIN, THEODORE - Local - Jul 24, 1881 Theodore Tobin a saloon keeper died from a sunstroke.

TODD EDW. S. - A Card - Jul 5, 1878 Thanks to friends and neighbors for what was done during the illness and at the death of sister Mary.   Edw S. Todd.

TODD, JOHN D. - Died - Dec 7, 1882 Died at his home in Keene township of paralysis preceeded by typhoid fever, John D. Todd, 62 years old. Born Charleston, Clark County Indiana in 1820. Moved to this county 1840 (about), settled in Camp Point township on to Honey Creek and on to Keene. Was good husband and parent.

TODD, MARY L. - Died - Jul 5, 1878 Died at her home in Camp Point on Friday eve June 28th of typhoid fever, sick 2 weeks, Mary L., daughter of R.S. and Mary A. Todd age 20 years 2 months. Body taken to Quincy and buried in Woodland Cemetery Sunday June 30th.

TOLBERT, MR - Neighborhood News - Aug 2, 1878 A man named Tolbert while cutting logs near Alexandria, Missouri last Tuesday was crushed beneath a tree, recovery considered improbable.

TOPLIFF, MARY E.
    SEE: SMITH, PETER

TORRENCE, DR A. - Liberty - Jul 22, 1880 Died, Dr A. Torrence at about midnight Thursday, buried at Columbus Friday afternoon.

TORRENCE, DR ALBERT - Local - Jul 22, 1880 Died, Dr Albert Torrence of Liberty. Died on the 16th inst, age 42 years.

TORRENCE, DR JOHN
    SEE: PRENTISS, MRS ALWILDA

TOTTEN, MARIA N. - Death of Maria Totten - Aug 31, 1882 Died, of typhoid fever August 27th at the home of her sister, Mrs Anna Hedgecock near Plymouth, Miss Maria N. Totten 30 years old. Was a teacher 8 years at Maplewood School, Camp Point.

TOTTEN, MARIA N. - Local - Sep 7, 1882 Died, typhoid fever August 27th at the home of her sister, Mrs Anna N. Totten in her 30th year. For 8 years she had taught school at Camp Point. Her sisters name was Mrs Anna Hedgecock, lived near Plymouth.

TOURNEY, J.B. - Liberty - Oct 27, 1881 Died, J.B. Tourney Saturday 22nd of typhoid fever. Buried Sunday.

TRACY, JAMES W. - Hash - May 25, 1877 Died James W. Tracy a lad about 12 years old, son of John Tracy living near Bowensburg was kicked by a horse Tuesday, died about an hour later.

TRAVER, ALICE - Liberty - Apr 25, 1879 Died, Alice, daughter of Simeon Taver on the 19th inst.

TRESSLER, PROF. DAVID - Local - Feb 26, 1880 Died, Prof David Tressler, pres. Of the Carthage College died last Tuesday.

TRIMBLE, A.H. - Mendon - Feb 24, 1881 Died, Hon A.H. Trimble died last Wednesday night. Buried Friday.

TROTTER, REV W.D.R. - Local - Aug 5, 1880 Rev W.D.R. Trotter died at Jacksonville last week, age 73 years.

TURNER, MRS CLEMENTINE - Local - Nov 23, 1882 Died, Mrs Clementine Turner, wife of Ex-mayor Turner, of Quincy died Sunday afternoon.

TURNER, FRANK - Local - Dec 5, 1879 Died, Frank Turner of Quincy died Tuesday afternoon from an overdose of morphine (symptoms of insanity).

TURNER, JOSEPH - Died - Mar 24, 1876 Died at Mendon, Ill. on the 16th inst Joseph Turner, Esq. 77 years old. He was a native of the state of Maine and came to this county 40 years ago. Was a member of the Methodist Church.

TURNER, JOSEPH - Supplement - Sep 1, 1876   Died since last years meeting of Old Settlers of Adams and Brown counties, Joseph Turner of Mendon.

TURNER, MARGARET S. - Local - Mar 17, 1881   Mrs Margaret S. Turner, mother of Rev P.L. Turner died at Frederickstown, Missouri on the 2nd, age 70 years.

TURNER, NANCY - Died - Dec 2, 1880   "Grandmother" Downing died November 26th age 97 years.   Nancy Turner was born October 29, 1783 in Charles County Maryland and went with parents when 4 years old to Virginia.   There she married Rezin Downing September 8, 1809 and they moved to Clark County Indiana in fall of 1822.   Stayed there until 1835 when they came to Camp Point township. They had 12 children, 8 are still living and living in this vicinity, one died in infancy and 3 having families at the time of their deaths.   Has 101 grandchildren, 63 still living, 3rd generation there was 193, 161 still living, 15 in the 4th generation all living.   Her husband of 71 years survives her.   Funeral at Hebron Church on the 27th by Rev W.A. Crawford and buried in the cemetery.

TURNER, RUDOLPHUS K. - Local - Dec 23, 1880   Rudolphus K. Turner of Quincy died Saturday, 44 years old and son of Prof. J.B. Turner of Jacksonville.

TUXFORD, NANCY
         SEE: GARLETTS, DAVID

TUXFORD, WILLIAM - Local - Jan 6, 1881   Died, William Tuxford, of Big Neck, fell dead while at play at school Tuesday.

TUXFORD, WM - Sudden Death - Jan 13, 1881   Received from W.H. McIntyre teacher of school in Big Neck where the accident happened.   Wm Tuxford age 16 years fell to the ground at school and died there.   Buried in Mendon in the family burying ground on Thursday.

TYLER, MRS - Bowen - Jul 29, 1880   On the 10th inst Mrs Tyler gave birth to tripletts, 2 are living and 1 was still born.

TYLER, FRANK - Riceville - Oct 27, 1881   Died, Frank Tyler, of South Richfield.   Died Sunday from typho malaria.

TYLER, H.B. - Richfield - Mar 3, 1881   Died, Mrs Tyler,

wife of H.B. Tyler. Leaves a number of motherless children.

TYNDALL, EDWARD
    SEE: ROBERTSON, MRS

TYRER, JULIA M. - Hash - May 7, 1875 Miss Julia M. Tyrer, a young lady employed as teacher of the school situated on the Fabius river, near West Quincy was accidently drowned in that river last Friday.

UNDOLT, JOHN - State News - Aug 26, 1880 Double funeral at LaGrange, Sunday Mr John Undolt's two youngest children, Louisa age 11 and Sherman age 9.

UTT, AARON H. - Neighborhood News - Feb 22, 1878 Aaron H. Utt, of Plainview, Macoupin county committed suicide on the 8th inst.

VALENTINE, NELSON - Probate Notice - Dec 15, 1881 Nelson Valentine 1st Monday of February (6th) Wm L. Oliver, adm.

VALENTINE, NELSON - Personal - Dec 1, 1881 Died, Nelson Valentine died Wednesday A.M. of pneumonia.

VANCIL, MARTIN - Death of Martin Vancil - May 12, 1881 Died Martin Vancil an old citizen of Adams County died at his home in Liberty township last week. Born in Montgomery County Virginia February 4, 1809. Came to Illinois in 1821 and first located in Union County. In fall of 1829 he came to Adams County and located in Columbus township for 3 years and then to Liberty, father of 8 children all survive him. Had 70 grandchildren, some 30 great grandchildren. Was a member of Dunkard Church for 50 years.

VAN DOORN, JOHN K. - Obituary - May 7, 1875 Died, John K. Van Doorn, of Quincy at his home Tuesday eve May 4th age about 61 years. Came to Quincy in 1838 where he manufactured chairs and then into the lumber business. He was Grand Secretary of the Order of Good Templars.

VAN DOORN, MRS JOHN K. - Local - Dec 21, 1882 Died Mrs John K. Van Doorn of Quincy died Sunday, 61 years old.

VAN DYKE, JOSEPH
    SEE: MANARD, WM G.

VIAR, MARY
    SEE: SKAATS, JAMES H.

VICKER, MRS
    SEE: WILKES, DANIEL

VICKERS, EDITH - Livingston - Feb 19, 1880 Died, Edith, infant daughter of H.J. and Ann Vickers on the 10th. Funeral at the church by Rev Hawker of Newtown.

VICKERS, EDITH - Burton - Feb 19, 1880 Died, February 10th little Edith, only child of Howard and Ann Vickers in her 3rd year.

VON GOETZEN, BARON FRITZ
    SEE: GERHARD, MR

WADDELL, J.O.
    SEE: POWELL, MARY WADDELL

WADDELL, L.
    SEE: POWELL, MARY WADDELL

WADDELL, O. - Death List - Sep 7, 1877 Old settlers death list since last meeting: O. Waddell, Melrose, age 80 years.

WAGNER, JACOB
    SEE: REEDER, JOHN J.

WAINLY, EDWARD - Neighborhood News - Jul 6, 1877 A steam pipe on the Red Wing bursted Saturday afternoon while the boat was near Dallas. The steward Edward Wainly is missing, probably drowned.

WALCOTT, ELIZABETH J.
    SEE: GARLETTS, DAVID

WALKER, MR - Mendon - Feb 9, 1882 Died - News received Sunday of the death at Kinderhook, Illinois of Mr Walker, father of Mrs B.F. Stout of our village. Also the death at Lansingburg, New York of the mother of Mrs Brown, widow of the late Dr Brown of Mendon.

WALKER, MRS - Mendon - Jul 20, 1882 Died, Mrs Walker, mother of Mrs B.F. Slack of our village, yesterday A.M.

WALKER, REV - La Prairie - Mar 21, 1879 Died, the only daughter and youngest child of Rev Walker of this place died Sunday A.M.

WALKER, GEORGE - Local - Oct 17, 1879 Died, George Walker, one of the oldest citizens of Hancock County died a few days ago at his home in Walker township.

WALKER, MRS H.C.
    SEE: POLING, MRS

WALKER, LUZENA - Death List - Sep 7, 1877 Old settlers death list since last meeting: Luzena Walker, North East, age 55 years.

WALLACE, MRS - Clayton - Mar 31, 1881 Died, old mother Wallace who was a pioneer in this section died last week.

WALLACE, ALLEN - Obituary - Jun 11, 1875 Died at his home in Camp Point of paralysis Allen Wallace, age 65 years 11 month 28 days. Born in Madison County Kentucky June 18, 1809. Married Miss Alma Smith Dunwidie 1835 and they came to Missouri in 1836. Wife died in 1857 he married second to Mrs Mary Armstrong, nee Cromwell in 1859. Leaves his wife.

WALLACE, JAMES A. - Died - Apr 9, 1875 Died, in Adams County Iowa April 1st, 1875 of lung fever, James A., infant son of W.K. and Julia W. Wallace age 1 year 2 months 18 days.

WALLACE, JANE A.
    SEE: MOREY, SETH J.

WALLACE, JASON - Clayton - Feb 19, 1880 Quite a few attended the funeral of Jason Wallace of Bear Creek last Sunday.

WALLACE, JASON - Died - Mar 13, 1873 Died at this place on Monday eve March 3rd of asthma, Jason Wallace, age 64 years. He was one of 4 stalwart brothers who emigrated to this state from Kentucky in 1839 each of whom, with 3 other brothers preceded him to the grave. At the time of his death he was the oldest resident of Clayton.

WALLACE, JASON - Notice of Sale - Nov 25, 1880 William Wallace and Daniel Smith, adm's of the estate of Jason Wallace deceased will sell land to pay debts VS Sarah J. Wallace, James A. Wallace, Mason R. Wallace, Elizabeth R. Wallace, Lizzie Griffith and Oliver Griffith.

WALLACE, JASON I. - Local - Feb 19, 1880 Jason I. Wallace of Clayton township 2 miles south of Keokuk Junction died suddenly last Friday.

WALLACE, JASON S. - Probate Notice - Mar 4, 1880 3rd Monday of April Jason S. Wallace, deceased Wm Wallace and Daniel Smith, adm's.

WALLACE, MRS MARGARET - Died - Oct 14, 1880 Died at her home near Keokuk Junction, Illinois of dropsy, Mrs Margaret Wallace, nee Lyle, September 19, 1880. Born in the County Derry, Ireland August 15, 1836. Came to America with parents when 9 years old. Stayed 2 years in Lehigh County Pennsylvania and on to Illinois. Married Wm Wallace March 29, 1855. He survives her. Also daughters survive her. Married in Clayton Church.

WALLACE, MRS MARGARET - Local - Sep 23, 1880 Died, Mrs Margaret Wallace, wife of Wm Wallace of this township died last week and buried Sunday.

WALLACE, MARGARET W.
    SEE: SEATON, RICHARD

WALLACE, MRS MARY ANN - Clayton - Feb 3, 1881 Died, Mrs Mary Ann Wallace, mother of William A., John L. and James A. Wallace died at the home of her son W.A. last week of congestion of the lungs in her 73rd year.

WALLACE, NANCY I. - Probate Notice - Oct 6, 1876 Nancy I. Wallace 3rd Monday of December Wm Wallace, adm.

WALLACE, MRS NANCY T. - Obituary - Dec 15, 1876 Died in Clayton township, Adams County Illinois August 2nd, 1876 Mrs Nancy T. Wallace, wife of the late William M. Wallace, age 56 years 7 months 19 days. Services by Rev J.A. Edie, pastor of the United Presbyterian Church at Clayton of which she was a member.

WALLACE, MRS WM - Clayton - Sep 23, 1880 Mrs Wm Wallace of Bear Creek was buried Sunday.

WALLETT, JOHN - Fowler - Jan 24, 1879 John Wallett is not expected to live.

WALTER, MARTHA
    SEE: SLONEKER, ADAM W.

WALTON, RICHARD - Hash - Aug 11, 1876 Richard Walton,

of Payson, aged 81 was killed by the cars at Hannibal last week.

WALTZ, REV H.C. - Various Squibs - May 18, 1877   Died, Rev H.C. Waltz, pastor of Artus (M.E.) Chapel died in Quincy last Friday of consumption. He was a young man of much promise.

WARD, EDWARD - May 11, 1882   Died, at Glenwood, Iowa on Saturday the 6th inst, Edward Ward age 63 years. Mr Ward was an old and respected citizen of La Prairie for many years. Moved to Iowa last February. Native of Lancashire, England. Came to states some 30 years ago. Leaves a wife and family.

WARD, FOSTER - Local - Sep 26, 1879   Foster Ward age 20 years son of the late Dr F.D. Ward died at Golden, Colorado on the 15th inst from injuries received in coupling a freight train.

WARD, HENRY - Hash - Dec 21, 1877   Died, Henry Ward, 4 year old son of F.J. and Sadie Ward of Loraine drowned in Bear Creek on the 12th.

WARD, HENRY - Texas Tidings - De 28, 1877   A sad accident 5 miles west of Loraine Tuesday the 11th inst, 4 year old Henry, son of F.W. Ward drowned in Bear Creek. Body recovered the 18th, returning from visiting his grandmother.

WARD, J.W. - Local - Jul 27, 1882   Died, a little child of J.W. Ward Thursday of last week. Buried at Mounds on Friday.

WARD, MELINDA C. - Obituary - Jul 18, 1879   Melinda C. Ward born November 6, 1855 in Adams County Illinois moved to Marion County Missouri at the age of 12 years. Married Charles N. Ward November 5, 1874 and lived since in Shelby County Missouri. Died July 5, 1879. Was daughter of Henry C. and Nancy C. Marsh of Camp Point, member of ME Church.

WARD, WILLIE - Neighborhood News - Jul 5, 1878   Last Monday, Willie Ward of Macomb age 9 years was drowned while bathing in a creek near town.

WARRELL, ADAM - Local - Dec 23, 1880   Died, Adam Warrell, a Wabash engineer was found dead at Springfield on Thursday A.M. Was last seen on Friday the 11th. Body was partly decomposed when found.

WARREN, CALVIN A. - Feb 24, 1881 Died, at 6 A.M. today, Col. Calvin A. Warren of our city. Born in Essex County New York June 3, 1807, lived other eastern states and learned the printers trade from older brother Ansel. Lived Ohio where he married a daughter of Senator Morris, a sister of I.N. Morris, deceased. Came to Hancock county in 1836, located in Warsaw, on to Quincy in 1839. Was a lawyer in Quincy. Second wife was Harriett, 2nd daughter of J.P. Robbins and a sister of Mrs I.N. Morris and after her death he married Miss Boswell. Leaves 2 children, Charles of Chicago and Henry Warren of Santa Fe New Mexico. "News"

WARREN, CHARLES B.
    SEE: CURTIS, ELAM B.

WARREN, MRS LYDIA - Died - Feb 24, 1881 Died at the home of her daughter, Mrs John F. Linn, February 18, 1881 in the 66th year of her life Mrs Lydia Warren, relict of T.B. Warren. Born Onandago County New York September 29, 1815. Married may 13, 1834 and came to Illinois same year.

WARREN, WILKES
    SEE: CURTIS, ELAM B.

WASHBURNE, MRS H. - Exchange Notes - Apr 25, 1879 Inquest held on the remains of Mrs H. Washburne of this city, 63 years old. Died Monday eve. Lived Ursa township.

WASSON, CYRUS - May 22, 1880 Last Monday a single man named Cyrus Wasson was killed in a farm accident, about 30 years old. He had been drinking. Macomb Eagle

WATSON, THOMAS - Local - Sep 14, 1882 Died, Thomas Watson, formerly of Fowler died at St Augustine on the 7th inst at the home of N.B. Vertress. Remains brought back to Fowler. Born in Glasgow Scotland June 6, 1803. Came to U.S. in 1841.

WEBSTER, JOHN K. - Death of Ex Mayor Webster - Oct 5, 1882 Died, in Jacksonville, Mr John K. Webster, late Mayor of Quincy. Born in West Hartford, Connecticut in 1816 and moved when quite young to Florida until 1838 when he came to Illinois (Springfield) and on to Galena. In 1840 he came to Quincy, married Katurah C. Wood in

1843 who survives him. They had 6 children, 3 still living John Webster, Annie W. Roberts and Henry S. Webster who lives in Boston.

WEEMS, JESSE - Local - Nov 3, 1881 Died, Jesse Weems Sr. Tuesday at the home of his son Jesse Weems, Quincy at the age of 82 years. Buried at Augusta.

WEEVIL, HERMAN - Livingston - Aug 30, 1878 Herman Weevil died Saturday from the sting of a bumble bee.

WEILDER, SARAH
    SEE: THOMAS, PETER

WEISENBURGER, FRANKLIN - Liberty - Mar 30, 1882 Died, Franklin Weisenburger of Liberty township eve of the 25th of consumption. Sold his farm last fall and went to Kansas and bought land. Leaves a wife and 3 children. Wife had expected to move this spring to Kansas.

WEISENBURGER, DR. X. - Local - Oct 13, 1881 Died, Dr X. Weisenburger a dentist of Mt Sterling formerly of Liberty died October 1st.

WEIST, NEPOMUCH - Local - Aug 3, 1882 Nepomuch Weist, a German committed suicide in the river at West Quincy, Friday. He had some time ago worked in Liberty township.

WELLS, A.E. - Neighborhood News - Oct 12, 1877 A.E. Wells, a fireman on the C.B. & Q Railroad at Galesburg was fatally injured by the upsetting of a locomotive Friday.

WELLS, ED - Riceville - Aug 17, 1882 Died, a child of Ed Wells' on Saturday, July 29th, 1 year old.

WELSH, ELLA - Riceville - Aug 17, 1882 Died, Miss Ella Welsh, age 2 years on Friday July 28th.

WELSH, H.C. - Local - Oct 7, 1880 H.C. Wells, wife and child started out Saturday to visit friends at Keokuk Junction. Their child died on the way.

WELSH, JAMES T. - Local - Dec 29, 1881 Rebecca C. Welsh will sell all the personal property of the late James T. Welsh on January 5th at her home 1-1/2 miles SW of Golden.

WELSH, JAMES TAYLOR - Local - Dec 22, 1881 Died, James Taylor Welsh Monday night of typhoid fever at his home 4 miles northeast of Camp Point. Only leaves a wife.

WELSH, PATRICK - Ursa Murder - Apr 22, 1880 Body of Patrick Welsh who was at work in the bottom above the city about a year ago and never heard from again was found. He worked for Keen before he disappeared. Keen and woman who lived with him left Quincy and are thought to be in Iowa. "Herald 28th"

WELSH, WILLIAM - Local - Apr 13, 1882 Died, William Welsh who was injured at Bluffs last week died Sunday A.M. Remains brought here Sunday eve. Buried cemetery here Monday. Born January 18, 1869, 23 years old. Leaves a mother and family.

WELTE, HENRY - Liberty - Jun 27, 1879 On Thursday last Mr Henry Welte and son about 14 years, came to Liberty, his son procuring some ague medicine. They started home and when near Charley Bowers the boy fell over in the wagon, died a short time later.

WERTZ, MRS LUCY - Death of Mrs Lucy Wertz - Nov 9, 1877 Death notice of Lucy Wertz nee Howden taken from the Marysville, Missouri "Republican" Miss Howden was well known in Camp Point where her parents at one time lived. Wife of B.F. Wertz of Green township and daughter of T.L. Howden.

WESSEL, MRS JOHN - Keokuk Junction - Mar 25, 1880 Died, Mrs John Wessel, former resident of the Junction for about 10 years.

WHEELER, MRS BROOKS - Burton - Nov 12, 1880 Mrs Brooks Wheeler died November 18th.

WHEELER, LEROY - Died - Jun 15, 1882 Died, Friday A.M. June 2nd with scarlet fever, Leroy, infant son of Henry C. and Mary J. Wheeler age 16 months. Buried Saturday at Newtown.

WHEELER, THOMAS - Liberty - Jan 27, 1881 Thomas Wheeler buried his little boy last Wednesday. This is his 3rd in 5 weeks.

WHEELER, TOM - Burton - Dec 23, 1880 A little child of Tom Wheeler's died last Monday.

WHEELER, W.T. - Burton - Jan 13, 1881 A little girl of
W.T. Wheeler's died last Monday, age 9 years. Two other
children of his are very sick.

WHEELER, W.T. - Livingston - Jan 20, 1881 Two dear
little ones of W.T. Wheeler's have died with diptheria,
3rd very sick.

WHIPPRECHT, MR - Mendon - Dec 22, 1881 Died, a little
daughter of Mr Whipprecht formerly a citizen of
Coatsburg died this A.M. of diptheria and croup.

WHITCOMB, MRS E.K.
     SEE: HALL, E.D.

WHITE, MRS FRANK - Local - Nov 9, 1882 Died, Mrs Frank
White, nee Ida Chatten Sunday A.M. at her home in Quincy
of malarial fever. She was a sister of Mrs Z.S. Pratt.

WHITE, JOHN - Neighborhood News - Jul 13, 1877 John
White, a laborer of Quincy has fallen heir to property
in Springfield worth 1/2 million dollars.

WHITMORE, JONAS - Neighborhood News - Mar 8, 1878 Jonas
Whitmore living in Missouri township drowned in a creek
Monday. Mt Sterling "Democrat"

WHITNEY, HORACE - Local - Dec 28, 1882 Killed, Horace
Whitney an old citizen of Lima township (lived about 3
miles north of Lima) was accidently shot and killed by
his oldest son, age 20 years, in Hancock county about 9
A.M. Christmas day.

WHITTLESY, MRS
     SEE: PEARSON, MR

WIBLE, HANNAH - Mendon - Feb 5, 1880 Miss Hannah Wible
died at the house of her brother, Andrew Wible on Friday
A.M. last.

WIGGINS, CHARLES - Local Hash - Nov 29, 1878 Charles
Wiggins living east of Quincy was run over by a wagon
last week receiving injuries from which he died Friday.

WIGLE, MISS
     SEE: BROADY, JOHN C.

WIGLE, MR
     SEE: BROADY, MRS

WIGLE, SOLOMON - Clayton - Oct 31, 1879 Died, Solomon Wigle died last Saturday. Buried at Liberty with Masonic honors.

WIKE, GEORGE - Local - Mar 4, 1880 Died, George Wike of Barry, father of Hon. Scott Wike died last Saturday.

WILCOX, MRS CLEMENTINE - Died - Jun 4, 1875 Died on the 23rd ult, Mrs Clementine Wilcox, wife of Meshac Wilcox of consumption.

WILCOX, DANIEL - May 24, 1878 Died, Daniel Wilcox, prop. of the Quincy Whig died Sunday A.M. at his home in Quincy. Born in Providence, Rhode Island, September 1820. Came west to Janesville, Wisconsin in 1854 where he was connected with the "Gazette". 1870 he went to Milwaukee and managed the "Sentinel" on to Quincy and bought the Whig in 1874.

WILCOX, KATE
    SEE: HALEY, MRS JESSIE

WILCOX, MESHAC - Local - Jun 10, 1880 Meshac Wilcox a well known wagon maker in this village was found dead in his bed last Thursday A.M. Buried Mendon. Left 2 daughters, 1 grown and the other 10 years and a boy about 8.

WILCOX, MESHACH
    SEE: HALEY, MRS JESSIE

WILCOXEN, A.P. - Personal - Feb 12, 1875 Died, A.P. Wilcoxen, town collector of Payson, an old and respected citizen died at his residence last Wednesday.

WILHELMY, JOHN - Mar 2, 1882 Died at Nauvoo, Illinois Sunday afternoon at the home of John Wilhemy his two children when their home burnt. Mother was nursing a sick neighbor and attempted suicide.

WILHOIT, WILLIAM N. - Probate Notice - Sep 14, 1882 William N. Wilhoit, deceased 3rd Monday of November 1882 (20th) J.T. Myers and D.L. Wilhoit Ex.'s.

WILHOIT, WM N. - Coatsburg - May 4, 1882 Died, April 13th Wm N. Wilhoit 69 years old. Leaves mother Wilhoit and family. Services by Rev H.C. Coats.

WILHOLT, WILLIAM N. - Local - Apr 20, 1882 Died,

William N. Wilholt of Columbus, Thursday, at his
residence in Coatsburg where he moved last fall.

WILKES, DANIEL - Obituary - Jun 26, 1873   Daniel Wilkes
died at his home in this town last Sunday, 68 years old.
We think he was a native of Kentucky and came with his
father's family to Illinois in the fall of 1831, the
next year he married Jane Reaugh and settled on the NE
1/4 of section 33. He was at the time of his death the
oldest settler of the township except for Farrow
Hamrick, his brother in law who settled on the SW 1/4 of
the same section about the same time. He was a farmer
until 1864 when his whole family, except for 1 daughter,
Mrs Crippin, died in a few months of each other,
consisting of his wife, 3 sons and a daughter, two of
his sons John and William, having died in army in the
winter of 1862. He afterwards married a Mrs Vicker and
resided in town.

WILKES, DANIEL - Hash - Jul 3, 1873   James E. Downing
was named executor of the will of Daniel Wilkes.

WILKES, MARGARET - Local - Aug 25, 1881   Died, Margaret
Wilkes of Columbus the mother of John Wilkes died last
week, age 91 years.

WILKES, MARGARET - Probate Notice - Oct 27, 1881
Margaret Wilkes, deceased 3rd Monday of November, 1881
John Wilkes, adm.

WILKES, MARGARET - Probate Notice - Sep 29, 1881
Margaret Wilkes, deceased 1st Monday of November (21st)
John Wilkes, adm.

WILKS, MRS CORDELIA - Local - Apr 21, 1881   Died, Mrs
Cordelia Wilks, widow of the late Daniel Wilks died
Wednesday A.M. taken to Ursa where the obsequies will be
held.

WILKS, MRS CORDELIA
    SEE: CRAWFORD, JAMES M.

WILKS, CORDELIA - Death of Cordelia Wilks - Apr 28, 1881
Died at her home on Camp Point April 20th Mrs Cordelia
Wilks, age 60 years 3 days. Born in Calhoun but lived
most of her life in Adams County. Leaves 2 children
John T. Baker of Stanberry, Missouri and Mrs John L.
Peabody of Quincy.

WILKS, DANIEL - Probate Notice - Aug 7, 1873   Daniel Wilks, deceased   3rd Monday of September 1873   James E. Downing, Ex.

WILLARD, DAVID - Legal Notice - Jun 1, 1877   Margaret A. Willard adm for David Willard, deceased   VS James Willard, Virginia Hughes, William Henry Willard, Douglas Willard and Francis Willard defendants. Virginia Hughes lives out of state.

WILLARD, DAVIS - Legal Notice - Mar 26, 1875   Davis Willard, deceased   3rd Monday of May 1875   Margaret A. Willard, adm.

WILLARD, DAVIS - Adm Sale of Real Estate - Jul 27, 1877   Margaret A. Willard, adm of the estate of Davis Willard, deceased   George Simmonds solicitor.

WILLARD, DAVIS - Hash - Oct 5, 1877   The real estate of Davis Willard deceased was sold at public auction last Monday to William Owens.

WILLARD, DAVIS - Adm's Sale of Real Estate - Apr 22, 1880   May 15th will sell real estate belonging to Davis Willard, deceased   Margaret A. Willard, adm.

WILLARD, GEORGE F. - Probate Notice - Mar 10, 1881   George F. Willard, deceased   3rd Monday of April (18th)   F.M. Stump, adm.

WILLARD, MARGARET A. - Petition - Jan 23, 1880   Petition to sell real estate to pay debts of defendant Margaret A. Willard adm of the estate of Davis Willard, deceased   VS James S. Willard, William H. Willard, Stephen Douglass Willard, Francis Louisa Willard, Virginia Hughes, and Charles Steel, defendants.

WILLARD, OSCAR - Bowen - Nov 30, 1882   Oscar Willard is very low with typhoid fever and little hopes of recovery.

WILLIAMS, ALBERT - May 13, 1880   Accident on the Robert Ward farm. His hired man Albert Williams was killed in the accident. Funeral at the ME Church at Chili on Monday by Rev Swim. "West Point Correspondence" - "Carthage Gazette"

WILLIAMS, HENRY C. - Local - Sep 1, 1881   Died, Henry C. Williams, a brother of Judge Williams last week at

Topeka, Kansas. He was engaged in the postal service.

WILLIAMS, JAS. C. - Clayton - Apr 4, 1879 Jas. C. Williams was buried this week.

WILLIAMS, MAGGIE - Exchange Notes - Dec 13, 1878 A 3 year old daughter of Maggie Williams at Plymouth fell into a tub of hot water and died Friday night.

WILLIAMS, OLLIE G. - Obituary - Feb 8, 1878 Died, on February 2nd at the home of her parents 2 miles and a half SE of Camp Point, Miss Ollie G. Williams in her 20th year. Born Hancock County September 6, 1858. Moved as a baby with parents to Liberty until 5 years ago when they moved to Camp Point. Services at Pleasant View Church.

WILLIAMS, THEODORE - Died - Dec 3, 1875 Died at his residence in Clayton Saturday the 20th ult of heart disease, Theodore Williams, age 74 years.

WILLIS, G.M. - Tribute - Feb 9, 1877 G.M. Willis died January 29, 1877 age 66 years 11 months. Leaves a wife.

WILSON, JAMES - Capture of James Wilson - May 30, 1879 James Wilson was arrested for aiding his brother Zach Wilson in the murder of Thos. McDonald at Plymouth, Hancock County in 1876. Was arrested at his father in laws, Mr Swisegood two miles from Plymouth.

WILSON, JAS. - Death List - Sep 7, 1877 Old settlers death roll since last meeting: Jas Wilson, Adams County, age 40.

WILSON, JIM - Hash - Mar 16, 1877 Jim Wilson was sentenced to the penitentiary for 16 years at Carthage as accessing to the murder of Thos. McDonald at Plymouth last summer.

WILSON, LUCY - Fowler - Jul 28, 1881 Died, Aunt Lucy Wilson.

WILSON, MRS MARY C. - A Sad Death - Jul 20, 1882 Died, Mrs Mary C. Wilson near Paloma, Illinois July 12th. Born in Huntsville, Missouri January 14, 1859. On October 8th of last year she married Thomas W. Wilson. Her child was born on Tuesday and she followed it to heaven Wednesday. Leaves a husband. Funeral from their home Thursday by Rev A.M. Danely.

WILSON, WILLIAM - Homicide in North East - Sep 26, 1879 William Wilson of Northeast township was arraigned on the charge of murder of his step father, Samuel Hinkson, an old citizen of Northeast, lived a few miles from La Prairie. Killed him Wednesday A.M.. "Herald"

WILSON, WILLIAM - Clayton - Dec 12, 1879 William Wilson, formerly of this place had his neck broken by the falling of a log when raising a house in Missouri.

WILSON, WM - Court News - Feb 12, 1880 Wm Wilson charged with murder of Samuel Hinkston. Hinkston was step father of Wilson living in North East township (killed September 16th), found guilty, also found insane and sent to asylum.

WILSON, ZACHORIAH T. - Oct 20, 1876 Zachoriah T. Wilson, who is charged with the murder of Thomas McDonald on last August 14th was arrested near the west fork of White River on the border of Boston Mountains, Arkansas Wednesday the 11th inst.

WINE, S. - Accident - Aug 28, 1873 We hear that S. Wine was run over by the CB & Q train between here and Keokuk Junction Tuesday eve.

WINE, S. - Correspondence - Sep 4, 1873 Mr S. Wine that was reported dead last week is very much alive. It was Mr H. Oaxs who died.

WINGET, JAMES
    SEE: CADWALLADER, SAM

WINGET, MRS W.C.
    SEE: FELT, MRS ALEY

WISEHART, ED C. - Personal - Oct 3, 1879 Ed C. Wisehart died Wednesday night.

WISEHART, EDWARD C. - Obituary - Oct 10, 1879 Edward C., son of James C. and Eliza Wisehart born December 1, 1857 died October 2nd, 1879 age 21 years and 10 months. Leaves parents, 1 sister and 6 brothers.

WISEHART, EDWARD C. - Died - Oct 3, 1879 Died, October 2nd Edward C. Wisehart, son of James and Eliza Wisehart age 21 years. Funeral at Pleasant View Church Friday at 11 A.M.

WISEHART, EDWARD C. - Adjustment Notice - Oct 14, 1880
Any claims against the estate of Edward C. Wisehart,
deceased are requested to present before December 1st.
Wm N. Wisehart.

WISEHART, JAMES - Local - Feb 3, 1881 Died, James
Wisehart died Saturday A.M. age 67 years. Buried in
Pleasant View Cemetery Sunday.

WISEHART, JAMES - Obituary - Feb 10, 1881 Died January
29th, 1881 at his home near Camp Point, James Wisehart
age 68 years 10 months 19 days. Born in Jefferson
County Kentucky March 10, 1812. Came to Adams County in
spring of 1834. Married Eliza Curry in 1835. Leaves
his wife, 6 sons and 1 daughter.

WISEHART, JAMES - Probate Notice - Mar 17, 1881 James
Wisehart, deceased   3rd Monday of April (18th) William
N. Wisehart, adm.

WISEHART, JAMES - Local - Mar 3, 1881 Wm N. Wisehart
has been appointed executor of the will of James
Wisehart, deceased.

WITT, MRS - Personal - Mar 24, 1876 "Grandmother" Witt
residing in Big Neck died Sunday A.M. Mrs Witt, about
80 years old and was one of the early settlers. She
leaves a large family of children and grandchildren in
this county.

WITT, CATHERINE
    SEE: STRICKLE, STEWART

WOLF, DAN - Burton - Nov 24, 1881 Remains of Mr Dan
Wolf, who recently died in Quincy was transferred from
the cemetery at that place to the Burton Cemetery by
I.N. Enlow undertaker.

WOLF, DAVID
    SEE: LIMBAUGH, CATHERINE

WOLF, MRS EMMA - Liberty - Aug 8, 1879 Died, Mrs Emma
Wolf, wife of Jacob Wolf and daughter of Jonah Grubb
died August 1st. Buried in Burton graveyard. Received
medical attention from her Uncle Wm Kendall. Leaves a
husband, parents and 3 children.

WOLF, WM - Burton - Nov 25, 1880 A little son of Wm
Wolf died Sunday A.M. cause diptheria.

WOLFE, DAVID - A Good Man Gone - Oct 3, 1879 Died, at his home 2 miles west of Liberty September 14th Rev David Wolfe. Settled with his father on the farm he died on, on an early day. Married Permelia McKnight April 15, 1822 who survives him. Father was Rev George Wolfe. Funeral from his home on September 16th, age 66 years.

WOLFRED, GEORGE - Local - Dec 16, 1880 George Wolfred was run over by the train an killed Tuesday. Leaves a wife and 6 children. "Chapin Cor. Meredosia Enterprise"

WOOD, CAPT C.J.
    SEE: ROBERTS, MRS SUSIE F.

WOOD, CHARLIE - Accident - Jul 8, 1877 "Aurora Paper" Charlie Wood a brakeman on the C & I Railroad son of C.J. Wood, Grant Street, Aurora fell from a train at Rochelle Wednesday night. Funeral from his late home #5 Grant Street today (Friday) at 5 P.M. Charlie lived in this town (Camp Point) some years ago with his parents, then a stout lusty boy.

WOOD, COL H.H. - Local - Jul 14, 1881 Died Col. H.H. Wood of Jacksonville. Died in Quincy Saturday from a sunstroke.

WOOD, HARRY - Mendon - Sep 26, 1879 One of the oldest and best known of the citizens of Ursa township died last night, Uncle Harry Wood. Funeral tomorrow age 80 years.

WOOD, JAMES HERVEY - Hash - Feb 9, 1877 James Hervey Wood, a well known plow manufacturer of Warsaw died at Denver, Colorado on the 28th ult of small pox. He settled in Warsaw in 1837 and had many friends in Hancock county.

WOOD, KATURAH C.
    SEE: WEBSTER, JOHN K.

WOODRUFF, WM - Neighborhood News - Dec 30, 1877 Died, Wm Woodruff accidently shot himself at Lima Lake. Died a few days later.

WOODS, ELVY
    SEE: ANDERS, JOHN

WOODS, MRS MARTHA A. - Burned - Aug 14, 1874 Mrs Martha A. Woods, daughter of Stewart Strickler, who keeps house for her father was burned when her clothes caught fire. Her sister threw water to put it out. Mrs Woods is in great danger.

WOODS, WILLIAM J. - Probate Notice - Sep 18, 1873 William J. Woods 3rd Monday of November 1873 Stewart Strickler, adm.

WOODS, WM J. - Hash - Aug 28, 1873 We learn that Mr Wm J. Woods died at his home in Houston township Tuesday after a protracted and painful illness.

WOOLEN - Local - Jun 17, 1880 A boy named Woolen attempted to couple 2 cars in Quincy yards Monday and was caught between the bumpers and his head smashed.

WORLEY, ESQ. - Mendon - Jan 29, 1880 Died, Esq. Worley of Ursa died Friday A.M. He was probably the oldest resident of Adams County Born in what is now Ursa township December 26, 1828.

WORRELL, ELISHA - Local - Apr 27, 1882 Died, Elisha Worrell, at Chili on the 17th inst, 85 years old. Lived in Chili since 1835 and laid out the town.

WRIGHT, MISS ALICE - Mendon - Oct 18, 1878 Miss Alice Wright, daughter of John Wright, Esq. died on the 6th inst of consumption.

WRIGHT, J.C.
    SEE: GORDON, MRS O.

WRIGHT, JOHN - Mar 12, 1874 An old man was found Sunday A.M. named John Wright near the Amphitheatre of the fairgrounds completely exhausted. He was taken to the club house to recover. He says he owns a farm about 4 miles from Clayton and has a son near there. Later: He died at the club house Tuesday A.M., died from exposure. Son took charge of his remains.

WYLE, MRS JOHN
    SEE: NORTON, CHARLIE

WYLE, JOHN - Probate Notice - Jul 27, 1877 John Wyle 3rd Monday of September "77" Mary Wyle, adm.

WYLE, JOHN - Obituary - Jun 29, 1877 Died, at his home in Camp Point on the 22nd inst of rheumatism of the heart, John Wyle, 66 years old. Born in Ballimore

County Maryland September 8, 1811. Father died when he was a small lad. Married in 1840 to Miss Mary Hughes who survives him. Had 6 children only 2 are living. Came to Illinois in 1858 and settled near Burton, Adams County. Was a farmer.

YANCEY, JERRY A. - Local - Jul 7, 1881 Dispatch from Hannibal states that Jerry A. Yancey, agent of the Keokuk Packet Co. and A.H. Conner were run over in the railroad yards and killed Tuesday about noon. Mr Yancey is the father of Dr C.H. Yancey of Camp Point.

YARNEIL, WILLIAM - Died - Jan 19, 1877 Died, January 1st, 1877 William Yarneil, age 72 years an acceptable member of the Methodist Church.

YEARGAIN, EDWARD - Columbus - Nov 9, 1882 Died, Edward Yeargain Jr yesterday. Buried today. Funeral at Mt Pleasant.

YEARGAIN, EDWARD B. - Obituary - Nov 9, 1882 Died, Edward B. Yeargain November 5 at the home of his father Edward Yeargain of typhoid fever. Born March 26, 1860, was oldest son. Services at Mt Pleasant on Monday at 10 A.M. by Rev A.M. Danely.

YENG, JIM - Local Hash - De 27, 1878 Jim Yeng the chinaman was acquitted of the murder of his employer.

YOCHEM, MRS PETER - Hash - Sep 7, 1877 Mrs Peter Yockem, of Quincy committed suicide Saturday by drowning in a well. She was insane, age 30 years and mother of 5 children.

YOUG, MR - Local - Jan 2, 1880 Last Friday near Kinderhook, Pike County an old man named Youg dropped dead while sawing wood.

YOUNG, BILL - Acquitted - Oct 31, 1879 A telegram from Keokuk last night tells the Bill Young who is on trial in Kohoka, Missouri for murder of Spencer family near Luray, Missouri was acquitted yesterday by a jury. "Herald"

YOUNG, BILL
    SEE: LANE, FRANK

YOUNG, BRIGHAM - Latest News - Sep 7, 1877 Died, Brigham Young. Died at Salt Lake City August 29th, 76 years old.

YOUNG, FRANK - Local - Apr 20, 1882 Died, Frank Young who clerked last summer at Kelley's jewelry store. Died Tuesday of last week at Carthage of consumption.

YOUNG, JOHN - Neighborhood News - Jul 26, 1878 Tuesday eve David Nicholas 21 years old who had driven up the hearse from Mt Sterling with the body of Mr John Young was hit in the head by Garlic Angel. "Rushville Citizen"

YOUNG, MOSES - Mendon - Dec 12, 1879 Mr Moses Young, the father of Dr Young of our village is lying low and probably will not recover, 86 years old.

YOUNG, MOSES - Mendon - Jan 9, 1880 Moses Young died at the home of his son, Dr Young of this town Friday afternoon, age 87 years.

YOUNG, WM - Local - Oct 31, 1879 Wm Young, who was acquitted of the murder of the Spencer family near Keokuk last week was hung by a mob Tuesday. He had just arrived from Ohio where he had married a Miss Julia Bray.

ZEH, HARMON - Burton - Aug 15, 1879 Died during the past 2 weeks in Burton little son of Mr and Mrs Harmon Zeh Friday A.M., 3 years old.

ZIEGLER, HENRY - Local - Oct 19, 1882 Died, the little son of Henry Ziegler Tuesday A.M. of cerebro spinal meningitis.

ZIEGLER, MRS LORENTZ - Died - Dec 26, 1879 Died, Dec. 21st, Mrs Ziegler, widow of the late Lorentz Ziegler.

ZIEGLER, LORENZ - Died - Jul 11, 1879 Died, July 4th, Lorenz Ziegler age 68 years. Came to Camp Point in 1866.

ZIMMERMAN, DR - Hash - Jul 14, 1876 Dr Zimmerman, an old, well known doctor of Quincy died Saturday evening.

ZIMMERMAN, BAXTER - Neighborhood News - Nov 9, 1877 Last Thursday Baxter Zimmerman, a brakeman for QM & P road was run over by a car at Durham Station and killed.

ZIMMERMAN, JOSEPH - Local - Aug 19, 1880 Joseph Zimmerman of Quincy died last Saturday A.M. age 83 years. Settled in Quincy in 1839.

ZIPSE, LOUIS - Hash - Sep 8, 1876 Louis Zipse was
arrested in Quincy Wednesday for brutally beating his
wife. They had been seperated and she had returned to
see her child. She may not recover.

Other Heritage Books by
Mrs. Joseph J. Beals, Sr. and Mrs. Sandra Kirchner:

Births and Related Items Abstracted from The Camp Point Journal
of Camp Point, Adams County, Illinois, 1873–1903

Deaths Abstracted from The Camp Point Journal, *1873–1882,
Camp Point, Adams County, Illinois*

Deaths Abstracted from The Camp Point Journal, *1883–1892,
Camp Point, Adams County, Illinois*

Deaths Abstracted from The Camp Point Journal, *1893–1903,
Camp Point, Adams County, Illinois*

*Marriages (1895–1905) and Deaths (1895–1900) and Related Items Abstracted
from the* Golden New Era *of Golden, Adams County, Illinois*

Marriages and Related Items Abstracted from Clayton Enterprise
Newspaper of Clayton, Adams County, Illinois, 1879–1900

Marriages and Related Items Abstracted from the Mendon Dispatch
of Mendon, Adams County, Illinois, 1877–1905

Obituaries and Death Related Items Abstracted from Clayton Enterprise
Newspaper of Clayton, Adams County Illinois, 1879–1900, Volume I

Obituaries and Death Related Items Abstracted from the Hendon Dispatch
of Mendon, Adams County, Illinois, 1877–1905

CD: Births and Deaths Abstracted from The Camp Point Journal,
Camp Point, Adams County, Illinois, 1873–1903

CD: Marriages and Related Items Abstracts from the Golden New Era
Newspaper of Golden, Adam County, Illinois, 1895–1905

CD: Marriages and Related Items Abstracts from the Mendon Dispatch
of Mendon, Adams County, Illinois, 1877–1905

CD: Obituaries and Death Related Items Abstracts from the Golden New Era
Newspaper of Golden, Adam County, Illinois, 1895–1900

CD: Obituaries and Death Related Items Abstracts from the Mendon Dispatch
of Mendon, Adams County, Illinois, 1877–1905

www.ingramcontent.com/pod-product-compliance
Lightning Source LLC
Chambersburg PA
CBHW050802160426
43192CB00010B/1607